ROUTLEDGE LIBRARY EDITIONS:
AGRIBUSINESS AND LAND USE

I0124414

Volume 23

THE STATE AND
THE FARMER

THE STATE AND THE FARMER

PETER SELF
AND
HERBERT J. STORING

Routledge
Taylor & Francis Group

LONDON AND NEW YORK

First published in 1962 by George Allen & Unwin Ltd.

This edition first published in 2024
by Routledge
4 Park Square, Milton Park, Abingdon, Oxon OX14 4RN

and by Routledge
605 Third Avenue, New York, NY 10158

Routledge is an imprint of the Taylor & Francis Group, an informa business

© 1962 George Allen & Unwin Ltd

British Library Cataloguing in Publication Data
A catalogue record for this book is available from the British Library

ISBN: 978-1-032-48321-4 (Set)
ISBN: 978-1-032-47346-8 (Volume 23) (hbk)
ISBN: 978-1-032-47364-2 (Volume 23) (pbk)
ISBN: 978-1-003-38574-5 (Volume 23) (ebk)

DOI: 10.4324/9781003385745

Publisher's Note
The publisher has gone to great lengths to ensure the quality of this reprint but points out that some imperfections in the original copies may be apparent.

Disclaimer
The publisher has made every effort to trace copyright holders and would welcome correspondence from those they have been unable to trace.

THE STATE AND
THE FARMER

PETER SELF
*Reader in Political Science
in the University of London*

AND

HERBERT J. STORING
*Associate Professor of Political Science
in the University of Chicago*

London
GEORGE ALLEN & UNWIN LTD
RUSKIN HOUSE · MUSEUM STREET

FIRST PUBLISHED IN 1962
SECOND IMPRESSION 1971

ISBN 0 04 338032 8 Cased
0 04 338049 2 Paper

PRINTED IN GREAT BRITAIN
in 10 on 11 point Times Roman
BY REDWOOD PRESS LIMITED
TROWBRIDGE & LONDON

TO
PARTNERSHIP
properly understood

FOREWORD

THIS book deals with agricultural policies and politics in Britain between 1945 and 1961. The distinctive feature of this period has been agricultural 'partnership'—a close and pervasive pattern of co-operation between the Government and the principal agricultural organizations. The power of the state was enlisted to support British agriculture, to guide its development, and to supervise its efficiency. The actual programmes were worked out, at both national and local levels, with the close participation of the agricultural organizations.

The period with which we are concerned started with ambitious post-war plans for placing agriculture upon a stable and efficient basis, and.ended with the emergence of new problems presented by the prospect of closer European integration. In the first half (until 1954) agricultural policy was dominated by problems of economic stringency and food rationing; in the second half policy has been increasingly affected by the very different problems of greater abundance. Labour Governments ruled for most but not all of the first nine years, and Conservative Governments have continued in office during the latter seven. Throughout the whole period, however, the state's programme of support and guidance has continued, and despite many strains the agricultural 'partnership' (typified by such an event as the annual price review) has also survived. The post-war edifice still stands at the time of writing, although some serious cracks have now appeared in the structure.

In this book we have explored the character and history of this co-operative endeavour to support and strengthen British agriculture. We have described the character and policies of the agricultural organizations, and the many problems and conflicts which have arisen over the administration of public policy. We hope that our approach has certain advantages. At present, studies of a subject such as this are generally concerned either with political pressures and techniques or else with an economic assessment of Government policy. We have tried to show what actual effects the organizations have had on political and administrative decisions, and what influences have caused Governments to act as they did. The results should help to illuminate the actual power of interest or 'pressure' groups in the modern world, and to assist conclusions about the possible and desirable limits of co-operation between Government and private organizations.

At the same time, the quest for a satisfactory and viable policy for British agriculture has a continuing interest, as relevant today as in 1945. We have tried to give a reasonably full account of the development of agricultural policies throughout the period, and to offer some comments about the success or failure of particular measures. This account may at least serve to point to some of the pitfalls which need to be avoided, if the stability and prosperity of agriculture is to rest upon sound foundations.

The authors would disclaim any intention of turning the National Farmers' Union into the villain of an agricultural drama. While we have plenty of criticisms to make of the Union's policies and activities, we also have ample sympathy with the special problems of farmers in the modern world. In most modern states, and not only in Britain, agriculture has become highly dependent upon state support. The achievement of the Farmers' Union in this country has been to help to persuade the state to involve itself particularly closely with the welfare of agriculture and itself to become the chief consultant of Government in the administration of public policy. Such a position invites and here receives a full and critical examination, made from the viewpoint not only of public interest, but of the interests of agriculture also. It is only fair to note, however, that other organizations can often get much of their way with less fuss and more secrecy.

It may be useful briefly to describe the design of the book. The first chapter deals with the post-war circumstances of British agriculture, and can be omitted by anyone familiar with this subject. The second chapter deals with the rise and character of the National Farmers' Union, and the two following chapters give an account of the annual price review encounters between Government and Union and of the tortured controversies over agricultural marketing. Chapters V and VI deal with the experiment in 'sanctions' against incompetent farmers and with the activities of local agricultural committees. Chapters VII and VIII describe, on a smaller scale, the activities and problems of the organized farm workers and of the country landowners. Chapter IX examines the political strength and weaknesses of British agriculture, including the significance of the farmers' vote. The last chapter offers an assessment of agricultural policy and of the partnership between Government and farmers. The first section of this chapter may be omitted by anyone not interested in theoretical questions about the relation between interest groups and the state.

Mr Self took primary responsibility for Chapters I, III, IV, VIII and IX, and Mr Storing for Chapters II, V, VI and VII. The last chapter was written jointly. Mr Self was the final editor. We are grateful to the London School of Economics and Political Science for a research grant in connection with this work, and to the University of Chicago for a travel grant and other assistance to Mr Storing. Chapter V of this book first appeared as an article in the

Winter, 1960, issue of *Public Law*, and is included with due acknowledgement to that journal.

We are indebted to the Ministry of Agriculture, Fisheries and Food; the National Farmers' Union of England and Wales; the National Union of Agricultural Workers; and the Country Landowners' Association for their courteous and helpful replies to our enquiries. We have been greatly helped by conversations with various persons who have been active in Government positions or in the principal agricultural organisations, as well as with many Members of Parliament. We have had the benefit of advice on certain matters from Mr Charles Hardin of the Rockefeller Foundation, Mr George Allen of St Edmund's Hall, Oxford, and Mr David Butler of Nuffield College, Oxford. None of these organizations or individuals has any responsibility for the accuracy of our facts or the soundness of our opinions.

May, 1961

CONTENTS

CHAPTER I

AGRICULTURE AND THE STATE

1

IN Britain, since 1945, the state has assumed an unprecedented degree of responsibility for the functioning and welfare of agriculture. It has done so at the behest of agricultural interests with which it has closely co-operated in devising and administering programmes of support, advice and control. A close and wide-ranging partnership has grown up in which the Government has provided agriculture with a high degree of support and protection, and agriculture has accepted in return an unusual amount of supervision and regulation.

Superficially, British agriculture seems an unlikely candidate for the close attentions of government. Except in wartime its importance in the national economy has steadily declined to a point where it employs about 4 per cent of the working population and produces a similar proportion of national output.[1] Compared with its position in almost all other states, agriculture in Britain is quantitatively and economically unimportant. In some ways this small size is not really a disadvantage since it at least makes practicable a degree of state-aided prosperity which could not be contemplated for the larger, poorer agricultures of many other countries. But to realize this possibility, the interest of government in agriculture must be effectively secured; and until recent times there seemed little prospect of doing so.

What C. S. Orwin has called the 'second agrarian revolution' started in the mid-eighteenth century and gradually transformed British farming.[2] It consisted in new methods of land reclamation, striking advances in crop strains and rotations and in the breeding of livestock, and the invention of new machines, all of which combined to bring about a steady increase in agricultural productivity. This scientific progress, in which the best British landlords and farmers led the world, was accompanied by sharp changes in the agricultural system. The 'enclosure movement' of the late eighteenth century overwhelmed the traditional 'open-field' system, enabled the

---

[1] In 1958 agriculture, forestry, and fishing combined employed 1,090,000 of the UK working population of 24,635,000. Their gross output was £865 million in a gross domestic product at factor cost of £19,861 million. *Annual Abstract of Statistics for 1959*, HMSO, pp. 104 and 243.
[2] C. S. Orwin, *A History of English Farming* (London: Thomas Nelson & Sons, 1949), pp. 35–74.

new inventions to be efficiently applied, and displaced from the land large numbers of yeomen and peasants. Agricultural progress was the essential concomitant of industrial development, releasing the labour required for the new factories and mills and providing most of the extra food required to feed a rapidly growing population.

Both the Whig and Tory political aristocracies were composed predominantly of landed gentry. Industrialization took a long time to shake the political power that was rooted in land. Of the 5,034 members who sat in the House of Commons from 1734 to 1832, fully three-quarters had their principal economic interest in land.[1] It was an easy matter for landlords to secure the passage of private Enclosure Bills through so pliable an instrument as the unreformed Parliament; and it was equally natural for Parliament to enact strong measures of protection against imported grain.

The Repeal of the Corn Laws in 1846 bore witness to a decline in the political power of land, but it did not quickly affect the prosperity of British agriculture, which at that time was not closely dependent on protection. British agriculture, in fact, reached its highest level of production in the 1870's. Up to then, it had secured the lion's share of the rising demand for food of an urban population growing both in numbers and in spending power. Thereafter it was subjected to successive waves of competition from overseas producers practising more specialized and extensive forms of agriculture over vast areas of virgin land. The first great dent in farm prices and prosperity came from the mass importation of cheap grain from the prairies of North America. The second was made by the arrival of refrigerated meat and dairy products from Argentina and Australasia. These developments spelled disaster for the old 'high farming' with its basis in arable production and the folding of sheep and cattle, and with its intensive use of capital and labour.

British farmers still had one major asset in their proximity to a rapidly growing urban market. To utilize this advantage, however, they had to change their traditional methods, and this they were slow to do. The successful invasion of the British bacon market by Denmark, which enjoyed few of the natural economic assets possessed by virgin territories overseas, revealed the vulnerability of home agriculture to efficient competition from any source. Many home farmers preferred to distribute their risks between several small enterprises and to concentrate on survival, rather than to try and meet overseas competition on its own terms in an effort to be prosperous.

The political influence of agriculture sharply declined between 1868 and 1900. In the former year, 44 per cent of the total economic

[1] S. H. Beer, 'The Representation of Interests in British Government: Historical Background,' *American Political Science Review*, September, 1957, p. 623.

interests held by Members of the House of Commons could still be attributed to land, but by 1900 the corresponding figure was only 23 per cent.[1] The agricultural leadership of the landowning class began to falter, as their numbers became diluted by industrial and commercial parvenus; although such dilution was nothing new, it now occurred on a much larger scale. Moreover, it became difficult for agriculture to mobilize such political power as it still retained. Its well-being had been linked for so long with the social and political power of its aristocratic sponsors that the need for giving organized expression to agricultural interests as such was not easily grasped.

In any event, the economic interests of the nation were running strongly against agriculture. Britain was enjoying the benefits of free trade practised under very special conditions. A vast and rapid development of agricultural resources was occurring in countries with which Britain had close political and financial links, and for which Britain provided the principal market. Nothing like this peculiar pattern of trade between one small, industrialized state and major agricultural regions distributed over four continents had occurred before or will probably recur. The pattern, while it lasted, was highly advantageous to British consumers. It was not surprising that their interest and that of manufacturers, aware of the utility of cheap food for limiting wage claims, should be politically dominant. What British farmers did with their land and resources, and whether they sank or swam, mattered to few save themselves.

In 1870 those employed in agriculture, including both farmers and workers, enjoyed a rough parity of income with those in urban occupations. This unusual state of affairs emphasizes the degree of prosperity which the old style of farming had managed to attain. The ratio of agricultural to non-agricultural income is estimated to have fallen to 63 per cent by 1900 and to 61 per cent by 1930.[2] The importance of agriculture in the national economy declined still more dramatically. The proportion of the occupied population working in agriculture fell from 19.1 per cent in 1871 to 6.8 per cent in 1931, whilst agriculture's share of the national income fell still more steeply from an estimated 20 per cent to a mere 4 per cent.[3] Concern and regret were widely voiced about this 'drift from the land'; but the actual measures taken to retain the rural population were inconsiderable. The one economic concession of substance made to agriculture was a reduction in 1896 in the basis of its assessment for local rates.

The first change in the state's attitude towards agriculture occurred

[1] J. A. Thomas, *The House of Commons. 1832–1901* (University of Wales Press Board 1939), p. 18.
[2] E. M. Ojala, *Agriculture and Economic Progress* (Oxford University Press, 1952), p. 135.
[3] *Ibid*, pp. 85, 134.

as a consequence of the First World War, although it was very short-lived. In this war, unlike its successor, the general pattern of farming was not greatly altered. Livestock production was not much affected at any point, and it was only in 1917 that guaranteed prices for cereals, followed by compulsory cropping orders, were hastily intro-duced. Compulsory cropping was abandoned before the war ended in the following year, but the guaranteed prices, which had originally been enacted for six years, were re-enacted on a revised basis by the Agriculture Act of 1920. This Act was suddenly repealed the next year, farmers were given compensatory payments on an acreage basis for the 1921 harvest only, and agriculture was abandoned to the rigours of an intense post-war depression.

This incident still lingers in the lore of British farming as a cynical political betrayal. Cynical it may have been in the speed with which the Government repudiated its promises. The cause was a sudden fall in food prices which meant that any special aid to British agri-culture would prove expensive. Successive Governments (Coalition, Conservative, Labour) toyed with the idea of a subsidy of £1 per arable acre to relieve the extreme agricultural distress, but all rejected it.[1] Throughout the 1920's even the Board of Agriculture remained unreceptive to proposed measures of economic relief, although one such (the sugar-beet subsidy of 1925) was enacted. Before this inci-dent Lord Ernle had stated what he, like most well-wishers of agri-culture, accepted as an immutable fate: 'Nothing seems to me more certain in politics than that British agriculture will be neither subsi-dised nor protected.'[2]

However, a drastic change in public agricultural policy occurred as a result of the great economic depression which started in 1929. From this point can be dated the modern period of state interven-tion, assistance, and control; but its objectives and methods in the early 1930's were quite different from those which came later. Agri-culture was treated as one of a group of depressed basic industries, and the same general recipes (taxation relief, import control, and internal re-organization) were prescribed for it as for coal, steel, and cotton textiles. Complete relief from local rates had already been accorded to agriculture during the 1920's before partial derating was applied to industry generally. Like the leaders of other basic indus-tries, the National Farmers' Union's main demand was for protec-tion against foreign competition; and, as with coal and steel and textiles, the Government made the grant of such protection condi-tional upon an internal reorganization.

In the case of agriculture, the instrument for internal reorganiza-

[1] E. M. H. Lloyd, 'Some Thoughts on Agricultural Policy,' *Journal of Agricul-tural Economics*, February, 1957.
[2] Lord Ernle, *The Land and Its People* (Hutchinson & Co., 1925), p. 222.

tion was the Agricultural Marketing Acts of 1931 and 1933. The producer-elected boards which were established for milk, potatoes, and hops under these Acts succeeded to some extent in stabilizing prices through the regulation of supplies and markets. Substantial tariffs for certain horticultural products were introduced in 1931. However, the main instrument for protection against overseas competition was not tariffs but import quotas, which were imposed, by agreement with overseas suppliers, upon bacon, ham, mutton, and beef. There were also experiments with international agreements for the regulation of supplies of wheat, beef, and sugar. Finally, price subsidies were introduced gradually for a wide range of products, including sugar beet, wheat, barley, oats, and fat cattle. The most important was the wheat subsidy which was financed by a levy on imported flour and paid on a sliding scale of guaranteed prices which varied with total output.

Some of these measures, particularly those relating to marketing, have had a lasting influence upon the techniques of agricultural support. All the same, the legislation of the 1930's was permeated with a depression psychology and a disposition towards restrictionist devices which have proved less lasting. Nor was the apparatus of protection, except in the case of horticulture, of much benefit to home producers. Price subsidies were more efficacious, but four-fifths of the £104 millions paid out in the inter-war period related to wheat and sugar-beet and was primarily of value to the arable farmers of Eastern England.[1] This concentration of support on arable production protected the remains of the old 'high farming' and inhibited the shift to livestock products which was economically desirable. There was a small rise in agricultural incomes during the 1930's, but even with the help of these numerous state measures, agriculture as a whole remained in a very depressed condition.

The history of agriculture in the second world war need only be briefly mentioned.[2] Almost from the outset the state assumed a far-reaching control over agricultural production through the medium of local representative committees. Their main task was to supervise a great expansion of crop production aimed at saving the maximum amount of shipping-space. Compulsory cropping orders were issued, neglected and derelict land was reclaimed, inefficient farmers were evicted. Large numbers of pigs, poultry and cattle had to be slaughtered because feeding-stuffs could not be spared to keep them, although milk production was maintained for nutritional reasons. The great plough-up brought the arable acreage back to its record peak

·[1] Keith Murray, *Agriculture* (History of the Second World War, U.K. Civil Series, HMSO, 1955), p. 37 and appendix Table 3.
[2] For a full account, see *Ibid.*

of the 1870's, although (because of the slaughter of livestock) total net output never increased by much more than 20 per cent. The whole pattern of farming was drastically changed, and unusual efforts and sacrifices demanded of farmers. On the other hand, their prosperity was greatly increased by the introduction of fairly generous guaranteed prices. They ended the war with a considerable preference for a full system of guaranteed prices, even with its concomitant of state control, over the kind of economic conditions under which they had been farming before the war.

2

A greatly altered prospect confronted British agriculture as the second world war drew to its close. In the first place the restrictionist mood of pre-war days had given way to a faith in expansion, typified by plans for maintaining full employment, expanding consumption, and liberalizing world trade. At the Hot Springs conference of 1943, forty-four states endorsed the objective of raising nutritional standards by governmental action. The international Food and Agriculture Organization, whose foundation followed, set out to bring about on a world scale the proposed 'marriage' between nutrition and agriculture. Secondly, agriculture plainly stood to benefit from the widespread acceptance of the idea that it was the state's responsibility to correct the causes of economic instability and depression; and it was also the gainer from egalitarian notions that all groups were entitled to a 'fair share' in the general wealth of the community. Finally, and more concretely, the serious deterioration in Britain's trading position strongly suggested the need for a permanently increased output of home-grown food.

Thus there were motives enough for offering a 'new deal' to British agriculture. It must be admitted that these motives contained a large admixture of loose idealism and generalized benevolence which grew easily out of the wartime atmosphere of shared sacrifices and suspended competition. This mood was nourished by admiration for the farmers' wartime achievements and by somewhat loose inferences about the strategic and economic value of keeping agriculture prosperous. The assertion of agriculturists that their industry had been shamefully neglected before the war, although far from being strictly true, received remarkably little questioning. Further, assessment of the most specific new reason for developing British agriculture—namely, Britain's changed position in the world economy—became seriously confused with the necessity of overcoming serious but temporary food shortages.

The principles of agricultural policy which were eventually adopted emerged from two main sources. First there were the policies advocated by a large number of agricultural and political organizations, mostly between 1943 and 1945. Besides advancing their own individual proposals at different dates, eleven agricultural organizations, including all the main interest groups and the principal professional, educational, and scientific bodies, agreed on a joint policy statement.[1] This advocated a system of guaranteed prices for agriculture, bearing a 'definite relation' to the costs of production and sufficient to yield 'a reasonable return to the producer and on the capital to secure a standard of living comparable to that of urban workers'. In return for this guarantee, 'all owners and occupiers of rural land must accept an obligation to maintain a reasonable standard of good husbandry and good estate management, and submit to the necessary measure of direction and guidance, subject to provisions for appeal to an impartial tribunal'. It was also proposed that permanent governmental machinery should be established for the control of imports and for the marketing of those foodstuffs subject to overseas competition.

This policy statement revealed the unanimous wish of agricultural organizations for a comprehensive system of state guarantees, and their complete willingness to accept state control as a corollary. Rather similar proposals—for guaranteed prices, a national minimum wage, and a more limited 'reserve' of state control—had been put forward by a sub-committee of the Ministry of Reconstruction in the First World War.[2] But important differences lay both in the unanimity and determination of the principal agricultural interests on the second occasion and in the endorsement of their aspirations by the political parties. Proposals for guaranteed prices related to an average level of efficiency were produced by the Labour Party and the Tory Reform Committee.[3] The Conservative and Liberal policy statements, while their actual suggestions were rather different, were sympathetic to the same general aims.[4] It is also significant that all

[1] The organizations were the National Farmers' Union; Country Landowners' Association; National Union of Agricultural Workers; Transport and General Workers' Union (which has an agricultural section); Royal Agricultural Society of England; Councils of Agriculture for England and Wales; Chartered Surveyors' Institution; Land Agents' Society; Land Union; Land Settlement Association. A group of Peers who had published a policy statement was also represented. The meeting was convened in April–May, 1944 by the Royal Agricultural Society. Many of the policy statements issued at this time are out of print. *Staples' Reconstruction Digests: Agriculture* contains a useful summary.

[2] Murray, *op. cit.*, p. 14.

[3] Labour Party, *Our Land, The Future Of Britain's Agriculture*. November, 1943. Tory Reform Committee, *The Husbandman Waiteth*, May, 1944.

[4] Conservative Party, *Agricultural Reconstruction*, April, 1943. Liberal Party *Food and Agriculture*, June, 1943. It needs to be remembered that some of the documents here quoted were only interim statements by committees which did not necessarily carry the full endorsement of the organizations concerned.

parties, not excepting the Liberals, advocated the supervision and, where necessary, the dispossession of inefficient farmers; and that Conservatives as well as Labour were prepared to apply the same medicine to incompetent landlords.

The consensus upon post-war agricultural policy extended also to business and to the press. In view of the free trade traditions connected with Manchester, a particularly significant event was a 1943 resolution from that city's Chamber of Commerce in favour of permanent Government support for agriculture. The British Chamber of Commerce followed suit in 1945. Even *The Economist*, the strongest, almost the only, critic of these generalized proposals, was prepared to accept a social case for substantial support though it questioned the economic *rationale* for providing it.[1]

Of course, it would be misleading to imply that there was complete unanimity in agricultural and political circles about the correct course for public policy. The Conservative Party and the Country Landowners' Association favoured a levy on imported food as a means of supporting domestic farm prices,[2] whereas the Liberal and Labour Parties, and also the Tory Reform Committee, were opposed to any form of taxation on food. The more right-wing groups attached great importance to subsidized wheat-growing for keeping the land in good heart, whereas left-wing groups were more concerned with the development of 'protective' foods such as milk, eggs, and vegetables. There was also disagreement about the desirable extent of landlords' control over their tenants.

Several policy statements also dwelled strongly on the case for import 'planning' as a device for protecting and supporting British agriculture. This even more than guaranteed prices was the main theme of the National Farmers' Union which advocated the maximum expansion of home agriculture to meet dietary needs, coupled with the allocation of residual requirements among overseas suppliers.[3] Protectionism of some kind was also advocated by the Conservative Party, by an influential Group of Peers, by the Country

[1] *Post-War Agriculture* (Extracts from *The Economist*, 1942). This pamphlet contains a lucid and interesting debate on the subject between *The Economist* and Lord De La Warr.

[2] Central (later Country) Landowners Association, *Post-War Rural Reconstruction Problems*. The Conservative Party put prime emphasis on a guaranteed price for wheat, related to individual quotas of output, as a means of pursuing the 'tradition of arable farming' in the eastern counties. A Group of Peers (*A Post-War Agricultural Policy for Great Britain*, February, 1943) advocated import quotas to give protection to those commodities whose production was essential for 'the proper farming of our land'.

[3] National Farmers' Union, *Agriculture and the Nation* (Interim Report, February, 1943); and *The Basis of Economic Security* ('A Permanent Policy for the Nation's Greatest Industry'), November, 1945.

Landowners' Association, and by the Council of Agriculture,[1] and it was also implicit in the combined statement already quoted. These views did not have any practical relevance until state trading and controls were wound up some ten years later, but they showed the persistence of protectionist sentiment in agricultural circles.

The second main source of agricultural policy-making was governmental. Early in the war the Ministry of Agriculture put forward certain proposals about post-war policy which were considered, in confidence, by 'a small number of persons of influence in the agricultural world', but these received a 'less than tepid' reception from the War Cabinet.[2] In 1943, following a dispute with the National Farmers' Union about prices, the Minister of Agriculture (Lord Hudson) got the Cabinet's consent to discuss future policy with the Union and other interested organizations. This energetic Minister was himself instrumental in urging the agricultural organizations to prepare their joint statement, which had much in common with the Ministry's own earlier proposals. Questions of import planning and control were outside the Ministry of Agriculture's scope, but the other two main recommendations relating to guaranteed prices and state control over farming standards provided an immediately practicable programme for this Ministry to sponsor.

Thus when the Labour Government came to power in 1945, it found the outlines of a legislative measure ready in the Ministry's files. With only one substantial change of policy relating to landlords,[3] the Government enacted this measure as the Agriculture Act, 1947. The Act was built around the 'twin pillars' of stability and efficiency. It required the three Agricultural Ministers[4] to conduct each year a general review of the economic condition and prospects of agriculture, in the light of which economic guarantees would be provided for a stated list of commodities.[5] These accounted for about four-fifths of total agricultural output. The Act limited the guarantees to 'such part of the nation's food and other agricultural produce as in the national interest it is desirable to produce in the United Kingdom', but stipulated that they should be sufficient to provide 'proper remuneration and living conditions for farmers and workers in agriculture and an adequate return on capital invested in the industry'.[6]

[1] Council of Agriculture, 'Memorandum from the Standing Committee,' May, 1943.
[2] Murray, op. cit., p. 348.
[3] See Chapter VIII.
[4] Agricultural policy in Scotland is the responsibility of the Secretary of State and the Home Secretary holds a watching brief for Northern Ireland.
[5] Wheat, barley, oats, rye, potatoes, sugar beet, fat cattle, fat sheep, fat pigs, milk, eggs. Wool was added in 1950. Horticultural products are excluded.
[6] Agriculture Act, 1947, sec. 1 (1).

These provisions were designed to provide 'stability'. The Act pursued the other goal of 'efficiency' by requiring all farmers and landowners to observe rules of 'good husbandry' and 'good estate management' respectively. It continued the wartime emergency powers of control over inefficient farmers and owners, hedged with closer safeguards, and it reconstituted the wartime County Committees on a more representative basis. Additional provisions were concerned with the creation of more smallholdings, to improve the ladder of opportunity for farm workers, and the establishment of an Agricultural Land Commission, to farm land acquired by the state and to investigate problem areas of poor farm lay-outs.[1]

The Agriculture Act set the general goals for state policy, but left most of the details to be settled by administrative action. It specified which products would be supported by the state, but it did not say how that support would be given, or what quantity of the farmers' output would qualify for support. This legislative vagueness was deliberate. The Government was anxious to avoid the risk of another such débâcle as had followed the highly specific legislation enacted in the First World War. However, the Act did indicate a method for settling such questions in the form of co-operation between Government and the principal agricultural organizations, especially in the annual economic review and in the administration of sanctions. The spirit of 'partnership' was strongly evident in the genesis and passage of the Agriculture Act and proved equally significant in its operation.

Before proceeding to the main part of this book, it may be helpful to consider briefly the difficult problems of state support and guidance to agriculture which were hidden beneath the generalized phraseology of the Agriculture Act. A full review of these problems would go well beyond the bounds of this book, and for fuller information about the economic and social circumstances of agriculture other sources must be consulted.[2] However, a brief survey should help to illuminate the problems with which both the agricultural organizations and the Government have had to grapple since 1945. We will deal first with the general question of agricultural support and then with the special circumstances of British agriculture.

3

To start with, it is useful to draw a distinction between the narrower and wider objectives of state agricultural support. The narrower aim is simply to 'iron out' the chronic instability of the prices of many agricultural products. One reason for this instability is that the supply of some products fluctuates sharply while demand for them is rela-

[1] *Ibid.*, Parts II, IV, V.
[2] See Appendix E, Note on sources.

tively inelastic. The yield of crops varies with weather conditions, but consumers do not eat much if any more bread or potatoes when production is high and prices fall. Another reason is the tendency of producers to over-react to market changes, through decisions being taken independently by hundreds of thousands of farmers. There are cases when an increase in price leads to a sharp expansion of output, followed by a collapse of prices and an excessive contraction of output. In the case of pigs, for example, a regular cycle of this kind has been shown to exist.

There is now widespread agreement that these price fluctuations are often more violent and unpredictable than is necessary. Not only is the farmer's security undermined, but his technical efficiency and financial standing suffer from his inability to plan his operations with a reasonable degree of confidence in the outcome. Various methods can be used to regulate prices so as to reduce fluctuations, although care is needed to ensure that they do not insulate farmers from changes in consumer tastes and requirements.

In theory stabilization schemes should not require any permanent financial support by the State. The scheme works by 'averaging out' prices over a period of time. Generally, however, producers do not find this average price acceptable, and the state comes under a strong pressure to aid farmers when times are bad without imposing any balancing charge at other times. In farmers' eyes, indeed, conditions are rarely good enough to warrant such a balancing. Thus it is that the 'stabilization' aim melts easily into a wider objective, which is to achieve a permanent increase in the level of agricultural incomes and not just to prop them up when markets are temporarily depressed.

This second, broader objective does raise very critical issues of policy-making. The reason for it is easily understandable. In most countries the disparity between agricultural and non-agricultural incomes is very marked, and agriculturists naturally resent and deplore their position somewhere near the bottom of the economic ladder. To many people outside agriculture also it appears both paradoxical and unjust that so skilled and socially useful an occupation should be relatively ill-paid. In modern times agricultural groups have increasingly looked to state action to remedy their situation. The purpose of raising farm incomes held a central place in the conception of the British Agriculture Act, even though it was only loosely defined.

One of the principal handicaps of agricultural producers is their naturally weak bargaining power when compared with other economic groups. Agriculture is carried on in a vast number of small, dispersed units, a circumstance which makes effective joint action by producers much more difficult than in most occupations. Control over output and prices is a great deal easier in manufacturing industries than in agriculture. This situation has already been noted as a cause of price instability, but its effect upon the relative level of farm incomes is equally important. In an economic depression, for example, manufacturers cut back production so as to maintain prices, often utilizing joint action for the purpose. Farmers, however, cannot easily manipulate their output in this way and often respond to falling prices by actually producing more. In most countries the depression of the early 1930's dealt a heavier blow to the incomes of agricultural producers than to those working in urban occupations, and the gap between their respective earnings was widened. The counterpart of urban unemployment was rural poverty.[1]

Up to a point, state support of agriculture represents a form of compensation for the intrinsically weak bargaining power of primary producers. It brings into play the kind of 'countervailing power' against stronger economic interests which has been described and commended by J. K. Galbraith.[2] The relative poverty of agriculture is not simply due to the weak bargaining power of its producers, however. Agricultural incomes are low partly because of an over-concentration of labour on the land. This situation stems from the historical position of agriculture as the principal occupation of mankind and as the main reservoir of labour for other industries. Technical progress causes a steady reduction in the amount of labour which an efficient agriculture actually requires, but unless men leave the land rapidly enough its full benefits cannot be exploited. This problem takes the form not of actual unemployment but of an excessive amount of labour for the work to be performed. Moreover, the small family enterprise, in which agriculture is mainly organized, often finds it difficult to secure adequate capital, while the size and layout of farms are often unsuitable for modern techniques.

State aid which leaves these causes of agricultural poverty untouched is liable to be self-defeating. It stops up the economic forces which would in time attract labour into other occupations (assuming jobs are available) and which would stimulate more efficient forms of agricultural organization. Insofar as this occurs it will also fail to

[1] This account postulates an opposite type of response to falling prices from that described earlier, but the reactions apply to different situations and can in fact proceed simultaneously. A fall in the price of one commodity can cause a sharp contraction in its output, assuming the farmer can switch to other products. On the other hand, a general fall in prices can cause a general expansion of output as producers strive, generally unsuccessfully, to maintain their incomes. The former phenomenon is largely generated by intrinsic characteristics of agriculture. The latter is generally set off by industrial depression, and its cure has to be sought largely through a revival of the general economy. Thus any improvement in the farmers' bargaining power can have only limited effect in overcoming the dependent position of agriculture within an industrial economy. See T. W. Schultz, *Agriculture In An Unstable Economy* (McGraw-Hill, New York, 1945).

[2] J. K. Galbraith, *American Capitalism: The Theory of Countervailing Power* (Hamish Hamilton, London, 1957).

raise agricultural incomes adequately; state support will be expended upon keeping more men on the land, practising less efficient forms of farming, than would otherwise be the case. Of course these consequences may be accepted and even sought. Farming may be deliberately nourished by the state, just as it is practised by many farmers themselves, as a way of life which has values transcending economic criteria.

Generally, the effects of state aid will be more complex. This aid need not simply prop up the incomes of inefficient farmers, but can also increase agricultural efficiency, at least in a technical sense, by providing funds for new investment and the introduction of new techniques. It may be deliberately allocated so as to further these objectives. Even so the improvement in farm efficiency and incomes may still be open to the objection that it is absorbing resources of capital, materials, and labour which could be better utilized in other sectors of the economy. The state, therefore, has always to strike a balance between its support of agriculture and its concern with the general functioning of the economy; and if it is to apply its aid to much effect, it will also be increasingly drawn into measures for improving the technical and economic efficiency of agriculture. This, as we have seen, was the presumption of the 1947 Agriculture Act. The problem was how to pursue it.

It should also be noted that state support to agriculture can take either or both of two forms. The state can itself provide price guarantees and other forms of assistance. Alternatively or additionally, it can help farmers to help themselves by lending its authority to the formation of producer-controlled organizations armed with statutory powers for the regulation of production, supplies, and prices. The former method of direct state aid is at least capable of providing farmers with a considerably broader and more effective level of support than they can usually achieve by collective action even on a statutory basis. This advantage is particularly important where competition from overseas producers reduces or eliminates the bargaining power of a 'farmers' monopoly'. The latter method of collective organization, on the other hand, enables farmers to pursue their advantage, upon a collective basis, without so direct a dependence upon state assistance. This advantage is subject to the important qualification that the use of statutory powers by a producers' organization may well be thought to require considerable public supervision.

4

In the case of British agriculture, any programme of support and guidance had to be related to special external and internal circumstances. As a great trading and food-importing nation, Britain could not base its agricultural policy upon a narrow conception of self sufficiency.

Before the Second World War, about 70 per cent of the nation's food supplies, as measured by wholesale value, were imported. In the period 1934–8, the proportion of total supplies which were imported amounted to 91 per cent for butter, 88 per cent for wheat and flour, 84 per cent for sugar, oils and fats, and 50 per cent for meat.[1] The most important food produced wholly in Britain was liquid milk which had a naturally protected market. However, milk and livestock production in Britain drew heavily upon imported feeding stuffs, which had increased to almost nine million tons annually immediately before the war.[2]

To British farmers 'stability' has little meaning unless it provides an effective shield against this overseas competition. The case for protection has also its narrower and its broader aspect. The narrower case consists in protection against excessive price instability and clear examples of unfair competition. One cause of instability is fluctuations in the world supply of food due to the variable bounty of nature. A more important cause is the efforts of other states to support *their* agricultures, leading to the production of food for which no regular markets are available. There are plenty of hungry people in the world, but they have not the purchasing power to buy these surpluses, whose existence depresses world food prices, sometimes below the costs of production. So far as Britain admits such surpluses, home producers are bound to be injured.

The reasonableness of protection against these types of competition has been generally recognized since the last war. Export subsidies or bounties are prohibited under the terms of the General Agreement on Trade and Tariffs (GATT). If subsidized 'dumping' does occur, governments are entitled to impose special duties on the products in question or to take other protective action, and Britain has instituted machinery for doing so in appropriate cases.[3] Moreover, certain international commodity agreements have been devised as a means of supporting world food prices and of securing an 'orderly' disposal of food surpluses.[4] These measures are not always effective, but they

[1] R. J. Hammond, *Food: The Growth of Policy* (*History of the Second World War*, UK Civil Series, HMSO 1951), p. 394.

[2] Murray, *op. cit.*, p. 385. Average for 1936–9.

[3] Customs Duties (Dumping and Subsidies) Act, 1957.

[4] An important example is the International Wheat Agreement, whose vicissitudes illustrate very well the limitations to which this kind of international economic planning is subject. Governments are less willing than domestic taxpayers to tolerate artificial prices, and for a time the UK, the largest wheat importer, withdrew from the Agreement. However, the Agreement has had some success as a device for stabilization.

help to supplement other more direct forms of agricultural support. Consumers certainly are deprived of occasional supplies of very cheap food; but their loss can reasonably be held less serious than the damage to agricultural stability which would otherwise occur.

British farmers are not satisfied with this minimal degree of protection, however. They claim protection also against overseas farmers who can produce profitably at lower prices than themselves. This disparity arises partly from the advantages of various overseas countries for particular forms of production. British farmers do not possess the advantages of the North American prairies for wheat production, of the Argentine pampas for the raising of cattle, or of the year-round grassland of New Zealand for dairying. Even where they suffer no natural disadvantages, they seek protection against overseas producers whose economic efficiency is superior to their own, as is the case with Danish bacon producers. They also seek enlarged markets, even if these can only be secured by the exclusion of regular supplies of much cheaper imported food.

The extent to which this wider protection should be conceded is much more questionable. The natural and other advantages of overseas agricultures are factors in the international division of labour which have contributed to the development of mutually profitable patterns of trade. On the other hand, the revival and development of such trading patterns has been impeded since the war by balance of payments difficulties. These difficulties have supported the case for aiding the development of British agriculture, but the strength of this case, from a national economic standpoint, depends upon a complex variety of factors. These include the relative costs of home-grown and imported food, the scope for industrial exports whereby food can be purchased, the return to be expected from investment in British agriculture, and the general prospects of international trade.

It is not our purpose here to assess these complex factors, but to point out the general problem which had to be faced by the administrators of the Agriculture Act. In terms of the national balance of payments, the utility of support to British agriculture was bound to vary considerably at different times and for different commodities. The national economic purpose was therefore best served by considerable flexibility in both the level and the distribution of Government support to agriculture. However, if 'stability' was to have any real meaning and if agricultural development was to be wisely planned and executed, frequent or large variations in the support programme had to be avoided. At the same time the Government faced the difficulty of persuading farmers that even a moderate measure of flexibility was necessary. The Farmers' Union could not be easily wooed from its view that imports should be used simply to supply any physical balance of requirements that a developing British agriculture could not satisfy.

A protective shield for British agriculture can be provided in two principal ways. One method is to limit overseas competition by the use of tariffs or import quotas. The other method is to support the position of home producers through price guarantees or direct subsidies. While the term protection is usually reserved for the first alternative, both methods equally provide it. The most important difference between them is that tariffs or quotas increase the price of food, while direct support has to be paid for out of taxation. The question, in other words, is whether the cost falls upon Britons as consumers or as taxpayers.

In the period of the 1930's, British agriculture was protected by both methods through a variety of tariffs, import quotas, and subsidies. In the post-war period with which we are concerned the main emphasis has been placed upon the second alternative of direct support. Tariffs have been used mainly for horticulture, which is not covered by price guarantees, and import quotas have been used when it was essential to conserve foreign exchange but not usually as a means of preventing overseas' competition. The principal reasons for this preference for direct support have been the social disadvantages of raising food prices through tariffs, and the need to honour Commonwealth and international trade agreements.

Internally, the chief problems for agricultural policy derive from the diverse circumstances of British farming. Concepts of the 'average' farm and the 'average' farmer have very little meaning. A farm can be anything from a great mechanized unit of 700 acres with a a capital of £100,000 to a tiny subsistence holding. The gradation is continuous and every intermediate stage is represented. There is also a great variety of farming systems and methods for so small a total area. No general formula of state aid and control will easily fit these varied circumstances.

There are over 500,000 agricultural holdings of over one acre in the United Kingdom, but according to official sources there are not many more than 300,000 full-time farmers.[1] The difference is explained by large numbers of spare-time and part-time occupiers. The former group do not depend upon agriculture for their livelihood, but possess a small holding as a subsidiary occupation. Most holdings of under 5 acres are in this category, as are many larger holdings. By contrast, 'part-time' occupiers are those who do depend primarily upon agriculture for their livelihood, while possessing some supplementary occupation. The size of this group cannot be defined with any precision, since it tails off at each end into the 'spare-time' and the 'full-time' categories. However, the existence of this group increases the number

[1] *Assistance for Small Farmers*, Cmnd. 553, 1958, p. 6.

of those who depend primarily on farming to at least 350,000.[1]

PRINCIPAL FARM GROUPS (1952–3)
(England and Wales)

Area of Holding (Acres)*	Percentage of Total			
	No. of holdings	Land Acreage	Gross income†	Net income‡
5– 99	74	30	42	45
100–299	21	45	39	38
Over 300	5	25	19	17
	100	100	100	100

* Excludes rough grazings.

† Including value of produce consumed on farm, farm rent value, and government subsidies.

‡ Return for medium- and short-term capital, and for labour and management by farmers and their wives.

Based, with acknowledgement, on J. R. Raeburn, 'Agricultural Production and Marketing' in D. Burn (ed.), *Structure of British Industry*, Vol. 1 (1958), Table 1, p. 2.

The structure of farming in England and Wales is illustrated by the table. There are only 13,000 holdings with more than 300 acres, 64,000 with 100 to 300 acres, and over 200,000 with 5 to 100 acres. Possibly a third of this last group are not worked on a full-time basis,[2] but even if these are excluded the numerical preponderance of this group remains. The small farms cover under a third of the agricultural area, but they account for a considerably higher proportion of total output. Shortage of space compels the small farmer to work his limited area more intensively to earn a livelihood. Larger farms tend to become progressively more extensive, as interests shifts from output per acre to output per worker.

In managerial terms farms can also be divided into three main groups. About half the farms in England and Wales rely almost

[1] The 1951 Census (1 per cent sample) showed 317,000 'farmers, graziers, and crofters' in Britain. Adding an estimate for Northern Ireland, the total on this basis would have been about 370,000. The number is slowly declining.

[2] It has been estimated that there are about 80,000 holdings in England and Wales which do not provide adequate full-time employment for their occupiers. (B. E. Cracknell and H. Palca, 'Farm Size and Farm Business', *Agriculture*, March, 1959, Table 3). Many of these are spare- or part-time occupiers as defined above, but an unknown number depend exclusively on agriculture. In Scotland as many as 45 per cent of holdings, a figure which includes many crofts, are in the same category. (G. F. Hendry and O. J. Beilby, 'The Small Farm in Scotland', *Scottish Agricultural Economics*, Vol. 8, HMSO, Edinburgh).

wholly on family labour and employ no regular male worker. The middle group consists of those farmers who employ a few (1 to 4) regular workers, with the farmer often working in the field alongside his men. These farmers are often thought of, and with some justification, as the core of the farming community—the Dan Archers of England. Finally there is the small but important group of farms (about 5 per cent of the total) who employ more than five regular men workers.[1] Their farmers are mostly the managers of substantial enterprises and have incomes and outlooks to match.

In terms both of average size and of productivity per head, British farms fall somewhere between the more peasant economies of most European countries and the much more extensive farming systems of North America and Australasia. British farms are in general highly mechanized, but the quality of their equipment (particularly fixed equipment) is very variable and many farms are too small to take full advantage of modern machinery and techniques. Some of the smaller farms are highly efficient, but on most farms below 100 acres, the farmer is in effect working for the value of his own manual labour and getting a negligible or even negative return upon his capital and managerial skill, while on the smallest farms his income is frequently below the farm worker's.[2]

The typical qualities of a yeomanry—a strong family sense, attachment to locality, and an innate conservatism—are still much in evidence among working farmers. Their mobility is low, and many small farms have been handed down within the same family for many generations. Often they carry on until a ripe old age before passing on the farm to their sons, and the high average age of farmers is naturally a conservative influence.[3] The plentiful supply of farmers willing to work for a low return bids up the price of such small farms as come on the market. Many farmers are also reluctant to expand the scale of their enterprises, preferring a simpler, poorer, but easier life to the problematic quest for economic gain. While this may partly reflect a lack of the necessary skills to manage larger enterprises, it is also connected with their difficulty in securing capital.[4]

Farming involves a high capital investment in relation to turnover,

[1] Figures of labour distribution are based on G. P. Hirsch and K. E. Hunt, *British Agriculture* (National Federation of Young Farmers' Clubs, 1960, p. 61). Holdings of under 5 acres have been excluded.

[2] *Scale of Enterprise in Farming*, a report by the National Resources (Technical) Committee, HMSO, 1961, pp. 64 and 67. This report charts the nature of small farmers' problems, but it also points out that farming profits vary greatly among small (as among large) farmers.

[3] The traditionalism of a small farming community is well described in *The Sociology of an English Village* (Gosforth), by W. H. Williams (Routledge and Kegan Paul, 1956).

[4] Raeburn, *op. cit.*, pp. 21–30.

and modern technology has increased the capital required for efficient production. The organization of agriculture in numerous family enterprises makes it difficult for many farmers to secure enough capital on acceptable terms. The traditional solution to this problem in Britain has been for landlords to supply fixed capital for the land and buildings and for tenants to provide working capital in the form of livestock, machinery, seeds, etc. On some of the larger private and public estates this system still works reasonably well, but it has been greatly weakened by reductions in the landlords' powers and responsibilities. At the same time the proportion of farms which are owned by their occupiers, which was only 11 per cent in 1913, has steadily increased and is now about 40 per cent.[1]

In Britain there is also a great diversity of farming systems. The number of specialized farms which concentrate on one major end-product (such as milk or vegetables) is increasing, but most farms are 'combination-enterprises' growing several main products in varying proportions. The Ministry of Agriculture's classification of seventeen principal types of farming in England and Wales distinguished five 'pasture types' where dairying and livestock enterprises are dominant, six 'intermediate types' which produce both livestock and crops, and six 'arable types' where the production of crops is of major importance.[2]

This pattern reflects the considerable natural variations of rainfall, topography, and soil types. There is a broad distinction between the drier and flatter East, where farms are larger and arable production is important (particularly in East Anglia, the Yorkshire plain, and the Eastern Lowlands of Scotland), and the wetter and hillier West where small livestock farms are the general rule (particularly in the South-west, Wales, and Western Scotland). There are also, however, great regional and local variations in farming conditions—for example, most of the major farming systems are found within a twenty-mile radius of Sheffield.[3] Superimposed upon natural geography is the influence exerted by large markets, illustrated by the importance of market-gardening in the Lea valley and of dairying in the proximity of Liverpool, Manchester, and Glasgow. Again, a

[1] J. T. Ward, *Farm Rents and Tenure* (Estates Gazette, 1960), pp. 14–15. Total investment in British agriculture (at 1955 prices) has been estimated at £1,750 million in land and buildings and £1,500 million in crops, livestock and machinery. Both figures are approximate and subject to various qualifications. (S. C. Hooper, *The Finance of Farming in Great Britain* (Europa Publications, 1956), p. 30 and ch. 4.) This compared with an annual gross output of about £1,300 million (*Annual Review and Determination of Guarantees*, HMSO, 1955).

[2] L. D. Stamp, *The Land of Britain: Its Use and Misuse* (Longmans, Green & Co., 1950, 2nd ed.), ch. 15.

[3] A. M. Duckham, *The Fabric of Farming* (Chatto and Windus, 1958), pp. 72–78.

long and complex history of land use has left its imprint on farming patterns. It has shaped the size and lay-out of farms, factors which change only very slowly and which affect what individual farms can conveniently produce.

This diversity of farming systems interacts with variations in the skill and enterprise of the farmers themselves and in their access to capital to produce a highly heterogeneous pattern. Even where there are two adjacent farms of similar size and fertility, one may well have three times the output of the other, and be producing different products, because of large differences in management and capital. These differences are reinforced by the social and educational divisions of British rural life. Between those farmers who have been to public school, University or agricultural college and the great majority who left school at fourteen or fifteen there exists a considerable social gulf, although a fair number of substantial farmers belong to the latter category. The number of farmers who have had any formal agricultural training is extremely small.[1] There also exist special groups such as the landed aristocracy, many of whom carry on an active agricultural tradition, and the 'hobby-farmers' who farm (often through an agent) for interest rather than profit and whose agricultural activities are partly governed by complex calculations of tax liability.[2]

The more straightforward and usual forms of Government aid, such as general price guarantees, ignore the circumstances of individual farms and farmers. As a consequence the largest amounts of aid go to successful farmers, while the poorest farmers get least.This arrangement can be defended on the grounds that it does not bolster up inefficient farmers, but directs aid where it will be used most effectively. The policy helps agriculture generally, but does not distort its detailed functioning. However, it is far from certain that the market is always the most efficient method of allocating resources,

---

[1] A 1944 survey found that the proportion of farmers who had attended an agricultural college or farm institute was only about 3 per cent, but the proportion going to institutes (not colleges) has since increased. *Scale of Enterprise in Farming*, op. cit., p. 60.

[2] Because of the conflicting passions which this group arouses a brief description may be of some interest. According to the wartime National Farm Survey there were about 3,000 farms (1 per cent of the total) being run by a paid manager or bailiff on behalf of some business or professional man who visited the farms at weekends or occasionally. Many of these farms are technically progressive, although the owner's approach may tend towards showmanship and display rather than commercial farming. Often, however, he stays well in the background. A further 7,600 (2·6 per cent) were 'hobby' farmers proper whose occupiers farmed the land themselves primarily for a non-commercial reason. Many of these latter farms were unimportant agriculturally, often consisting of a paddock or 'small gentleman's estate'. *National Farm Survey of England and Wales: A Summary Report*, HMSO 1946, pp. 8–14. Since the war the agricultural significance of both types of hobby farming has grown.

especially in the case of British agriculture. Many larger farmers will continue to increase both their output and efficiency, whatever the state does, but many smaller farmers require help in overcoming intrinsic disadvantages. If help is not forthcoming, they will not necessarily make way for better farmers.

Another point is that the large differences in the profits of farmers are not due simply to differences in efficiency. Natural advantages (i.e., soil, climate, topography, location, etc.) also play a considerable part. According to classical economic theory, these natural advantages are equalized through the operation of rent. Farmer A whose land will grow 50 per cent more wheat per acre than Farmer B, pays a higher rent which offsets this advantage. In practice agricultural rents do not follow this theoretical model but are governed by legislation and traditional conventions which are difficult to change. Consequently, if state aid is unselective, Farmer A not only has the better land but also gets a higher subsidy in virtue of that fact.[1]

In any event the purposes of state aid are wider than that of giving general economic support to agriculture as a whole. State policy is also concerned with helping particular groups of farmers to overcome poverty and to farm better. This seems to call for a more selective system of aid, which does not allocate the bulk of public support to farmers who may not need it. The difficulty with selective aid is that it involves the state in deciding which farmers should get special help and on what terms. There is also the problem of limiting the extent to which selective aid promotes an uneconomic distribution of resources. For example, aid to the poorer farmers may produce an over-development of agriculture in remote and upland areas where many such farmers are congregated.

Thus both methods of aid are subject to considerable drawbacks. If generalized aid is to help the weaker and smaller farmers to much effect, it has to be fixed at a level which will entail a large and probably wasteful use of public funds. In these circumstances it seems prudent to make at least some use of selective aid, despite the administrative and economic difficulties which are certain to arise.

This brief review has shown that the 'stability' and the 'efficiency' propounded by the Agriculture Act are far from simple concepts. In administering the Act it was necessary to give concrete meaning to these concepts and to strike a balance between the often conflicting requirements of stability and efficiency. Naturally enough, the interpretations favoured by the farmers' leaders were bound to differ

---

[1] Of course, if surplus values did accrue to agricultural landlords, it would be possible to recoup a large proportion by a special rate of taxation. This procedure would combine the older case of the land-taxers with the newer case for taxing state-assisted profits.

considerably from those which seemed good to the Government. The circumstances of British agriculture set the background against which the post-war experiment in agricultural 'partnership' was to be played out.

CHAPTER II

FARMERS UNITED

1

THE National Farmers' Union is not only the most powerful organization in British agriculture but one of the most prominent trade unions in the nation. The great majority of farmers in the United Kingdom belong to the Union or to its Scottish and Ulster counterparts.[1] Its leaders are widely accepted as speaking for agriculture, even though this acceptance is tinged in some quarters with a certain scepticism. Internally, it manages to maintain a remarkably successful cohesion among the varied interests of Britain's farming community. Externally, its strategy lifts it for the most part above the level of party warfare and enables it to function, as Union leaders sometimes point out, almost as an arm of the state.

During the early part of the nineteenth century there were numerous agricultural societies and farmers' clubs scattered over the countryside, but in spite of occasional political forays, they remained true to their original object of promoting technical development.[2] In 1865 the Central Chamber of Agriculture was formed with the explicit purpose of looking after the welfare of agriculture in Parliament, and it remained the dominant agricultural organization for fifty years. It was led mainly by large landlords and, while not confining itself to their interests, tended to see the problems of agriculture from their point of view. It was especially active in matters immediately affecting landlords, such as local taxation; but much of its programme was of general benefit to agriculture, for example its successful efforts to promote stricter regulation of cattle disease. The Chamber even ventured into the extremely delicate field of landlord-tenant relations and gave its support to some modest changes in favour of tenant rights.

[1] Except when otherwise stated all references are to the National Farmers' Union of England and Wales, which is the largest of the three unions and which takes the lead in all matters affecting farmers throughout the United Kingdom.

[2] The official historian of the Central Chamber of Agriculture, A. H. H. Mathews, says of the farmers' clubs of the 1830's and 1840's: 'It was taken for granted that, with "the Squire" in Parliament, their political interests were safeguarded, and that all they had to do was to improve their methods of production; the idea that some machinery was required to spur their Member into doing his duty by them never entered the heads of these worthy farmers; such a suggestion would have been looked upon as little less than profane.' *Fifty Years of Agricultural Politics, Being the History of the Central Chamber of Agriculture, 1865–1915*. (London: P. S. King & Son Ltd., 1915), pp. 2–3.

Other agricultural groups also began to organize. In 1879 the Farmers' Alliance was formed to protect the interests of tenant farmers. As a defensive alliance, speaking only for tenants, it accepted the established order and did not aspire to a position of agricultural leadership. It never reached a position of influence and gradually died out.[1] In the 1890's the Earl of Winchilsea launched the National Agricultural Union in an effort to combine agricultural workers with landowners and farmers into a comprehensive organization. Its active leaders, however, were still drawn from the landed interest. The Central Chamber of Agriculture, conscious of the need for the landlords to broaden their basis of support but fearful of losing its position of leadership, maintained a cautious liaison with the new organization. Lord Winchilsea's group foundered soon after his death in 1898 and was eventually transformed into a central organization of agricultural co-operatives.

The founders of the National Farmers' Union acted on the belief that the three branches of agriculture, while interdependent, ought to have their own unions. Formed in 1908, the Union was at first composed mainly of tenant farmers and was especially concerned with their problems. It criticized those organizations purporting to represent all agricultural groups on the grounds that in such organizations (as its first secretary mildly put it) 'the tenant farmer would necessarily have but a limited chance of speaking his mind'.[2] In these early years the Union sometimes referred to itself as a body of 'practical tenant farmers'. However, by inviting as members all 'farmers in actual practice', the Union made the general interests of farmers, not only their interests as tenants, the basic principle of its organization. Thus, knowingly or not, was laid the organizational basis for the transfer of rural leadership from landowner to farmer.

Circumstances were ideal for the growth of the organization. Agriculture was slowly emerging from a long depression, and both recent hard times and prospective improvement served as incentives to united action. The landlords' power was gradually being broken by the application of death duties and by a series of Acts restricting their control over their tenant farmers.[3] The number of owner-occupiers was growing; and farmers, whether owner-occupiers or tenants, were coming to think of themselves as having a common interest. With its exclusively farmer basis the Union quickly out-

[1] Mathews remarks that the Farmers' Alliance was 'a sectional movement' based upon 'the supposed interests of tenant farmers . . . as apart from the general interests of the industry as a whole'. He notes, with some satisfaction, that the tenants' organization broke up over the Protection issue. A similar organisation, the Federation of Farmers' Associations, was initiated in the 1890's, 'but it also soon died a natural death'. *Ibid.*, p. 7.

[2] National Farmers' Union, *Yearbook*, 1910, p. 6.

[3] See below, Chapter VIII, pp. 178-9.

distanced its main rivals. In 1915 the chairman of the Central Chamber of Agriculture wrote that 'the loyal cohesion of agriculturists of all classes for the protection of themselves and their industry is more than ever essential'. In performing this task the Chamber welcomed the assistance of 'other and younger organizations formed for a like purpose' and reminded them of its own contribution for over half a century. This was perhaps the last time the landed interest could speak with such supreme confidence in its own leadership.[1]

The First World War brought prosperity to agriculture, and 'agriculture' was coming to mean farmers rather than landowners. Almost accidentally, the Union found itself a major force in agricultural politics as it was called upon to play an important role in policy formulation and execution. Its membership leaped from 20,000 in 1913 to more than 100,000 in the early 1920's. Even with the subsequent agricultural depression, the Union managed to conserve much of its strength. Membership figures become rather vague for this period—as they have a tendency to do during times of organizational stress—but it appears that after suffering a decline in the mid-twenties, membership again began slowly to move upward toward the end of the decade and reached 120,000 by 1935.[2]

First in the field as a general farmers' organization, the Union was remarkably free from serious competition. During the 1920's it did face a potential challenge from a statutory organization which it had helped to found. The Ministry of Agriculture and Fisheries Act of 1919 required county councils to establish agricultural committees. Each of these committees, in turn, appointed two members to a Council of Agriculture for England, which also contained direct representatives of the industry appointed by the Minister. The Council had no executive powers, but it held periodic public meetings and it advised the Minister on agricultural questions.[3] The Union had helped to promote an unofficial body which served as a model for the new Council, and it supported the launching of the new organization and accepted representation on it; but it was always somewhat dubious about the possible implications of this statutory 'parliament of agriculture'. It might become a useful instrument managed by the Union, but it might on the other hand become a rival of formidable proportions. When, in 1924, the Council 'adopted a report which

[1] Mathews, *Fifty Years of Agricultural Politics*, p. x. The Chamber continued in existence for many years, its affairs finally coming to a close in 1959 with the donation of its trust fund to the National Farmers' Union and the Country Landowners' Association. *The British Farmer*, August 22, 1959, p. 27.

[2] On membership figures see the Union's annual *Yearbook*s and its official journal, *The British Farmer*, for January 31, 1949 and February 1, 1950.

[3] See Sir Francis Floud, *The Ministry of Agriculture and Fisheries* (G. P. Putnam's Sons Ltd., 1927), pp. 17 ff. The 1919 Act also raised the old Board of Agriculture to Ministerial rank.

claimed that this statutory body expresses the authoritative opinion of agriculturists', the Union became seriously alarmed and recommended that all of its members on the Council relinquish their positions.[1] The boycott was successful, and the Council dwindled into insignificance.

The second and largest growth in the Union's membership occurred during and after the Second World War. Membership rose steadily from 125,000 in 1939 to a peak of 210,000 in 1953, but then fell back to 194,000 in 1957, the last year for which membership figures have been published. This membership figure can be compared with a total of about 220,000 full-time farmers in England and Wales. Membership does not consist exclusively of full-time farmers, since some retired farmers and farmers' sons belong, and since part-time farmers and smallholders are eligible for membership. The Union has no acreage qualification and no national records of its members' holdings by size, but it is unlikely that many part-time farmers are members while a fair proportion of the smaller full-time farmers have not joined either.[2] Many of these are intrinsically difficult to recruit and are less inclined than the larger farmers to equate their interests with Union policy. Indeed, some of them belong to the workers' union. For these reasons, the National Farmers' Union was never justified in claiming to have reached 90 per cent of its potential membership, and a fair estimate for 1961 would not put the figure higher than 75 or 80 per cent.[3] Even so, the degree of unionization which has been achieved is extraordinarily high for so dispersed, heterogeneous, and individualistic an occupation.

2

Throughout most of its career the Union's major problem has been to evolve a successful political strategy. Its rise in membership was accompanied by a growing influence in parliamentary and governmental circles, but the political influence of farmers, wartime apart, remained rather weak until 1945. Only in recent years has the Union

[1] National Farmers' Union, *Yearbook*, 1925, p. 217.

[2] A survey of small farmers in an industrial part of Yorkshire revealed that only 38 per cent of full-time farmers belonged to the Union. J. B. Butler in *The Small Farms of Industrial Yorkshire* (University of Leeds Department of Agriculture, 1958), p. 29. The low level of farm incomes and the industrial character of this area doubtless account for the poor membership record. The Union's decline in membership between 1953 and 1957 was greater in the north-west and south-west, where there are many small farmers, than elsewhere.

[3] This is roughly consistent with an estimate by the chairman of the Union's Organization and Assessment Committee that something less than 50,000 'working farmers' do not belong to the Union; however, the definition and number of 'working farmers' on which this estimate is based is not given. *The British Farmer*, June 4, 1960, p. 6.

at last found—it may be only temporarily—an effective solution to its basic political problem.

The early aspirations of the Union were modest and limited. 'What is to be done? How are we to better ourselves?' were the questions said to have been asked by Colin Campbell and his fellow Lincolnshire farmers in 1904. 'And nobody had any idea how they could better themselves until a few of them met together and said they would have to form themselves into a Union if they were to make themselves heard.'[1] 'Defence Not Defiance' was the motto adopted by the Union which was formed under Campbell's leadership four years later. The Union's first programme included requests for further relief for agriculture from local rates; increased appropriations for roads, education, and the Board of Agriculture; the abolition of preferential railway rates on imported produce; and greater security for agricultural tenants. No radical changes were demanded, either in the organization of the agricultural industry or in government policy. The Union at that time carefully avoided taking a position on the fundamental political issues of the day, even where the interests of agriculture were directly involved: 'It is not the farmers' business to tell the nation what our national agricultural policy should be. . . .'[2]

The influence of farmers in general, and of the Farmers Union in particular, will depend on there being as little intrusion as possible upon those issues of Free Trade and Protection, of extensive and intensive culture, of combined or individual development which legitimately excite party interest and economic schools, but which are not vital to a working dividend on the farm.[3]

During these early years the emphasis was very much on self defence in a struggle of each against all. Farmers were informed of the progress made in other industries by means of trade unions and urged in strong language that they had no choice but to support one of their own.

The question we propose to ask you is whether you think you are safe, at a time when every trade is combining AGAINST EVERY OTHER, in remaining outside your own Farmers' Union. Against every other, mind you. Every trade in the world is combined against yours. Dare you risk isolation?[4]

[1] W. Howard (a founder of the National Farmers' Union), quoted in Tom Tiffin, *The Origins of the National Farmers' Union* (Watersale, North Lincolnshire: *Lincolnshire Chronicle*, 1949), p. 25.
[2] National Farmers' Union, *Yearbook*, 1926, p. 99.
[3] *Ibid.*, 1917, p. 68.
[4] 'Dare You Risk It? Plain Facts for the Outsider,' National Farmers' Union propaganda leaflet, quoted *Ibid.*, 1913, p. 114.

As part of this struggle the Union immediately turned its attention
to the problem of parliamentary representation. One of the major
reasons given for the Union's establishment was that the interests of
farmers were too generally ignored by both major political parties.
The Lincolnshire Union reflected in 1907 that,

> however bitterly the two great parties of the State were opposed on
> many questions, as regards agriculture they were equally indifferent;
> the one side counting on the unreasoning support, and the other side
> on the bitter opposition of the farmers. The one felt confident they
> would not lose support, and the other that they were unlikely to gain
> any.[1]

Although intensely interested in parliamentary affairs, the Union
had no intention of making an alliance with one party or the other.
It aimed to 'place agricultural questions above party, and so keep
the Union free from all party questions; in other words, to lift politics
out of agriculture, and uplift agriculture above politics'.[2] The specific
objective was to promote in the House of Commons a bloc of
Members who would be independent of party ties so far as agriculture was concerned. By setting out a programme for which it invited
pledges of support and by sponsoring the candidatures of a few
practical farmers, the Union hoped to be in a position to manipulate
the balance of power on any agricultural issue coming before the
House: 'we can hold the key to the situation and the balance of
parties in our hands that will make it impossible for any Government
to turn a deaf ear to the just and reasonable and legitimate wants of
the agriculturists of this country.'[3]

In 1909 the Union approached the party whips in an effort to find
constituencies for farmer candidates, but no arrangements could be
made. In the Parliament elected in 1910, however, sixty-eight Members (including fifty Unionists, sixteen Liberals, and two Labour
Members) pledged their support of the Union's programme. The list
grew slowly, but the pledged members did not act in concert. In 1913,
the Union appointed its first paid Parliamentary lobbyist to put forward its views and to maintain contacts with Members who had
promised their support.[4]

[1] Quoted by A. W. Palmer (general secretary), 'Programme and Policy of the
National Farmers' Union Briefly Reviewed,' *Ibid.*, 1910, p. 7.

[2] *Ibid.*, p. 6. One of the Union's criticisms of the Central Chamber of Agriculture was that its two presidents, one a Conservative and the other a Liberal
Member of Parliament, thought as party politicians first. *Ibid.*, 1917, p. 69.

[3] Seth Ellis Dean (chairman of Lincolnshire Farmers' Union), 'A Plea for
Combination', *Ibid.*, 1912, pp. 1, 13.

[4] Of its lobbyist, Mr G. Weller Kent, the Union reported that 'though he did
not lay claim to agricultural knowledge, he possessed intimate acquaintance with

In 1917 the Union went on record in support of proportional representation as a means of assisting a distinct agricultural representation, and in the General Election of the following year it sponsored six independent 'agricultural' candidates recommended by county branches, all of whom were defeated in what were mostly three- and four-cornered fights.[1] Much better progress seemed to be made, however, in constructing a bloc of friendly party Members. At the same Election, no less than 143 of the successful candidates (mostly Unionists and Coalition Liberals but with a sprinkling of other parties) had pledged their full support to the Union's programme. These members proceeded to form an all-party agricultural committee, but the success proved superficial. The programme for which so much support had been found was not sufficiently concrete to induce united action among its supporters, and it proved in practice completely ineffective.[2] When the Union made its next programme much more detailed and specific the number of parliamentary supporters fell to forty-five. The Union took what comfort it could in a more reliable knowledge of who were its friends and of the constituencies where organizational effort was especially needed.[3]

In the 1922 election four 'direct representatives of the Union' were elected, 'the first occasion on which the organized working farmers of England and Wales have secured representation by men from their own ranks'.[4] Direct representatives they may have been, but they were, like all succeeding Members sponsored by the Union, Conservatives—though one or two listed themselves as 'independent on agricultural questions'. Besides the four successful Conservatives, the Union had also sponsored three 'agricultural independents' who all lost.

The Union published a list of the names of its Parliamentary friends for the last time in 1924, remarking the following year that thirty of the members returned for agricultural constituencies in the recent General Election had given full support to its programme and ninety-four had given partial support. 'In view of the great preponderance of Conservative representation of agricultural constituen-

many members of the House of Commons, and methods of Parliamentary procedure which should prove of great advantage to the National Farmers' Union'. *Ibid.*, 1913, p. 68.

[1] *Ibid.*, 1917, pp. 41–42; 1918, pp. 98 ff. In addition to the six independent candidates, the *Yearbook* for 1918 listed six other Union members who had contested seats without official Union support: two Liberal, one Labour, one Labour-Agricultural, and one Coalition candidate. Only the last was successful.

[2] The programme consisted of five broad points calling for greater security of tenure, revision of local taxation, better and cheaper transport facilities for home-grown produce, better housing and living conditions for the agricultural labourer, and a 'fair return' to farmers for their capital and labour.

[3] *Ibid.*, 1919, p. 57.

[4] *Ibid.*, 1923, p. 196.

cies, it was not thought worth while to publish an analysis of the support given to the Union's programme, but the information will be used by Headquarters as occasion arises.'[1] The plain truth of the matter was that the effort to build and maintain an independent force in the House of Commons had failed, and at about this time the all-party agricultural committee broke up. It was found far more difficult to get politicians to agree on concrete measures than to give verbal support to a broad programme.

This same situation had earlier caused the Central Chamber of Agriculture to attempt to launch an independent agricultural party, but the project was (in the words of the historian of the Chamber) 'completely destroyed by the obstruction of a small group of members' who opposed linking the new party to the Chamber.[2] The Union's promotion of independent candidates was sometimes seen as a way to create the nucleus of such a party, but the major aim was the narrower one of securing direct Union representation. Although the subject continued to be discussed right up to the 1940's, the Union generally regarded a separate agricultural party as impracticable and over-ambitious—as indeed it was.

In the Union's early years its leadership had a considerable colouring of liberal and radical political opinion, in spite of the predominantly conservative views of the countryside. One of the post-war Presidents had been an unsuccessful Liberal candidate for Parliament, and another was known to hold 'pronounced Liberal and Free Trade views'.[3] By the late 1920's most of the leaders were Conservative, although in 1926 the Union unsuccessfully opposed the by-election candidature of the new Conservative Minister of Agriculture because of disappointment with his party's policies and his own unsatisfactory reply to a questionnaire submitted by the county branch.[4] Even great irritation with the way the Union was treated by the 1929–31 Labour Government seemed not to shake headquarters' neutral resolution. No candidates were recommended by branches for endorsement in the election of 1931, and the Union again professed its lack of concern in party politics. Although it was in fact happy to see the end of the Labour Government, it sought to discourage its branches from becoming associated with an 'Agricultural Party' that was being promoted as a rural wing of the Conservative organization.[5]

[1] *Ibid.*, 1925, p. 247.
[2] Mathews, *Fifty Years of Agricultural Politics*, pp. 340–48 and Appendix 5. Mathews quotes the report of a special committee of the Chamber which indignantly catalogued the failure of the eighty Chamber members in Parliament to give any help to their organization.
[3] National Farmers' Union, *Yearbook*, 1917, p. 85; 1919, p. 3.
[4] *Ibid.*, 1929, p. 207.
[5] *Ibid.*, 1933, p. 408.

Nevertheless the Union found itself drawn increasingly into the Conservative camp by the failure of alternative policies. At the county level, particularly with the decline of the Liberal Party, the Union's branches saw little point in neutrality, and many of them established more or less open alliances with local Conservative groups. In Parliament the Union continued to be represented by one or two Conservative Members, one of whom (Major, later Sir Reginald, Dorman Smith) was its President at the time of his election and subsequently became Minister of Agriculture. Union headquarters continued to profess a rather precarious political neutrality, defending its sponsorship of Conservative candidates on the grounds that in no other way could it obtain direct influence in Parliament. This non-partisan claim was never abandoned, but it could not during the 1930's be taken very seriously. During this period, as Sir Ivor Jennings remarks, the Union's politics consisted of 'discriminating support to the Conservative party'.[1]

The Union's vacillating strategy during the inter-war period was uncomfortable and frustrating, but it was not without some modest success. The Union was instrumental in securing, for example, the important subsidies for sugar beet and for wheat which were especially beneficial to the East Anglian farmers who at that time dominated the Union's councils.[2] It also successfully insisted that agricultural marketing legislation should be coupled with controls over agricultural imports. Once its initial doubts about the desirability of marketing boards had been resolved, the Union played an active part in their creation and operation.[3] For a time it looked as if agriculture's salvation was to be sought in the direction of state-supported schemes of self-help.

Developments in the Second World War, however, shifted the Union's general strategy to different lines. The Government needed

[1] *Parliament* (Cambridge University Press, 1939), p. 178. Jennings's emphasis on the farmer-Tory alliance, however, leads him to miss the ambivalence of the Union's strategy during these years. It was not correct, even between the wars, to say that 'the Union cannot pretend and does not pretend that it is impartial in the party sense' (p. 212). The Union never abandoned precisely that claim. Jennings repeats these remarks in the second edition (1957, pp. 189, 221), by which time they were without any foundation whatever.

[2] An exaggerated but not entirely incorrect view of these farmers is provided by A. G. Street: 'They might not be able to produce either grain or meat profitably at time's prices by their old methods, but they could produce noise. And they did. Somehow or other there had grown up in London and most of England's large towns an agreed opinion that farming in England meant wheat first, East Anglia second, and the remainder of agricultural England nowhere at all.

'So the farming community of this district played up to this fallacy. Its members produced noise all over East Anglia, noise in London clubs, noise in the headquarters of the NFU, and noise whenever and wherever possible.' *Farming England* (B. T. Batsford Ltd., 1937), p. 74.

[3] See below, Chapter IV, pp. 88-90.

the Union's assistance in the conversion of agriculture to a wartime basis. Regular consultations between the Minister of Agriculture and representatives of the Union were begun in 1939 and continued throughout the war. The Union co-operated in exhorting farmers to greater efforts and became the recognized 'mouthpiece of the farmers' point of view in respect to the many and varied food production problems which arise in wartime.'[1] Almost without realizing it, the Union abandoned its old cautious policy of 'defence not defiance' and instead shouldered widening responsibility for agricultural policy in exchange for an increasing measure of influence over it. The decisive and most significant example of the new 'partnership' was the price review, which is discussed in the next chapter. But in other matters of high policy as well, such as agricultural marketing and import controls, the pattern of consultation became much closer than ever before. In hundreds of matters of detail, from the supply of binder twine to the acquisition of land for military purposes, and on dozens of official advisory committees, Whitehall and the Union's old headquarters at Bedford Square were drawn together.

These developments pointed the way to a new orientation of Union strategy. Formerly the Union's main aim had been to use farmers' organizational strength to increase their power in Parliament. This power was not only difficult to manipulate; it was intrinsically extremely weak. The farmers' voting strength was too small for them to make much direct Parliamentary impact, while politicians had generally assumed that the great majority of farmers would vote Conservative anyhow. In Whitehall, however, the Union could make a much greater impact. Here among the guardians of tradition and precedent, a pattern of close consultation, once established, tended to perpetuate itself. Here the Union's privileged consultative position, its professional staff, and its well-briefed and experienced leaders could have their greatest effect. The Union therefore accorded priority to its connections with Whitehall, regulating its relations with Westminster in the light of this paramount aim.

This strategy required the Union to make at last a reality of its long professed principle of political impartiality. This the Union set out to do after the war, and it was favoured by a most fortunate set of circumstances. During the General Election of 1945 it took a position of strict neutrality between the parties, but there is no doubt that many of its leaders were uneasy about the advent of a Labour Government. The Union reiterated its neutrality and hoped for the best: 'agriculture while of necessity in politics, must be above the plane of party conflict; and . . . the Union, a non-party body, must work as far as possible with the Government of the day'.[2] Any fears

[1] National Farmers' Union, *Yearbook*, 1940, p. 23.
[2] *Ibid.*, 1946, p. 84.

the Union had soon proved unfounded. It was possible to work with the Labour Government far more closely and satisfactorily than any of the farmers' leaders had expected. Mr Attlee, the first Prime Minister ever to speak at the Union's annual dinner, emphasized in 1946 the Government's desire to continue the 'close consultation between the Government and the industry' on which wartime policies had been based.[1]

In the closely fought elections of 1950 and 1951, the Union adhered firmly to its political neutrality. Although one of its leaders, Mr G. R. H. (later Sir Richard) Nugent, became a Parliamentary Secretary to the Ministry of Agriculture in the new Conservative Government, there was now no question at all of the Union's surrendering its independent position as the farmers' spokesman for that of junior associate of a political party. In point of fact, the Conservative approach to agriculture was less to the Union's taste than that of Labour, although the pattern of close consultation continued. A mead of disappointment with Conservative policies was thrown into the balance against the time-worn propensities of most of the Union's rank and file. The result was to keep the Union firmly non-partisan again in the General Elections of 1955 and 1959.

Few Union leaders imagine that their slogan, 'Keep agriculture out of politics,' means that agricultural policy can be uncontroversial or non-political. Its practical meaning is that agriculture should be kept as far as possible out of *party* politics and that the principal matters of concern to agriculture should be settled in Whitehall and not in Westminster. Guaranteed prices, the Union insisted in 1955, 'are not a matter of party politics but of common sense' and 'a matter of national interest'.[2] The Union much prefers that these questions should be discussed and settled in statesmanlike conclave between itself and the Government of the day.

3

As the Union's national power has increased, its internal structure has undergone a metamorphosis. Its traditions of decentralization and amateur leadership have given way to centralized policy-making by a small professional leadership, while it has steadily consolidated and strengthened its claim to speak for the whole body of English and Welsh farmers.

The Union originated as a kind of federation, and its local units

[1] *NFU Record*, February, 1946, pp. 101–2.
[2] 'NFU Bulletin', Cyclo. No. 1029/155, May 3, 1955 (mimeo). Many Liberals would not agree with these sentiments, and the Union's neutrality does not extend so far as to ignore Liberal criticism which it has attacked as 'a diversionary attack on the entire system of support for agriculture. . . '. *The British Farmer*, May 31, 1958, p. 53; see July 5, 1958, p. 9.

continue to feel that the national organization is, or ought to be, their creature. Each county branch is composed of area and specialist branches, and a farmer becomes a member of the Union by joining one of these. His subscription is paid to the county office, not to headquarters, and at one time the counties set their own subscription rates. Within limits (which before the Second World War were very broad), the county branches make their own rules and settle their own organization. They select their own staff quite independently of headquarters.

Formally the county branch is governed by an executive committee, composed of delegates of the local and specialist branches, but this body tends to be large—an executive of over a hundred is not uncommon—and the active leadership is to be found within a much smaller group. The almost universal practice of changing the county chairman every year or two means that he shares leadership with a group of 'elder statesmen' and committee chairmen, some of whom may have far more influence in the organization than he. The other elected positions of importance are the delegates to the Union's national council, but they often suffer from the stigma of being associated more with headquarters than with the county.

The power behind the throne is likely to be the county secretary. His is a peculiarly independent position, for once appointed by the executive committee he enjoys in practice almost permanent tenure. He is paid partly by the county, partly by funds from headquarters, and partly by the Mutual Insurance Society which is described below. Servant of all, he is mastered by none. Often a man of no agricultural experience prior to his Union employment, he soon acquires more knowledge of Union affairs and influence in the county branch than all but the most exceptional lay leaders.

A principal source of the county secretary's influence is his responsibility for the local administration of the Union's numerous services to members. He is assisted by a number of full-time group secretaries, each of whom serves several local branches. In its early years the Union laid heavy emphasis on its legal services. The theme of its propaganda, characteristic of the formative stage of organizations of this kind, was that the individual's environment consisted largely of hostile forces ready to involve him in legal disputes which he certainly could not afford and probably could not win. 'How do you think you will stand if one of these big corporations should come up against you?' non-members were asked. 'You will simply go under. You cannot afford to fight. You will be at the mercy of every aggressive corporation which finds out you are silly enough not to belong to your Union.'[1] Ominously, the Union added that many

[1] 'Can You Afford It? A Plain Word to the Unorganized Farmer,' propaganda leaflet reprinted in National Farmers' Union, *Yearbook*, 1912, p. 76.

disputes are between farmer and farmer. If both were members of the Union, it was blandly explained, the dispute would be arbitrated in a friendly way; but if only one were a member the other might find himself with the great weight of the Union against him.

Legal services and quasi-legal advice, while still provided, are today much less important to members than assistance in finding their way around the complex governmental machinery on which they so greatly depend. Among the matters dealt with by a group secretary during one week were: five National Service deferments, compensation under the Town and Country Planning Acts, and local authority water charges. He also gave advice on a contemplated farm purchase, the settlement of a claim against a potato dealer, a rent dispute, an accident claim, a contemplated partnership, a company formation, a mortgage difficulty, and a rail damage claim; but he reported that he had not included 'the ordinary every-day calls affecting A[gricultural] E[xecutive] C[ommittee] matters, Deficiency payments claims, form filling, insurance, electricity supplies, F[at-stock] M[arketing] C[orporation], etc.'[1]

Another inducement held out to farmers has always been cheap insurance, which started with the negotation by county branches of reduced premiums for members. In 1919 headquarters succeeded in getting the rather reluctant approval of the branches for the establishment of the National Farmers' Union Mutual Insurance Society. This is a limited company, independently constituted and managed by its own board of directors. Only members of the Union are eligible to insure with the Mutual, and this service contributes much to the Union's hold on its membership. The Mutual also makes small contributions to the funds of county branches and the salaries of county secretaries. More important, the Union's field men, the group secretaries, are the sole agents for the Mutual in their areas. While they are pàid a small salary by the Union, they also receive commissions from the Mutual. Without this assistance the Union could not maintain anything like its present extensive local organization.[2]

In the past the branches' independence was protected by a very substantial finaпcial autonomy. The national organization was supported by an annual assessment of a portion of county subscription income (usually between 40 and 50 per cent), although some of the poorer counties were allowed remissions. In 1948 a suggestion from the Lincolnshire branch that a million pound 'fighting fund' be raised by voluntary means was transformed by headquarters into a proposal to increase the subscription rate and to change the basis of Union

[1] *The County Farmers' Journal for Cambridgeshire, N.W. Essex and S.W. Suffolk*, March 1956, pp. 16–18.
[2] See National Farmers' Union Norfolk County Branch, *Annual Report*, 1953–54, p. 4; *The Farmers' Weekly*, January 15, 1960, p. 45.

finance. The counties were asked to give up only 37½ per cent of their increased income but to turn over 90 per cent of any unexpended surplus to a national reserve fund. The Council accepted this proposal despite strong opposition from several branches, including Lincolnshire, which viewed it as a 'subterfuge' on the part of headquarters 'to camouflage their long-thought-of proposals for increasing subscriptions.'[1] Partly because of irritation with headquarters tactics, the counties' contributions to the reserve fund fell far short of expectation.

In 1955 the subscription rates were again raised, and another method of assessment was instituted, aimed at equalizing the services provided by the county branches, providing adequate revenue for the headquarters organization, and building up a reserve fund. The details of the scheme are exceedingly complex, but its essential feature is a series of judgments by headquarters of each county's 'ability to pay'. It represents a move in the direction of centralized finance, though mitigated by the Union's still powerful tradition of local autonomy. The new subscriptions did not produce the income predicted, and inflation and increasing demands for services further weakened the Union's financial position.[2] In 1960 the rates were again increased, this time very substantially, to a basic subscription of £3, together with 1s for every acre of a member's land.[3]

The most significant change in Union affairs has occurred in its national leadership. Headquarters is responsible for the co-ordination of the various field services, but its main task is to bring the farmers' organized power to bear upon public policy. Until 1945 this aspect of the Union's work, although greatly expanded during the war, was the responsibility of part-time amateur leaders. In that year the Council elected as president thirty-seven year old Mr James Turner (now Lord Netherthorpe), who served continuously until his retirement in 1960. In 1945 the Council also took the unusual step of appointing the previous president, Mr J. K. Knowles, to the position of general secretary. In Turner and Knowles the Union discovered a team ideally suited to the circumstances of the post-war period, and its members had the sense to keep the team together as long as they could. The Council gave official recognition to the virtual professionalization of its leadership when it decided in 1946 to pay the president a regular salary of £5,000 a year. It also offered in 1956 to provide him with a free residence near London, but the proposal was

---

[1] *The Farmers' Weekly*, October 22, 1948, p. 23; see October 8, 1948, p. 25; and *The British Farmer*, November 30, 1948, p. 3; April 30, 1949, p. 1.
[2] See *Ibid.*, January 10, 1959, p. 8; January 9, 1960, p. 21.
[3] *Ibid.*, January 7, 1961, pp. 24, 26. The acreage subscription for horticultural land is assessed at varying rates, ranging from 1s 6d to £3 4s per acre.

roughly treated by a section of the press and eventually abandoned at Turner's request.[1]

Dominant personalities are the usual pattern in some organizations; but in the old National Farmers' Union, once Colin Campbell had set it on its way, no commanding figures appeared for many years. Turner, in contrast, will be long remembered, and he set his stamp on the whole organization. Urbane enough to put the countryman's case in Whitehall, but rustic enough to assure members that his loyalties were sound, he was almost universally admired by farmers, even those who did not like his policy or were suspicious of the Union itself. He was once described by an irritated politician as the 'sacred bull' of British agriculture,[2] but farmers saw him rather as a sturdy John Bull, complete with broad Yorkshire accent, and full of the qualities they like best in themselves. Knowles was complementary in every respect. While Turner's character, like his figure, suits the public platform, Knowles is more comfortable behind a desk and behind the scene. Even aside from personal qualities, this team acquired more experience of high level policy-making than almost all of the public servants concerned with agriculture.

The Union's leadership has often been subjected to sharp questioning from branch delegates at the annual general meetings, but Turner was remarkably adept in managing these meetings. One suspects that the delegates were long back at their farms before they realized (if they ever did) the extent of the President's guidance, with his stern reminders, his stout platitudes, and his charming assurances. He customarily represented himself as a pliable instrument altogether in his members' hands; and in 1951 *The Farmers' Weekly* praised, apparently without irony, 'the democratic and easy way' in which the annual general meeting of that year had been conducted and Turner's 'constantly referring to it as "your meeting"'.[3] Nine years later the editor of *The Farmers' Weekly* had acquired a keener insight, assisted by the rather freer use that Turner was making of his characteristic technique.

... with that charming disregard of common procedure at general meetings which makes the NFU so beautifully different, the president was careful to point out that the resolution being lost did not mean that headquarters would not act upon the spirit which inspired it.

By the same token, it might have been said that had the resolution been passed it did not follow that headquarters would act upon it.[4]

---

[1] NFU 'Press Release' (mimeo), January 24, 1956.
[2] Sir L. Plummer, H. of C.O.R., Standing Committees, 1956/57, Vol. I, col. 28.
[3] February 2, 1951, p. 27.
[4] January 29, 1960, p. 43.

The formal policy-making body of the Union is not the annual conference but the Council, consisting of about 120 delegates elected by county branches and twenty-five co-opted members who are mostly past and present office-holders and chairmen of minor committees. This body provides an opportunity each month for broad discussion and for the ventilation of particular problems; but the ordinary Council member is not at the centre of decisive deliberations, however much, back in his county, he may pretend the contrary. Although Turner was always surrounded by a group of interested and capable counsellors, his very long tenure did inevitably restrict the opportunities open to leading Council members. In 1946 the office of deputy president was established as a rather unsatisfactory substitute goal for aspiring leaders.

During this time decisions generally emanated from President and general secretary, assisted by an inner circle of advisers on particular subjects. The old East Anglian predominance was replaced by a broader geographical distribution of leadership, though most of the leaders continued to be substantial farmers.[1] The members of this second rank of Union leadership held most of the strategic positions on the Council's numerous committees. In addition to the main commodity committees, there are a few committees of special importance, although no one of them qualifies as the nerve centre of the organization. The general purposes committee, consisting of all committee chairmen and a few co-opted members, deals with general policy; but it includes many members whose influence is confined to rather specialized fields. The small parliamentary committee analyses proposed legislation, organizes the presentation of Union views in Parliament, and watches over the administration of important statutes. The organization and assessment committee deals with internal affairs. The economics and taxation committee plays an important part in connection with price reviews. The labour committee decides Union tactics on the Agricultural Wages Board.

In view of the Union's tradition of frequently changed leaders, it is not surprising that the consolidation of leadership should have given rise to a certain amount of grumbling, forcibly expressed in the assertion of one farmer that 'a thing is not right merely because Sir James Turner says it is'.[2] No farmers' leader, including Turner, has ever had a placid following. Despite the usual complaints about poorly attended meetings,[3] the county branches continued to be active in forwarding their views, their complaints, and their apprehensions to headquarters and they remained extremely jealous of their

[1] See, for example, the series of articles in *The British Farmer* on committee chairmen, beginning June 4, 1960.
[2] *The British Farmer*, August, 1949, p. 8.
[3] *Ibid.*, March, 1957, p. 3; April 4, 1959, p. 4.

prerogatives. In 1957, for example, the Union's journal reported that the Council approved by a small majority a proposal that county secretaries be brought to London not more than twice a year to attend Council sessions, 'but not before delegates had had to be assured that headquarters were intending no sinister design for tightening their grip on the counties, and secretaries were not really wanted for brain washing'.[1]

In general, however, Turner's long tenure and large discretion were the result of a delegation seen to be highly advantageous and even necessary. The delegation having been made, he did acquire a kind of indispensability, but this did not grow, as it has in some organizations, out of a shortage of men competent to assume positions of responsibility; nor was it characterized by an absence of lieutenants and critics of some independent stature either at headquarters or in the counties. All of this was well understood by the president and other national leaders and even, in a more general way, by the rank and file. Turner's leadership received impressive annual confirmation; for, as a result of a rule suggested by himself, each re-election required a majority of 85 per cent of the Council members present when the vote was taken.[2]

While farmers were generally satisfied with the way their Union was managed, there did exist, especially as the years wore on, a certain amount of justified uneasiness about the long-term effects of Turner's rule, of centralization, and of the close relations between Union headquarters and government. A few went so far as to demand 'a reshuffle at NFU headquarters from the top downwards, and a resumption of the practice that there should be a new president each year, as this is the only method by which the NFU can retain its independence of the Government and freshen up its ideas'.[3] But to most farmers 'independence' and 'fresh' ideas seemed scarcely worth a return to the tradition of casting off leaders just as they were becoming useful. A more general opinion was expressed in one farmer's melancholy complaint that the Union's old vigour seemed to have departed, 'a fate which overtakes most people and organizations which become too prosperous and powerful'. 'Even though there are brilliant and talented people engaged in the work of the organization, its principles seem to have become too sterile and stagnant to compete adequately with the demands placed upon it.'[4] We shall return to this question in the last chapter.

[1] *Ibid.*, November, 1957, p. 11.
[2] These conclusions are supported by replies by Union members to a questionnaire submitted by Joseph Finklestein in connection with a study of the social history of British agriculture. See a preliminary report in *Ibid.*, July 2, 1960, p. 12.
[3] *The Farmers' Weekly*, December 24, 1952, p. 23.
[4] *Ibid.*, March 28, 1952, p. 39.

Upon Turner's retirement in 1960, the Council elected in his place fifty-four year old Harold Woolley, owner of a 500 acre farm in Cheshire. Woolley had been one of the most influential members of the inner group of Union leaders; he had served several times as vice-president and deputy president, and as chairman of the parliamentary committee and leader of the Union's delegation on the Agricultural Wages Board. The presidency continued to be a full-time job, as the Council recognized when it voted to continue the annual salary of £5,000, but the formal leadership was put into commission. General sentiment in the Union was moving in the direction of some kind of 'collective leadership' even before Turner's retirement, and for this reason the members accepted the departure of their leader with far more equanimity than they would have done even three or four years earlier.

The Union's affairs are now managed by a 'President's Committee', consisting of the main office-holders, the chairmen of the Horticultural and the Welsh Committees, and Sir James Turner (or Lord Netherthorpe, as he now is).[1] Woolley explained that 'the whole purpose is to bring Council more into the picture,' but he added the qualification that 'if we try to indulge ourselves in doing these things in huge assemblies, we are in fact going to see things going past us too fast for us to deal with them'.[2] Union leadership is more broadly shared, but it remains stable and centralized.[3] A new balance is being sought between democracy and 'business-like handling of affairs'.

Accompanying this extension of leadership is the growing importance of the Union's staff, a tendency which Turner's retirement both accentuated and made more visible.[4] Of course Turner's leadership rested on a solid foundation of administrative staff work; but it was emphatically *political* leadership, and Turner cast a long shadow. With his retirement, with the regularization of the Union's political relations with Government, and with the increased importance of technical and business competence in the management of Union affairs, there has been a distinct change of emphasis. It is significant that in a speech in early 1960 on the future of the Union, Knowles gave a prominent place to the work of the permanent staff. 'When—

[1] *The British Farmer*, March 4, 1961, p. 25. Turner continued to serve on the Union's price review team in 1960 and 1961.

[2] *Ibid.*, April 2, 1960, p. 31; See November 7, 1959, pp. 34, 36; August 22, 1959, p. 7; June 4, 1960, p. 14; *The Farmers' Weekly*, December 23, 1959, p. 24.

[3] The three major officers elected in 1960 were re-elected in 1961 without opposition.

[4] One manifestation of the bureaucratic tendency was the inclusion in 1957 of the secretary of the Labour Committee and the Union's chief economist, both paid officials, on the Union's delegation on the Agricultural Wages Board. The chief economist and the general secretary have gradually taken a more active part in the organization's public affairs.

at the celebration of our Jubilee [in 1958]—we talked proudly of the men who had inspired and led us, perhaps not enough was said of the demands that the attainment of our present status had put upon the Union's staff.'[1] There is little doubt that the staff will become both larger and more important in the years to come. Indeed, the most significant changes occurring in the Union's national organization are likely to be found not so much in 'collective leadership' as in bureaucratization.

4

Something less than two hundred and fifty thousand farmers among a population of forty-four millions have been impelled to speak with one voice, that they might be heard at all. The Union's achievement has been to translate this impulse into a disciplined and effective organization. There are numerous independent specialist and commodity organizations in agriculture, but virtually all of them recognize the Union's over-all responsibility for representing farmers' opinions to government. As we have said, the Union has never had a serious challenge from another general farmers' organization. Because it views the success of its post-war strategy as dependent upon its monopoly position, however, the Union has been jealous of any organization which appeared to threaten its primacy.

A relatively minor example can be found in the specialized field of poultry and egg production. Several organizations representing poultry and egg producers have joined the Union during the post-war period, but there remain two or three independent bodies. The strongest of these, the National Poultry Association of Great Britain, vigorously opposed the Union's egg marketing scheme, but the scheme's overwhelming approval in 1957 demonstrated the Union's superior strength.[2]

The specialist branch of agriculture causing the most difficulty in in post-war years has been horticulture. The Union's claim to represent horticulturists as well as farmers was strengthened in 1944 by its absorption of the National Growers' Association, which itself had been formed by a merger of a number of small societies. But horticulturists differ from general farmers in many important respects, not least perhaps in having on the whole a more commercial and business-minded approach,[3] and a few smaller horticultural societies

[1] NFU Press Release (mimeo.), January 8, 1960.

[2] See below, pp. 100-2, for the egg marketing scheme. Although it is a rather special case, an exception to the general rule of Union expansion in this field should be mentioned. The Chick Producers' Association, a small body representing hatcheries, joined the Union in 1945. It retained its identity, however, and distinguished itself by withdrawing in 1954.

[3] Agricultural Improvement Council for England and Wales, *Second Report* (London: HMSO, 1950), p. 3.

continue to resist affiliation with the Union. Horticulturists gained little from the direct economic guarantees provided for agriculture, although as primary producers they faced similar hazards. The Union made continuous efforts to increase the protection which horticul- turists possessed in the form of tariffs and import quotas, and it re- doubled these efforts as post-war trade began to be liberalized. Nonetheless many horticulturists argued that they would be better served by an organization devoted exclusively to their interests. The Union tried to counter-act this feeling by stepping up propaganda aimed at horticulturists and by making generous provision for the formal representation of horticultural interests; in addition to a cen- tral horticultural committee with numerous sub-committees, the Union has committees dealing with flowers, fruit, glasshouse pro- duce, and nurserymen.

'In this matter of justice for the horticulturist the NFU stands solidly together,' the President affirmed in 1950, 'I want you to know this and I want you to know too that the fight on your behalf is on.'[1] By the next year, the horticulturists' impatience with such generaliza- tions showed itself in exasperated complaints at the Union's general meeting. Turner was able to turn aside what might have become a serious rebellion by arranging for a deputation to visit the Chancellor of the Exchequer to put the growers' case.[2] Horticulturists were especially resentful of the 'soft' line taken by the Union on the Agricultural Wages Board; for while the increased labour costs of farmers were ordinarily made up by increases in guaranteed prices, the horticulturists had no such protection. In response to this feeling, the Union included in 1952 a horticulturist on its Wages Board delegation.[3]

In 1953 the Union's persistent efforts resulted in a stronger mea- sure of tariff protection, and in 1960 a system of improvement grants, totalling £8 millions spread over five years, was also made available to horticultural growers. This aid was meant as a more productive alternative to the further increase in tariffs which the Government at that time refused to grant. The Union was far from satisfied, but it did stress for the benefit of horticultural members that its 'exten- sive consultations' with the Government had been 'most fruitful'.[4] In 1960 the Union also obtained a further increase in the tomato tariff. Thus although overseas competition continued to press more

[1] *The British Farmer*, December 31, 1950, p. 7.

[2] See 'NFU "Annual": Growers in Revolt', *The Farmers' Weekly*, January 19, 1951, p. 30: January 26, 1951, p. 31.

[3] The Ministry of Agriculture had consistently turned down requests on behalf of the independent British Growers' Union for representation on the Board. See H. of C.O.R., 1945/46, Vol. 426, cols. 251–52.

[4] NFU 'News' (mimeo.), Cyclo. 2140/59, Press 50, November 5, 1960. See *The British Farmer*, December 5, 1959, pp. 20–21; January 9, 1960, pp. 31–34.

strongly upon horticulturists than upon farmers, the Union did secure for them a very substantial measure of relief. It is improbable that an exclusive horticultural organization could have done nearly so well.

As we have seen, horticulture was one of two special interests given representation on the 'President's Committee'; the other was Wales. Here in the winter of 1955 a 'revolt', centering in Carmarthen, resulted in the establishment of an independent Welsh Farmers' Union. 'The small farmers of Wales can never be assured of a living under the present set-up of the NFU,' its President asserted. 'It is being run by a small group of large farmers with no interest whatever in the small man.'[1] Fed on Welsh nationalism and the grievances of small farmers, the independent union was successful enough to maintain itself beyond the first burst of enthusiasm; but its membership remained small—and undisclosed. Its problem was to gain sufficient momentum and size to secure government recognition, but this was a remote prospect. The Minister of Agriculture rejected its claim for participation in the price review in 1958.[2] Meanwhile the Union staged a counter-attack, emphasizing that it had fought hard for small farmers, as indeed it had. In 1959 it reported that after 'three testing years' its membership income from Wales was higher than ever.[3] That did not mean, however, that membership had increased, and in fact between 1954 and 1957 the Union suffered losses in all but one of the Welsh counties. While these were generally of about the same proportion as losses elsewhere, drastic declines in Cardiganshire and Carmarthenshire (where membership declined by 20 per cent and 30 per cent respectively) can doubtless be attributed largely to the independent Welsh Union.

A struggle of a rather different kind occurred in the important field of agricultural co-operation. In some countries farm organizations have found their principal salvation in co-operation, but the Union has never seen the movement in this light. Its caution has been partly due to the supposed ideological links between farmers' co-operatives and the consumer co-operative movement with its Socialist affiliations.[4] In the main the Union's restraint reflected the belief that co-

[1] *Daily Mail*, December 6, 1955. An independent Welsh Union had existed until 1921 when it was absorbed by the National Farmers' Union. National Farmers' Union *Yearbook*, 1922, p. 188. Wales continued to have its own federation of co-operative societies, the Welsh Agricultural Organization Society.

[2] H. of C.O.R., 1957/58, Vol. 585, col. 827.

[3] *The British Farmer*, February 28, 1959, p. 42; see also June 27, 1959, pp 14–15.

[4] Allegations of such ideological links are the subject of periodic vigorous rebuttals (see, for example, *Ibid.*, November, 1957, p. 7; February, 1, 1958, p. 49; October 31, 1948, p. 6; *NFU Record*, August, 1946, p. 235). There is no doubt that British agricultural co-operation has been commercially oriented and that few farmers have much sympathy with any conception of co-operation as a social `

operation, however useful, could not solve the fundamental problems of farmers in a country where farming is so varied and so exposed to foreign competition. The Union looked to political means for strengthening the farmers' bargaining power rather than to the gentler and slower instrument of voluntary co-operation.

In 1924 the central organizations dealing with co-operation, the Agricultural Wholesale Society and the Agricultural Organization Society, were dissolved as a result of financial difficulties. Under some pressure from the Ministry of Agriculture, the Union set up a co-operation committee to take over responsibility for co-ordination and promotion of the movement. Although isolated Union members showed enthusiasm, the work of this committee ticked rather slowly. In the 1930's the Union's preoccupation with statutory marketing schemes reduced its interest in voluntary co-operation still further.

After the Second World War the Union participated in the creation of a new Agricultural Co-operative Association, and its own co-operation committee exchanged members with the new Association. But the Association grew and prospered, and the Union had second thoughts. By 1952 the two organizations had drawn apart, and the arrangements for mutual representation were abandoned. An informal liaison committee was set up to consider future relations, but while discussions were still going on, the Union took steps to establish a rival organization. The Association first guessed these intentions on discovering that the staff of the Union's co-operation committee was being augmented by methods which included the acquisition of one of its own key men. It responded by calling a special conference of delegates of co-operative societies where its President, Sir Frederick Brundrett, reported the position:

So the situation seems to be this. While we have been, unfortunately, in the position of imagining that we were conducting informal discussions with the NFU, they have in fact taken unilateral action. I don't like this. It sounds to me like the big stick, and I am not very fond of the big stick.[1]

The meeting supported Sir Frederick's proposal to uphold the Association, and many delegates, most of whom were also Union members, complained of the secrecy surrounding the Union's decisions. They also pointed out, however, that the Union was a very

movement or a way of life. There are a few, however, who deplore this commercial narrowness and who urge that agricultural co-operation should concern itself 'with its members as human beings with a fuller life to live. . . .' Harry Soan, 'The Real Soil of Co-operation', *The British Farmer*, April 4, 1959, p. 62.

[1] ACA broadsheet, 'ACA Receives Mandate', February, 1953; see *Farmer and Stockbreeder*, November 24; 1953, Barbara Castle, 'The Battle of Bedford Square', *The New Statesman and Nation*, September 18, 1954.

powerful body. 'We must not get cross with the NFU, whatever we do,' said one speaker, chilled by the prospect of an open conflict.

At this time the Association claimed to represent more than 100 societies, a high proportion of the total movement.[1] Many of them quickly transferred their membership to the Union's rival body, and although a majority were still loyal a year later, even the Association leaders could not hope to achieve more than 'honourable' surrender terms. Eventually the diplomatic 'Jim' Turner took over from Knowles as the Union's chief spokesman, and terms of agreement were arranged in 1956. A new organization, the Agricultural Central Co-operative Association, was established in which the Union commanded considerably increased influence. The Union appoints directly nine of the twenty-seven members of the Council of this Association,[2] and wields at its annual meeting a block vote equivalent to one-third of all votes cast, whereas it had no voting rights at the general meetings of the old Association. It also makes a substantial contribution to the Association's income.[3] The new Association is formally 'an independent body in full control of its own administration and finance', but the Union has largely achieved (at least for the present) its basic aim: 'that the ultimate responsibility for that central body must rest with the NFU.'[4]

The Union's sudden interest in the co-operative movement after so many years of scarcely disguised indifference appears strange. Its position had always been that there was plenty of room for both movements so long as they did not tread on each others' toes: 'the political activities of farmers—as represented by the National Farmers' Union—and the trading activities of farmers—as represented by the Agricultural Co-operative Association—were both fundamental to the success of the agricultural industry.'[5] The Union's ostensible concern was to maintain its supremacy in the political field, but the defeated Association never challenged this supremacy. On the contrary it was prepared to accept the proposition that 'whatever was the policy of the NFU we were ready to follow and adapt our own machine'.[6] This attitude extended even to the sphere of agricultural marketing, where the interests of co-operatives were directly, and sometimes adversely, affected by Union policy. In point of fact

[1] See *The Farmers' Weekly*, August 14, 1953, p. 37.
[2] Of the remainder fifteen are elected by the co-operative societies and three are co-opted by the Council itself.
[3] The Union's assessment is set periodically at not more than one-third of the subscription income from the individual societies, subject to a maximum limit.
[4] *The British Farmer*, January, 1953, p. 8.
[5] *NFU Record*, June, 1948, p. 123.
[6] *The Farmers' Weekly*, March 12, 1954.

it faithfully accepted the subordinate role that was assigned to its successor.[1]

Lying behind this organizational conflict was a vague fear by the Union that under changing economic and political circumstances the co-operative movement might raise a fundamental challenge. The leaders of the movement, although compliant enough with Union policy, were at least aware of the possibility.

It has been said of State control in wartime that, if British farmers had been organized on co-operative lines, as completely as Danish or New Zealand farmers, co-operative societies might then have exercized controls on behalf of the Government. Such a conception applies not only to wartime.[2]

Such a conception could scarcely have been to the liking of the Union; and while its realization was admittedly remote, the Union preferred to take no chances about the future location of agricultural leadership. While the organizational victory was the Union's, it is still possible that the co-operative movement may win the battle of ideas. The new Agricultural Central Co-operative Association inherited the plain-speaking chairman of its dispossessed predecessor, who in 1958 asked his supporters, 'Do you honestly think it reflects much credit on the advocates of agricultural co-operation that it has taken ninety years to sell it to the recognized representatives of the farming industry?'[3] Impatient with the Union's long disinterest and irritated by the Union's tactics, the co-operators nevertheless took hope that at last the Union's great prestige and resources might be effectively harnessed to the advancement of their cause.

A defence for the Union's organizational acquisitiveness can be sought in the importance which the idea of 'farmers' solidarity' holds for most British farmers. The agricultural interest tends to think of itself as engaged in a desperate many-fronted struggle for stability and prosperity. In this context unity seems all-important, since farmers are heavily outnumbered by vaguely identified 'urban interests' which are thought to be ignorant and ill-disposed. While some-

---

[1] 'The new association shall be recognized by the National Farmers' Union as responsible for the co-ordination and development of agricultural co-operation in England. . . . It will have the right of approach to Government Departments and other authorities on matters which concern the trading operations of agricultural co-operative societies or organizations so long as they have no implications on overall agricultural policy. In matters of overall agricultural policy, the association recognizes the necessity for the Union to act as the national organization speaking for all sections of the agricultural industry.' NFU Cyclo. 56/136, April 10, 1956 (mimeo.).

[2] Agricultural Co-operatives Association, *Co-operation in English Farming*, 1948, p. 6.

[3] *Co-operation*, No. 3, 1958, p. 4.

times slightly paranoic, the Union's pressure towards a monolithic organizational structure certainly represents a tenable interpretation of farmers' interests. Many of the Union's arguments, on small matters as well as large, are directed to the dangers of division. This theme has been repeatedly stressed, for example, in the Union's promotion of marketing schemes which is discussed in Chapter IV. In the same way the straying Welsh farmers were warmly exhorted to return to the fold.

The door is open. Come in. Let us see if there is room for improvement, if there are issues that require deviation from present procedures. . . . There are people who are laughing at this situation, looking on at us with the cleavage that exists. . . . We have a job to do and need the unity of purpose of a combined organization to do it.[1]

The Union has succeeded remarkably well in its aim of uniting farmers behind its banner. How wisely it has used this power must be reserved for further consideration.

[1] *The British Farmer*, May 31, 1958, p. 18.

CHAPTER III

THE QUEST FOR STABILITY

1

THE first and most crucial of the tasks of partnership facing Government and Farmers' Union was the quest for the 'stability' promised in the 1947 Agricultural Act. Nobody save the more intractable advocates of *laisser-faire* dissent from this goal in principle; but the problem is to reconcile stability for agriculture (with its implication, at least in farmers' minds, of a reasonable general level of prosperity) with the other demands upon the British economy. The main instrument of reconciliation was to be the annual farm price review or, to give its more technical definition, the 'annual review and determination of guarantees'.[1]

The farm price review had a wartime origin, and some of its features derive from wartime precedents. During the war the great bulk of agricultural output was purchased by the Government at fixed prices, and the farmer had an assured market and known price for all he was able to produce. The overriding need for stimulating production resulted in the determination in November, 1940 of a generous schedule of prices which (with one upward revision) proved generally acceptable for the next three years. The prices were not reviewed according to any regular procedure, but the Government promised to adjust prices from time to time 'to the extent of any substantial changes in cost of production'.[2]

In 1943, as a result of an increase in farm workers' wages, agricultural prices were reviewed in consultation with the Unions, and some increases were made. These covered only a part of increased costs, and the Government also took the opportunity to adjust the price schedule in favour of certain commodities. Farmers regarded this award as a violation of the 1940 pledge. The Government argued that it had never contemplated an automatic and equal increase in prices whenever costs rose but only that increases in costs should be fully covered over a period of years.[3] This broad requirement had certainly been met, but the Union claimed that the commitment was more specific. It did not get its way on the immediate questions, but

---

[1] Some of the support to agriculture is given by guaranteed prices, and some by direct grants, but the event is generally known as a price review and was so described by the Government until 1954.
[2] H. of C.O.R., 1940–41, Vol. 367, col. 92.
[3] *Ibid.*, 1942–43, Vol. 393, cols. 386–7.

it did achieve a much larger objective, the creation of regular price review machinery. At the House of Commons debate on January 26, 1944, held under the shadow of the farmers' indignation, Lord Hudson promised to discuss the whole question of price guarantees with the Union, and by the end of the year a complete agreement had resulted.

Its most significant feature was the introduction of a joint review of the economic conditions and requirements of British agriculture, held each February by the Government and the farmers' representatives. The full import of this arrangement only emerged slowly. One effect was to place the Government under strong pressure to attune its programme of support to the wishes of the Union. It is true that, from the beginning, the Government emphasized that the final decision over agricultural guarantees was exclusively its own, as constitutionally it was bound to be. Yet a convention soon emerged whereby the Union gave a formal endorsement of some kind to the final settlement. In the first year the Union could state simply that its proposals 'ultimately formed the basis of the Government announcement of agricultural prices'.[1] Such a halcyon state of affairs (from the Union's standpoint) did not last long, and as the years went by its annual endorsement became sometimes rather lukewarm or hedged with reservations; but not until 1956 was this confirmation actually withheld and then in rather unusual circumstances. At least until that date, Ministers were extremely reluctant to face the unpopularity which would result from a failure to reach agreement with the Union; and every time they defended the guaranteed prices in Parliament by pointing to the Union's endorsement, as they invariably did, the convention of an agreed settlement was strengthened.

Secondly, the Union's status as spokesman for the whole farming community was greatly strengthened. In the first few reviews the Milk Marketing Board took part in the negotiations, but the Union did not like the arrangement and it was discontinued. A later attempt by the breed societies to gain a foothold in the review was not successful either.[2] The presence of other organizations, whether friendly or critical, would weaken the Union's ability to present an authoritative, co-ordinated case on behalf of all sections of farming.

The advantages of partnership were not all one-sided. The Union became obliged both to reconcile sectional differences among far-

[1] NFU *Yearbook*, 1946, p. 9.
[2] In 1947, the breed societies, through their national associations, pressed jointly for recognition as a negotiating body at the annual review. They approached the Union first, but apparently encountered little sympathy there and the attempt was unsuccessful. Two years later, Sir William Price-Smith of the National Sheep Breeders' Association, attacked the Union ('and, to a lesser extent, the Ministry') for its indifference to the arguments put forward by the Association. *The Farmers' Weekly*, May 16, 1947; May 27, 1949.

mers and to explain and defend, at least in some measure, the price settlements which it helped to shape. Both these functions were a convenience to Government, even though they equally made the Union a more formidable opponent if crossed. The Government was no keener than the Union to include other participants in the review. In resisting an amendment to the 1947 Agriculture Bill, which would have given other organizations a definite right to be heard, the Minister of Agriculture referred to the confusion which such interpolations would produce and pointed out that the Unions 'are supposed to be representative of every phase and factor of the agricultural industry'.[1]

The post-war Labour Minister of Agriculture, Mr Tom Williams, was a miner by origins and Member for a mining constituency (the Don Valley, Yorkshire). He had been a spokesman for the Labour Party during pre-war agricultural debates, and had served during the war as one of the parliamentary secretaries to the Ministry of Agriculture, the other being the Duke of Norfolk. The team of miner and Duke was well-suited to the wartime mood and was no doubt picked with this in mind. It soon became clear that the sympathies which united the new Minister with the farmers were more important than the doctrinal differences which might have divided them. Like most other Labour Members, Williams was acutely conscious of the evils of economic depression and could easily appreciate the farmers' strong desire for stability. Like many other Labour members too, his experience disposed him to believe in the necessity of a more or less indefinite expansion of food production. Malnutrition and thin diets were social matters with which he was well acquainted, whereas the problems of 'overproduction' could be viewed, as they generally were in the Left Book Club days, as the result of faulty capitalist economics. In any case, in the austere conditions of the 1940's, the first concern of a Minister of Agriculture was to stimulate production, and to this end Williams needed to win the confidence of the farmers and their Union. By the time conditions had eased, such appetite as the Minister possessed for Socialist fire-eating had diminished under the influence of his popularity with the farming community.

However, Williams' first close contact with the Union took the form of an explosive disagreement. Under the 1944 arrangements the Government had agreed to hold a special price review whenever any 'sudden or substantial change of costs' occurred between the annual reviews. Accordingly, when farm wages were increased in June, 1946, a special review was held and the Government agreed to increase prices. As in 1943, however, all prices were not increased in equal proportion, which was contrary to the Union's view that the balance of profitability between commodities, once fixed for the year, ought

[1] H. of C. Standing Committees, 1946–47, Vol. 2, cols. 78–79, 94–109.

to be strictly maintained. The Union also wanted prices to be raised by more than the wage bill in recognition of the value of the farmers' own labour.

On these grounds, the Union refused to accept the award or to discuss the details of its allocation. A heated debate was held in Parliament at which the farmers' case got a highly sympathetic airing. Eventually, in a crisis atmosphere, a special augmented meeting of the Union's council was called in the middle of the harvest period. After some hesitation the Minister agreed to attend, and at the meeting he offered to open discussions about any 'defects or anomalies' in price review procedures which had come to light.[1] This olive branch was not accepted until Turner had first got a clear assurance that the discussion would cover the Union's particular claims. The outcome was a definite victory for the Union. The Government accepted the principle of full recoupment for cost increases at special reviews and agreed not to discriminate between commodities on these occasions. It did not go so far as to accept that extra value should also be placed on the farmers' own labour.[2]

The Minister extracted a 'full recognition' from the Union that the acceptance of these principles was not to be taken as tying his hand at annual reviews; but in terms of practical politics this hardening of the special review procedure inevitably strengthened the Union's hand at annual reviews. This was the more serious as in the next decade no fewer than seven special reviews were held, and two more were only narrowly avoided—in one case on a dubious pretext.[3] The 'Williams Convention' became heartily disliked in Government circles, but at the time the Minister acted under considerable pressure. The Union had hinted darkly that it might take 'such constitutional action as would demonstrate beyond the shadow of a doubt the feeling of the industry towards the award'.[4] A wholesale resignation of Union members from the county agricultural committees would have administered a severe blow to the food production campaign.

Until 1947 Government policy had been rather indecisive about the proper scale of agricultural production under post-war conditions. Following the severe dollar crisis of that year, the Government swiftly announced a four-year plan for expanding net agricultural output by 20 per cent. Without waiting for the next review, it raised the agricultural price level by between 15 and 20 per cent, partly in

[1] The *Daily Telegraph*, August 18, 1946. The Union had pressed strongly for the dispute to be settled by 'independent arbitration'.
[2] H. of C.O.R., 1946–47, Vol. 430, col. 1029.
[3] In 1952, when an increase in wages occurred in England and Wales but not in Scotland, the Government relied on this discrepancy to reject the Union's claim.
[4] NFU *Record*, September, 1946, p. 247.

compensation for a fresh wages award but mainly as a deliberate incentive to higher production. Farmers were also encouraged to rear more calves, plough up more old grassland, apply more lime and phosphates, and do various other things by the offer of special grants. Considered in purely physical terms the targets were not over-ambitious. Production did in fact increase very rapidly in the next two years; the general goal was reached roughly in time, although the aim of making agriculture more self-sufficient through the production of more feedingstuffs was not fully realized.

When the Minister announced his proposals to a special augmented meeting of the Union's Council, again held in mid-harvest but in a very different atmosphere from the previous year, he received a pledge of full co-operation. The Union pointed with satisfaction to the resemblance of the Minister's programme to its own policy announced two years earlier,[1] and its President congratulated the Minister and his Department for their receptiveness to the Union's suggestions.[2]

Inflation, however, soon began to reduce the value of the farmers' 1947 gains. The Government increasingly insisted that some part of rising agricultural costs ought to be met out of increased efficiency, instead of being added on to the schedule of guaranteed prices. The Union did not question the reality of rising efficiency, which was at least a good advertisement for British farming, but it did strongly stress the patriotic sacrifices which farmers were making in the interests of fighting inflation.[3] Moreover, Union leaders may have cynically observed that as time went on the Government tended to equate 'efficiency' with that portion of costs which agriculture could absorb without suffering an actual decline in its total net income. The truth was that the Government, having made one highly generous award to agriculture, was thrown on the defensive.

The annual price reviews were fought vigorously over the relationship between costs and prices. The 1949 review was described by the Chancellor, Sir Stafford Cripps, as the hardest ever, although it was mild compared with some later ones. The 1950 review was also very closely fought, but ended amicably. *The British Farmer* (the Union's official organ) noted that the result 'not only reflects credit upon the negotiators but also emphasizes the unique value of the review machinery',[4] but the working of this machinery was beginning to come under fire. In April, 1950, Stanley Evans, Parliamentary Secre-

[1] *The Basis of Economic Security*, November, 1945.

[2] *NFU Record*, September, 1947, p. 252.

[3] At the 1956 annual general meeting, Turner devoted his address to a long warning about the perils of inflation, although his remedy—to produce more home-grown food to put in the shops—was a curious piece of economic reasoning. *The British Farmer*, February 2, 1956.

[4] *The British Farmer*, March 31, 1950, p. 2.

tary to the Ministry of Food, made an outspoken attack upon what he regarded as the heavy subsidies paid to British farmers. His resignation from the Government was promptly demanded and secured, and the Prime Minister wrote to Turner stressing that there was no change in the Government's agricultural policy. Evans found himself isolated on the back benches, but his outburst (particularly his coinage of the word 'feather-bedded') was not without its effect upon public opinion.

Williams's term of office ran out on an inharmonious note, with the Union in 1951 entering for the first time a 'strong reservation' about the treatment of milk and eggs at the annual price review. However, the Labour Minister's personal popularity with the farmers was unshaken. His reputation was built upon a genuine sympathy for their problems and a considerable readiness to fight their battles at Cabinet meetings.[1] He was also, however, a prisoner of his own popularity, and he and his Ministry left unsolved the basic problems of aid to agriculture which were certain to become more pressing as 'normality' returned.

2

Throughout the Labour period food remained scarce, at one point even scarcer than in wartime, and controls and rationing continued in force. The Government bought the bulk of the nation's food, both home-produced and imported, organized food distribution, and controlled food prices. It incurred heavy financial losses on these operations, but for most of the period at any rate these losses could not be ascribed to agricultural support. They were the result of a social and economic policy of stabilizing food prices at a low level, and farmers were understandably indignant at suggestions that they were being subsidized.

Gradually the situation changed as more food became available and farm prices continued to be raised. An indication that British farmers were sharing in the food subsidies was provided by the widening gap between the subsidies paid upon home and imported food. The eventual dismantling of state controls and rationing in 1953–4 revealed the dependant state of British agriculture. The British farmer was asked again to compete in the open market with much cheaper imported products. The only means of enabling him then to do so without losing his prosperity was some form of direct subsidization. The transformation of the 'consumer' food subsidies

[1] Sir Stafford Cripps, at the Union's 1949 annual dinner, remarked, 'I don't think you have done so badly, and for that you largely have to thank the persistent advocacy of the Ministers responsible for agriculture.' *Ibid.*, February 1, 1949.

into overt 'producer' agricultural subsidies was a vexing and somewhat humiliating process to the British farmer.[1]

The 1952 annual general meeting of the Union had a crisis atmosphere, very different from those of the previous five years. Eleven
of the thirty-two resolutions complained bitterly about prices, 'drift'
in government policy and 'undermining of confidence'; one went so
far as to urge the Union to cease negotiations with the Government
if the farmers' views on prices were not accepted.[2] The subsequent
review was the hardest fought to date, reaching a deadlock which
was only broken, unprecedently late, towards the end of April. If the
Union was belligerent, so also it seemed was the Treasury. In the end,
however, a settlement was reached which won a fairly warm endorsement from the Union.

The Economist remarked caustically that 'the price review took so
long because Ministers put up some fight, but in the end they made
concessions rather than face the embarrassment of a public quarrel',[3]
but this explanation was certainly not the whole truth. The 1952
review was strongly influenced by a fresh dollar crisis which gave a
new impulse to the encouragement of 'dollar-saving' home products.
The Government announced a modest new four-year expansion
programme, whose aim was to increase total net output to 60 per
cent above pre-war (it was already 50 per cent higher), with particular emphasis upon meat, wheat, and feedingstuffs. Although not
satisfied, the Union was quick to point out that the new programme
'would require extra financing'.[4]

From this time, the approach of Government and Union began
sharply to diverge. At the Union's insistence discussions were held
forthwith to work out a new long-term policy, but the talks got nowhere. The Union wanted to continue the kind of production planning which had provided the foundation for price review discussions
since 1945. The setting of definite production targets, particularly if
they were high ones, was a strategic asset of great value to the Union.
If prices were not high enough the targets might be missed and the
Government could be blamed. The structure of British farming
helped these arguments. The small farmer's perennial problems of
credit and working capital, the slimness of his resources, the difficulties and risks implicit in expanding his turnover—all these could be
pointed to as a warning that if the nation did not furnish enough aid
it would not get the desired food.

[1] When the Government abandoned State trading and control, it continued to
provide certain subsidies for reducing the price of milk and bread, but these were
gradually eliminated, leaving specific welfare schemes as the only genuine 'consumer' subsidies.
[2] 'Farmers' Complaints', *The Economist*, January 19, 1952.
[3] 'Food Without Thought', *Ibid.*, May 3, 1952.
[4] NFU *Yearbook*, 1953, pp. 9–10.

The Conservative Government's approach was different. Its main aims were to abolish rationing and controls and to re-establish free markets. Initially it needed to stimulate a sufficient output of food to facilitate derationing, so that for a while its route ran fairly parallel to the Union's; but once markets were freed, the Government had a definite interest in checking the output of any commodity which entailed heavy subsidy. The desirability of expanding home production thus became dependent, in the Government's view, upon the competitive efficiency of British agriculture. However, the Union showed a singular failure to grasp these Liberal-Conservative policies, patiently as Mr Heathcoat Amory (Minister of Agriculture from 1954 to 1958) laboured to expound them.

While the Union was still pressing its ideas about 'long-term policy', the Government was engaged in a careful withdrawal from the limited degree of production planning to which it had subscribed. In 1953 Churchill had told the Union at its annual dinner, 'It is just as important for our future now to wring the last ounce of food from our acres year by year as it was in the dark days of the war.'[1] In 1954 the Government could say, for form's sake, that the 60 per cent target was 'still a major objective' (as production was still rising, the declaration mattered little); but it was no longer prepared to set objectives for individual commodities, and even under heavy Union pressure it would do no more than 'give some general indication of the direction in which it appears to be desirable that production should be developed for the time being'.[2] In 1956 the Government coolly remarked that 'the objective of production policy remains [sic] the most that can be produced economically and efficiently in accordance with market requirements, steadily increasing technical efficiency and diminishing unit cost'[3]—hardly a programme to gladden the Union's heart.

The dismantling of state controls and rationing took place mainly in 1953 and 1954. The Union's first concern was to make sure that it was fully consulted about the various decisions which had to be taken. At the end of 1952, the Government announced a date for the decontrol of eggs without first consulting the Union. The latter was highly indignant and extracted a promise before entering the next price review that this omission would not be repeated. The Union was in fact extremely anxious about Government policy for prices and marketing. The marketing issue is treated in the next chapter. So far as prices were concerned, the Government favoured the establishment of minimum or 'floor' prices for certain products and wanted to consider every commodity separately, according to its

---

[1] *The British Farmer*, February, 1953, p. 6.
[2] *Annual Review and Determination of Guarantees*, 1954, pp. 2–3.
[3] *Ibid.*, 1956, p. 4.

special circumstances. The Union, on the other hand, insisted strongly upon the unity of the agricultural guarantees. Previous price reviews had always concerned themselves with first determining any desirable change in the total value of the guarantees and then with breaking this down between individual commodities. Minimum prices or a 'commodity by commodity' approach would undermine this system.

In the end the Union largely won its way over this crucial issue. The new system of guarantees was extremely complex. For cereals (wheat, barley, oats) and fatstock (fat cattle, sheep and pigs) a system of 'deficiency payments' was introduced. Farmers sold their output for the best market price which they could obtain, but any difference between the average market price thus realized and the guaranteed price determined at the annual review was made good in the form of a Government bonus paid retrospectively on each unit of output sold.[1] This arrangement provided each group of producers with the same degree of support as previously, although *individual* producers might do better or worse than the average.[2]

The guarantees for milk, potatoes, and (from 1957) eggs were implemented through the agency of producer marketing boards, which received sufficient Government subsidy to honour the prices agreed at annual reviews. In the case of these products the Government did somewhat reduce the extent of its commitments. For eggs and potatoes, it introduced what were intended to be 'minimum' or 'floor' prices which should operate only when the market was depressed. While these were established at a rather lower level than the previous guarantees, the new 'minimum' price for eggs proved in practice to be consistently well above market prices. In the case of milk, a guaranteed price continued to operate on the old basis, but it was limited to a specified quantity of output. This was the first use by the Government of its power under the Agriculture Act to impose quantitative limitation.[3]

Under the new arrangements the Government divested itself of some of the burden of agricultural planning. In the case of cereals and fatstock, it became much more important for a farmer to study the

----

[1] *Guarantees for Home-Grown Cereals*, Cmd. 8947, HMSO, 1953. In the case of barley and oats sales were converted to an acreage basis.

[2] To meet the Union's argument that the operation of 'rings' of dealers, particularly at the smaller fatstock auctions, was likely to leave some individual producers with an unfairly low price for their beasts, a supplementary 'individual guarantee' (or floor price) was also operated for most classes of fatstock; but this extremely cumbersome arrangement was discontinued in 1956, over the Union's protest.

[3] Government policy was stated in Cmds. 8798, 8947 and 8989 in 1953 and Cmd. 9104 in 1954. For the effects of subsidy administration by marketing boards, see Chapter IV.

market in order to maximize his returns, which consisted of market price plus a variable subsidy. In the case of milk and potatoes some of the burden of support was shifted from the Government to producer marketing boards. From the Union's viewpoint, however, the significant achievement was that most of the traditional price review conventions would continue to apply under greatly altered market conditions.[1]

This achievement was not won without a severe struggle. Indeed, the Union President's olympian political neutrality almost snapped under the pressure of price and marketing controversies. At a stormy council meeting in late 1953, he came close to a denunciation of Conservative policy, although he refused to accept the implication drawn by his listeners that things were 'tougher' under the Tories; the situation, he said primly, was completely different.[2] The new price arrangements were largely settled at the subsequent (1954) review when Turner could remark with satisfaction that the price review had proved its adaptability to the needs of a freer economy.[3] After a year in which farmers' costs had for once decreased, it was possible to launch the new guarantees on a favourable breeze.

3

Any satisfaction the Union felt in weathering the transition to a free market was short-lived. By the mid-1950's, the old agricultural problem of over-production was beginning to re-appear. The emerging 'gluts' did not take the form of unsaleable produce, but of a larger output of some commodities than could be sold without heavy subsidization. The products affected were eggs, pigs and milk, and in each case over-production stemmed at least in part from past public policies.

During the hungry and rationed 'forties it seemed impossible to suppose that any measures which would bring back eggs and bacon to the Englishman's breakfast table could be anything but desirable. Accordingly, as the quickest way of invigorating the nation's dreary diet, a substantial stimulus was given first to egg and later to pig prices. By the time Labour left office, the output of eggs and pig-meat was slightly above pre-war levels. The incoming Conservatives con-

---

[1] Under the new system, producers might realize higher average prices than those guaranteed, thus improving their collective income and dispensing with support. In this sense, the new guarantees were minima which could be exceeded; but the fact that such extra earnings have proved (for farmers collectively) to be both rare and small is evidence of the continued importance and comprehensiveness of Government support.

[2] *The British Farmer*, October, 1953.

[3] *Ibid.*, April, 1954.

firmed this policy. In particular they looked hopefully to the pig as the main source of the 250,000 extra tons of meat which they needed quickly in order to end rationing. The prolific animal obliged, and the output of pig-meat soared from 315,000 to 757,000 tons within three years. But by then food supplies had greatly improved, and after decontrol market prices for both pig-meat and eggs turned out to be well below those guaranteed to farmers.

This was not a problem of excessive or unforeseen foreign competition. In the case of eggs, heavy subsidization of home producers nearly eliminated overseas competition and even caused an abortive attempt in 1957 to sell subsidized British eggs abroad. In the case of pigs, there was little foreign competition in the pork and manufactured pig-meat markets, while in the bacon market competition from Danish bacon was modified by a 10 per cent tariff imposed in 1956.[1] The mistake lay in the encouragement of home production at prices which proved to be unrealistic. The Government had to turn about and pursue a policy of retrenchment. Two cuts in the pig guarantee still left the pig subsidy costing a quarter of total Government support for 1955–6, which led the Chancellor to comment ruefully that on the national farm all animals might be equal but pigs were more equal than the others.[2] For eggs, a sharp reduction in 1953 was followed by cuts in the four successive years between 1957 and 1960. Because of new methods and rising technical efficiency, however, egg production continued to expand and the total cost of the egg subsidy for the decade 1950–60 was as much as £296 million. Even with heavy subsidies, many small farmers were forced out of egg production by the new mass production techniques of specialized producers.[3]

Milk production provided a larger and more serious issue. Milk was strongly favoured for nutritional reasons while rationing lasted, and by 1951 total liquid consumption of milk was almost twice as high as before the war. Milk accounted for almost one-third of net agricultural output, and with Government encouragement many farmers had gone in for milk even in remote areas which were traditionally concerned solely with stock-raising. Production continued to increase but the liquid milk market ceased to expand, so that a mounting surplus had to be diverted to manufacturing uses at heavy

[1] This tariff replaced Ministry trading which had made a profit on Danish bacon, with which to subsidize British bacon. It was abolished in 1961 as a consequence of the creation of the European free trade area.
[2] Further price cuts reduced the subsidy to more tolerable proportions, but pig production and market prices became extremely unstable. See Pig Industry Development Authority, *Report of Conference of Agricultural Research Workers and Agricultural Economists*, 1960.
[3] The number of birds carried in large flocks (over 500 adult birds) increased from 11·2 per cent in 1948 to 28·6 per cent in 1957. Rupert Coles, *Development of The Poultry Industry in England, Wales 1945–1959* (Poultry World Ltd., 1960).

financial loss. Government policy changed from encouragement to discouragement. In 1951 the Government recommended 'a dampening down of the present rate of expansion'; in 1952 it wanted the dairy herd to be stabilized at its existing level; in 1954 it was preaching the need for a reduction in the size of the herd, and further increases of production were disqualified for subsidy payments.[1]

In the Union's eyes these policies amounted to an unfair and paradoxical penalization of farmers for reaching targets which the Government had itself set. In any case, the Union had to stand up for its numerous members who were dependent upon income from milk, pigs, and eggs.[2] The Government's suggestion that some farmers should switch back to beef production was not very kindly received. Against this background the Union leaders judged that it was safest to oppose any 'discrimination' against the prices of particular commodities.

In 1951 and again in 1953 the Union entered the 'strongest reservations' over the milk price finally fixed. At the 1955 annual general meeting a motion of no confidence in Government policy was withdrawn after some honeyed words from the Chancellor of the Exchequer, who had been warned by the Union's President 'of the mood of today's meeting'.[3] The subsequent price settlement gave farmers full recoupment for their increased costs and was particularly helpful to milk producers, but to many this seemed no more than an election year respite; and so it proved to be.

In 1956 the first complete break occurred in the price review concordat, although initially it did not seem too serious. The Minister stated that the Union would have accepted the general award but for its disagreement with its distribution.[4] The Union was particularly eager to obtain a higher milk price, and Whitehall understood, or thought it did, that the Union leaders had to make a gesture in order to satisfy small milk producers. However, the Union's county branches proved to be more indignant than headquarters itself. Conservative Members of Parliament were summoned to attend very hostile local Union meetings, and the incensed agricultural com-

[1] See *Review White Papers*, Cmds. 8239, 8798, 9104. Monthly figures of liquid milk consumption were 130.2 million gallons in 1951 and 126.5 in 1958, and for the manufacturing surplus 19 and 52 million gallons respectively.

[2] Holdings of under 100 acres contain over two-thirds of all adult poultry, over one-half of all pigs, and nearly one-half of the national dairy herd. *Scale of Enterprise in Farming, op. cit.*, p. 63.

[3] *Manchester Guardian*, January 26, 1955; *The Times*, January 27, 1955.

[4] H. of C.O.R., March 15, 1956. The Union later repudiated this interpretation, asserting that it would only have 'considered' the total figure 'on the basis of a schedule which gave less harsh treatment to the smaller producer'. *NFU News*, May 17, 1956. The distinction was not really very significant.

mittee of the Conservative Parliamentary party turned on Turner and Knowles as the alleged instigators of a plot to bully the Tories into unreasonable concessions.

As on previous occasions an uproar was followed by overtures of peace. For some time both Government and Union had wondered whether the margin for conflict and disagreement in the annual price reviews might somehow be narrowed, to the relief of both parties. Now talks on this subject began in earnest, ending in an agreement which became the basis of the Agriculture Act of 1957. Under this Act, the Government undertook not to reduce the total value of its guarantees by more than $2\frac{1}{2}$ per cent in any one year, after allowing in full for any change in costs. Each individual commodity was similarly protected by the provision that the value of its guarantee could not be cut by more than 4 per cent annually, or in the case of livestock products by more than 9 per cent over a three-year period. These restrictions were designed to remove the farmers' fears of sudden large price cuts, particularly in relation to individual commodities such as milk.

The new Act did not inhibit the claims which the Union could make, except in the important matter of special price reviews. The circumstances in which these reviews would be held were closely defined and restricted to narrow limits.[1] This was a great relief to the Government which had been frequently embarrassed by requests for such reviews ever since the Williams' convention. The Union's acquiescence was helped by the Act's provision for making full allowance for cost changes at each annual review. The settlement was further supported by Government allocation of £50 millions, to be spread over ten years, for grants towards the cost of a wide range of capital improvements. This assistance was additional to that provided through the price review.[2]

The 1957 Act gave more concreteness to the statutory guarantee of agricultural stability of a decade earlier, to the Union's evident satisfaction. Its general secretary declared that 'the support price system has been placed at last on a more realistic basis'.[3] Nonetheless the Act's provisions suggested that the level of government support might continue to be steadily reduced, and this proved to be the case. During the four years following the Act, additions to the guarantees fell short of cost increases by a total of £85 millions. This reduction of support was, it is true, £39 millions less than the maximum which

---

[1] A special review could only be held if the effect of cost changes over the remainder of the year was sufficient to reduce (or increase) the full value of the guarantees by three-quarters of 1 per cent.
[2] Agriculture Act, 1957, Part 2. The normal rate of grant is 33⅓ per cent. (Section 13).
[3] J. K. Knowles, *NFU News*, January 8, 1957.

the Act permitted, but the difference was mainly due to Government leniency in the election year of 1959.

This medicine was after all too strong for the Union to stomach, and in 1958 and again in 1960 it refused to endorse a price settlement. After the latter occasion, the Union's new President (Mr H. Woolley) took the farmers' case to the Prime Minister, and secured a fresh round of discussions between Minister and Union which culminated in a rambling but reassuring statement of Government intentions towards agriculture. This White Paper indicated that the maximum cuts permitted by the 1957 Act would only be applied 'in exceptional circumstances' and that farmers would generally be left 'with a measure of the gains from increasing efficiency'. The question of what constituted a reasonable settlement would continue to be decided year by year.[1] With this statement, and the much more favourable price settlement of 1961 that followed it, amity between Government and Union was yet again temporarily restored.

4

In many ways the price review is like any hard-fought price or wage negotiation. There is a great deal of shadow-boxing between the participants, and the outcome can often be predicted fairly accurately by an informed observer. But in two ways the price review is perhaps unique. First, it closely governs the economic position of a large, complex, and vulnerable industry. Secondly, it is much more politically charged than most negotiations of this kind. To farmers the review has been the supreme test of the genuineness of the state's interest in their welfare. Their leaders have been extremely anxious to preserve the 'spirit' and conventions of the review and have been a little inclined to suspect some subtle political betrayal whenever the Government drives a hard bargain. The heavy commitment of farmers and of the Union leaders in particular to the principles of the 1947 Act also ties the Government. At no time does a Government relish the charge that it has broken its pledge to an important sector of the community, and the charge is particularly harmful when party fortunes are fairly evenly balanced and the Opposition stands ready to endorse and broadcast the indictment.

One Chancellor described the price review discussions as 'the most complicated with which I have to deal in the whole realm of the activities of the Chancellor of the Exchequer'.[2] The review itself usually lasts from three to six weeks, but preliminary preparations and the subsequent 'post mortem' occupy many months and take up

[1] *Agriculture. Report on Talks between the Agricultural Departments and the Farmers' Unions, June–December, 1960*, Cmd. 1249 (1960), p. 9.
[2] *Manchester Guardian*, February 8, 1955.

a high proportion of the time of Union leaders and of many Ministry officials. The Government has published since 1951 an annual White Paper outlining the main facts, problems, and decisions relating to each review. The first White Paper also gave a summary of review procedure, although this account is no longer wholly accurate.[1]

Prior to the review proper economists of the Agricultural Departments and the Farmers' Unions examine statistical material relating to farmers' costs, incomes, and profits. In the early years the Union possessed no independent sources of information, but after being chided in 1945 by the Minister of Agriculture for questioning his figures of costs of production[2] it established its own farm accounts scheme which covers a sample of five thousand farms. When the review begins, the statistical material already agreed is used to assess agricultural prospects; but since this material is complex and in varying degrees retrospective, there is plenty of scope for differing interpretations.

The price review itself has two main phases. The first aim is to reach a provisional decision upon what adjustment should be made in the total value of the Government guarantees. In the second stage, this global award is divided among particular commodities and direct subsidies. In practice, these two stages become interwoven. According to the first review White Paper, the Government sets production objectives which form the basis for the determination of guarantees. As already noted, these production objectives have become of decreasing importance. The main problems in the review hinge upon the conflicts between the farmers' claims and the 'broad considerations of national economic policy',[3] which the Government puts forward. In recent years, these considerations have involved complex considerations of international trade, which have applied to individual commodities as well as to the general size of the award.

The final price settlement takes the form of a 'global award' to agriculture which has been broken down into a detailed schedule of guaranteed prices and direct grants of various kinds. Until 1957 the new guarantees for livestock products came into force immediately after the review (on April 1), but livestock producers were also protected against abrupt changes by a system of 'minimum' prices covering the next three to four years. In practice these minimum prices were too low to have much protective value. The crop guarantees, on the other hand, applied to the harvest of the following year, so that farmers could sow their crops knowing what prices they would receive. The long-term assurances provided by the 1957 Agriculture Act made it possible to end these rather cumbrous

[1] *Review and Fixing of Farm Prices*, 1951, Cmd 8239.
[2] H. of C.O.R., 1943–4. Vol. 396, col. 713–718.
[3] Cmd. 8239.

arrangements and to bring all guarantees settled at the price review into immediate operation.

Believing as it does in an expanding agriculture, prices related to costs and fair shares for all the different kinds of producer, the Union's case is usually fairly straightforward. It gives wide discretion to its negotiating team. This team is naturally aware of Union opinion as voiced by county branches, headquarters committees, and the annual general meeting, but it is not tied by any specific instructions. The Union's Council is sometimes summoned during the talks so that the team can be sure of its support, but special meetings are avoided if possible and the council's final endorsement of the team's decision is largely a formality.[1] The Union's review team normally includes the president, deputy president, and vice-president; the chairman and vice-chairman of the economics committee; several officers, including the general secretary and the chief economist; together with the leaders of the Scottish and Ulster unions.[2] Chairmen of commodity committees are excluded from the team, even though this once meant the exclusion of the vice-president. During the course of the talks, the President may informally consult some of these committee chairmen or the chairmen of the appropriate marketing boards to find out the minimum terms which they would accept. When the Government is wielding the axe the spokesmen for the better-placed commodities are expected to come to the rescue of their less fortunate colleagues, and they have been quite prepared to do so.

The determination of Government policy at price reviews is a more complex problem. An important part is played by an interdepartmental committee which advises Ministers on general policy before the review begins and which reviews all proposals for new grants or subsidies.[3] Until 1956, this committee was principally concerned with reconciling the often divergent views of Agriculture, Food, and the Treasury. As a result of the increasing significance of foreign trade decisions for agriculture the Board of Trade now sends a representative to some meetings. The Scottish Department and the Ministry of Agriculture for Northern Ireland also participate on this committee and in the review itself, but the complications of policy which they introduce are relatively minor.

The wartime disputations between the Ministries of Agriculture

---

[1] For example, the Council did not discuss in advance the breach with the Government at the 1956 review. It only ratified the team's decision not to endorse the award.

[2] Scotland and Ulster are heavily represented in proportion to their importance; for example, they accounted in 1958 for twelve of the twenty members of the team. In practice these mainly serve the purpose of useful ballast.

[3] See *Sixth Report from the Select Committee on Estimates, Treasury Control of Expenditure*, Session 1957–58, HMSO, p. 122.

and Food have been recounted elsewhere[1] and after the war these controversies continued. Whilst the Ministry of Agriculture was well conversant with producers' problems and in close touch with the Unions, the Ministry of Food had little contact with farming. As 'consumers' champion', Food wanted agricultural production to be subordinated to nutritional and social objectives to a greater extent than Agriculture thought practicable. After 1949, when the food sub-sidies were pegged, Food became more strongly opposed to farm price increases, since these had to be passed to consumers. The com-position of the two Ministries emphasized their different concerns. Agriculture was an old and unusually inbred department; Food was a wartime makeshift, with a nucleus of established civil servants, a large intake from the distributive trades, and a leavening of Univer-sity dons.

In 1956 most of the remaining functions of Food were transferred to Agriculture which became the Ministry of Agriculture, Fisheries and Food. Theoretically the senior department had devoured the upstart, but the result was not, as some had feared, a victory for the producers' over the consumers' viewpoint. The new Ministry's price review team was reconstituted in part from ex-Food personnel, and contained commodity experts who were directly concerned for the first time both with home production and imported supplies. The result was a more integrated and economically expert handling of the price negotiations.

In relation to the price review, the Treasury has acted in its usual capacity of an informed and objective critic before whom depart-ments must justify their expenditure. Whilst the size of the agricul-tural subsidies has made them an obvious target for periodic pressure of a general kind, Treasury influence has been limited by the estab-lished conventions of the price review. Since decontrol, the Treasury has been particularly concerned that the price guarantees should be honoured in the least expensive way, and its influence can be clearly seen in the policies of retrenchment applied to pigs and eggs and in the encouragement given to beef production.[2] Treasury control is normally expected to avoid detailed or technical analysis and to con-fine itself to broad 'lay' evaluation, and the limitations as well as the virtues of this approach have been apparent in its application to agriculture.[3]

[1] See the contrasting accounts given by the two official civilian war histories, Murray, *Agriculture*, and Hammond, *Food*.

[2] *Sixth Report from the Select Committee on Estimates*, 1957–8, p. 130.

[3] Perhaps the neatest definition of the purpose of Treasury control is that offered by a Ministry of Health witness to the Select Committee on Estimates: 'to satisfy themselves we are properly satisfying ourselves about the economics and soundness of particular schemes'. (*Ibid.*, c. 1092). The difficulty is to see how the Treasury can really perform this function unless it occasionally makes a detailed

While the civil servants who represent the Government can settle minor differences with a minimum of reference to political authority, the Union generally remains unsatisfied; and it is quite usual for the formal talks to reach a deadlock which can only be broken at the political level. The Union's President then has a private talk with the Minister of Agriculture and has been known to see the Chancellor of the Exchequer as well. Concessions may be forthcoming on both sides, but in the end it is the Cabinet which must decide whether or not to pay the necessary price for the Union's endorsement. The record suggests that Cabinets have often made substantial last-minute concessions sooner than face an open disagreement with the Union. In this context, suggestions sometimes made by Union members for entrusting their case to a 'competent businessman' seem strangely ingenuous. No businessman could command one tenth of the influence of a farmers' leader like Turner.

Of course, the Union's bargaining ability stimulated the Government to adopt protective camouflage. This was particularly so before the amalgamation of Agriculture and Food, when the Treasury was sometimes instrumental in producing a 'tough' initial offer which left plenty of scope for subsequent concessions. The Union leaders often stressed to their followers their success in weaning the Government from its original intentions.[1] Success of this sort has repeatedly been achieved, but only a part of it represented real gains to be ascribed to Union persuasiveness. The amalgamation of Agriculture and Food altered the pattern. The new Ministry, strengthened in skill and headed by a Minister who is able to play off his 'other responsibilities' to food consumers against his traditional obligations to farmers themselves, has proved much more of a match for the Union negotiators.

At a more strategic level, the Union's record also appears to be one of conspicuous success. On almost every occasion when it *has* openly disowned the results of the price review it has lost a battle to win a war. In 1944, the 'broken pledge' complaint led to the negotiations which forged the price review machinery. In 1946, the quarrel with Williams over special price review procedure led to important Government concessions. In 1956, the angry reaction of milk and egg producers led to the 1957 Agriculture Act, while in 1960 Union dis-

review of the economic and social value of some individual scheme. Otherwise its 'control' will not get beyond a gentlemanly stimulus to economy and reflection applied by one group of civil servants to another. Such a system is not without its virtues, although they are not perhaps so considerable as S. H. Beer's informative and courteous book, *Treasury Control* (Oxford University Press, 1956) might suggest.

[1] See, for one example, Turner's account of the 1951 negotiations as reported in *The British Farmer*, January 31, 1952.

satisfaction with the working of this Act led in turn to fresh Government assurances. In each case the principle of 'partnership' was triumphantly reaffirmed.

The reluctance of Governments to contemplate an open quarrel has provided the Union with its one trump card. The card has been played to good effect on several occasions, but if played too freely its effect will be lost. The Union's influence within consultative machinery which it was continually repudiating would steadily grow less. If a final breach should occur, the Union would naturally suffer the most. The shock to the Government's political standing would almost surely prove temporary, but the Union would lose the privileged consultative position upon which its whole post-war strategy has been built.

It has therefore been necessary for the Union, apart from its occasional outbursts of overt criticism, to accept the force of the various considerations of national interest. It has had to attend Government lectures on the cost of subsidies, the dangers of inflation, and the advantages of liberalizing world trade. If it has not been converted, it has certainly been educated. Its President has often grumbled that farmers are being treated as 'scapegoats' or singled out 'as the most convenient victim for an austerity axe',[1] yet he has also taken pride in stressing the 'statesmanship' which he and his farmers have shown in accepting 'sacrifices' in the general economic interest.

On the other hand, the Union's tractability is circumscribed. Its county delegates have never been backward about expressing their discontents with Government policies, and its leaders have often had a hard time convincing them that it would be better, so to speak, to go quietly. In recent years, discontent among Union members has become greater. The Union broke with the Government over no less than three of the five price settlements from 1956 to 1960, though not in two successive years. The result is that the Government is becoming rather less concerned, save in general election years, to reach an agreed settlement.

It is also true, however, that price review decisions are themselves becoming less important. The scope for adjustments and compromise was narrowed both by the 1957 Act and by the Government's policy of requiring agriculture to meet some portion of cost increases from its own resources. Government guarantees remain of basic importance to British agriculture but the farmers' protection has come to be based at least as much on statute as on annual negotiation.

5

Ultimately the important question is not who has 'won' the series of

[1] Reported in *The Times*, January 24, 1956.

annual negotiations but what content has been given to the general objectives of the Agriculture Act and how well the review machinery has served the long-term interests of agriculture and the country at large. We will briefly examine the effect of the review upon farmers' collective earnings, and then its effect upon the general wellbeing and efficiency of British agriculture.

Changes in aggregate farming net income are set out in the following table which gives three alternative estimates. In each case, the figure being calculated is the total *earnings* left to UK farmers, after deducting all costs including, in the case of owner-occupiers, an allowance for rent. What is left is the return for the farmers' own labour (manual and managerial) and for his investment of tenants' capital.

YEAR	'Departmental'* Calculation (£ million)	Do, Adjusted to normal weather conditions (£ million)	'Raised Sample'* Calculation (£ million)
1937–38	56	—	68½
1946–47	191	212	190
Average 1948–51	290	288	248
Average 1951–54	332	325	295
Average 1954–57	318	331	302
Average 1957–60	348	361	358

Source—Price Review White Papers
* The 'departmental' calculation treats agriculture as one large farm, multiplying total sales of each commodity by the average price realized and subtracting total expenditure. The 'raised sample' calculation is based upon 3,600 actual farm accounts collected by the provincial agricultural economists.

This table reveals that two sharp increases occurred in aggregate farm earnings, one during the war and the other after the 1947 expansion programme, and that they were followed by a much slower rise in earnings. These calculations do not allow, however, for changes in the value of money. In 'real' terms, the value of farmers' total earnings probably declined slightly between 1950 and 1960.[1] On the other hand, the gains generated by the expansion programme were largely retained, and the objective of stability in the general level of farm income was certainly fully met.

[1] On the basis of the 'departmental calculation', the decline in the real value of farm income between 1948/51 and 1957/60 appears to be about 10 per cent. If the alternative 'raised sample' calculation is taken, however, there was no decline in real earnings. These results have been reached by adjusting the figures to allow for changes in the cost of living as measured by the consumers' expenditure average value index of the London and Cambridge Economic Service. Calculations on the same bases show an increase in real earnings of at least 10 per cent between 1946/7 and 1957/60 (average).

The Union's complaints at price reviews have been broader than the question of stability, however. The basic grievance is that farmers have not shared in the rising prosperity of the last decade, despite achievements in output and efficiency which, by the Government's own admission, compare very favourably with other occupations. This contention is reasonably accurate, but its force depends upon what the price review can be expected to achieve. In the face of economic trends which have been highly adverse to agriculture, it is perhaps not surprising that farmers should have had to work hard to maintain the exceptional prosperity which they reached around 1950. Even this has only been possible with the support, since 1954, of Exchequer subsidies of between £240 and 280 millions a year. Without this support, the prosperity of British agriculture would have quickly collapsed. If a Government error was made it lay in inflating farm incomes to an unnecessary extent in 1947, without reflecting upon the painful difficulties which any degree of retrenchment would subsequently produce.

The producers of individual commodities have inevitably enjoyed a good deal less stability than agriculture generally. Price settlements have steered a middle course between the flexibility wanted by the Government and the rigidity demanded by the Union. Here again the chief Government error lay in over-stimulating the production of certain commodities without enough attention to costs. As a result of Union opposition, subsequent adjustments were made only slowly and with difficulty. It is difficult to judge the reasonableness of price shifts between commodities, because the efficiency of different branches of production changes at different rates. For example, repeated cuts in the egg guarantee have been consistent with fair profits for technically progressive producers, but not for those who have not changed their methods. The problems of price differentiation have increasingly become entangled with the special difficulties of the poorer farmers, but price rigidity is hardly a rational way of tackling their problems.

The basic problem which the Price Review has failed to tackle is that of the wide variation in standards and incomes between farmers. Probably something like two-thirds of the price subsidies are received by one third of the full-time farmers, most of whom are relatively prosperous.[1] Since 1954, smaller farmers have suffered from the curtailment of support for milk, pigs and eggs, and from the partial removal of fixed guaranteed prices. While the system of deficiency payments has increased the responsiveness of agriculture to market requirements, smaller farmers have become more absorbed in buying and selling and have been able to give less attention to improving

[1] See the analysis by E. M. H. Lloyd 'Some Thoughts on Agricultural Policy', *Journal of Agricultural Economics*, February, 1957.

their production methods.[1] The complexity of some of the new guarantees (particularly for pigs) has also overtaxed the understanding of many farmers.[2]

A considerable and increasing proportion of Government aid has been given in the form not of price guarantees, but of various direct subsidies. In 1959–60 fourteen principal subsidies were being distributed at a cost of £95 millions or about 40 per cent of total agricultural assistance. They included subsidies for fertilizers, lime, field drainage, water supply, farm improvements, silos, the rearing of calves, and the ploughing of grassland.[3]

This direct aid is often believed to have a more beneficial and egalitarian effect than price guarantees. For example, the Committee of Public Accounts was 'glad to learn' that as much assistance as possible is given 'in the form of direct and selective subsidies which are applied where they are most needed'.[4] In fact, however, only a very small proportion of these grants represented special aid to the less fortunate or more needy farmers. Until 1958 the main examples of special aid were the hill farming and livestock rearing grants, which were restricted to geographical 'problem' areas and were not provided from price review monies, and a part of the small marginal production scheme which was first introduced in wartime. The great bulk of direct subsidies are available to all farmers, and naturally enough it is the larger and more successful farmers who use most fertilizer and lime, plough up most land, and undertake the greatest number of capital improvements. Thus the extensive use of direct subsidies made very little difference to the distribution of Government support.[5]

Originally, direct subsidies were introduced to stimulate production. With the passing of this need, they were extended largely because they met the demand for action to raise agricultural efficiency, without raising the awkward political problems of more selective forms of aid. Some subsidies certainly have had a widespread effect in improving farming practice, although they are open to the objection that particular techniques may be subsidized beyond their economic value. From the Government's viewpoint, aid for agricultural improvements could be expected to improve technical efficiency, and

[1] The Agricultural Improvement Council, Second Report, HMSO, 1950, p. 3, gave strong and possibly exaggerated testimony to the value of fixed prices in increasing farmers' technical efficiency.
[2] See N. S. Thornton 'A Note on the Influence of the Annual Price Review on Pig Producers' Decisions', Journal of Agricultural Economics, December, 1958.
[3] See Appendix A.
[4] 1951–2 Session, Third Report, HMSO, p. 21.
[5] In 1957, receipts from subsidies per £100 gross output varied considerably with type of farming, but hardly at all with size of farm. Scale of Enterprise in Farming, p. 54.

thus to reduce the need for price support.[1] In practice, however, those who most needed to improve their methods were often least able to take advantage of the grants.

At last the growing difficulties of small family farmers caused the Government to introduce in 1959 a Small Farmer Scheme of rather modest dimensions. Only £9 million a year (about 3 per cent of total agricultural support) was allocated to the scheme. The principle, however, was a novel one, since it offered assistance only to those farmers whose businesses were not economic yet were capable of becoming so.[2] The scale and type of assistance was related to the needs of the individual farm, on the basis of a farm business plan worked out in conjunction with the district advisory officer.

The Union promised co-operation in working the scheme, but it was not enthusiastic. It wanted the scheme to be more widely drawn and asked for help for those small farmers failing to qualify, but its main fear was that the scheme would reduce the efficacy of the general guarantees. It deplored the fact that its cost was subtracted from the price review total, instead of being treated as additional assistance. Schemes of selective aid, it pointed out, 'inevitably involve discrimination between farmers and the hardship of borderline cases'.[3] Whilst (it was implied) such aid might be necessary up to a point, the Union would oppose the transfer of any sizeable proportion of aid to a selective basis.

Here indeed was the essence of the problem. The price review had been built upon a basis of undiscriminating aid to farmers generally, and so long as its level was fairly generous, the system worked smoothly even if wastefully. But once the level of aid began to be reduced, the less successful farmers found themselves in difficulty. It increasingly became in the interest of these farmers to receive special

[1] The Committee on Grassland Utilisation (the Caine Committee) stressed the contribution of many direct grants to the objective of grassland improvement. However, it also pointed out that the grants partly served to compensate for an unsatisfactory relationship between price guarantees. Cmnd. 547, HMSO, 1958, pp. 31–39.

[2] The scheme applied to those farms of between twenty and 100 acres which were judged capable of providing reasonably remunerative full-time work for their occupiers. This was defined as a minimum of 275 standard man-days a year, and farms already absorbing more than 450 standard man-days were not eligible. Assistance was limited to a maximum of £1,000 per farm and was available for a wide variety of improvements and operations directed towards raising the farm's productivity. At the same time, the marginal production scheme was abolished and a temporary scheme was introduced to help those small farmers who could not utilize the main scheme. *Assistance for Small Farmers*, Cmd. 553, 1958. Legislation was provided by the Agriculture (Small Farmers) Act, 1959. Over 21,000 farm plans were approved for assistance in the first twenty-one months. (Ministry of Agriculture, Fisheries and Food.)

[3] *NFU News*, October 30, 1958.

assistance, and in the interest of the Government to give it to them, provided such assistance could be effectively linked with improved efficiency. The Union could scarcely oppose this development without seeming to sacrifice the interests of the many small farmers to those of the few large ones, but it could oppose any attempt to convert agricultural support into a series of special grants for special groups of farmers. The Union's whole post-war strategy and its very considerable success in reconciling internal differences among farmers depended upon a generous level of overall support distributed as 'objectively' and steadily as possible. By 1958 the case for some measure of selective aid could no longer be withstood. Though Union vigilance and Government caution ensured that the first instalment should be an extremely modest one, it represented a significant new departure in the distribution of agricultural support.

CHAPTER IV

MARKETING MONOPOLIES

1

THE most curious and complex aspect of post-war agricultural politics has been that of marketing. Passions run high and numerous interests are involved. The determination of the organized farmers to maintain and extend their pre-war control over the marketing process has been met by opposition from distributive and processing interests and from sundry consumers' champions, and by the critical dissent of independent committees and economists. The political parties have hesitated over their policies, but both Conservative and Labour have been prepared to support at least a large part of the farmers' claims. Successive governments have been concerned with agricultural marketing in conflicting capacities: as farmers' friend, consumers' champion, and taxpayers' guardian.

Confusion stems from the fact that there are two aspects to the 'marketing problem'. There is, first, the problem of inefficiency in the presentation, handling, and distribution of the output of British farmers. That such inefficiency does exist on a serious scale has been the general verdict of a long series of official committees of enquiry, some of which, like the Linlithgow Committee in 1922 and the Lucas Committee in 1947,[1] reported on marketing in general, while others examined the marketing of particular commodities. A principal conclusion of most of these reports has been that the gap between farm price and shop price is unnecessarily wide, and their general tone reflects the still unproven opinion of the Linlithgow report that 'taken as a whole distributive costs are a far heavier burden than society will permanently consent to bear'.[2]

The second aspect of the 'marketing problem' raises somewhat different issues. As the Linlithgow report put it, the farmer 'stands alone at the end of a long line of distributive agencies'.[3] The multiplicity of agricultural units and their remoteness from their final markets places farmers in an unfavourable position in relation to the stronger and more organized interests with which they must deal. There is certainly a tendency for other groups to obtain much of the

---

[1] *Final Report of the Departmental Committee on Distribution and Prices of Agricultural Produce*, Cmd. 2008, 1924; *Report of the Committee Appointed to Review the Working of the Agricultural Marketing Acts*, HMSO, 1947.
[2] Cmd. 2008, 1924, p. 11.
[3] *Ibid.*, p. 28.

benefit from increased efficiency in farming, while farmers are left to carry the major burdens of price and market fluctuations. Collective marketing arrangements represent one of the main methods for strengthening the intrinsically weak bargaining power of primary producers. By banding together to establish a measure of control over the marketing process, farmers can build up (as Chapter 1 indicated) a kind of countervailing power against the bargaining strength of their customers and suppliers.

These two aspects of marketing are of course interrelated. Agricultural marketing is a continuous process which entails a mutual adjustment between farms and markets. Farmers often view it as a matter of utilizing and distributing their output as economically as possible, but it is also a matter of getting them to adapt their production to market requirements. In the past British agriculture was undeniably less successful than its overseas competitors in studying and meeting the requirements of Britain's mass urban market. The latter achieved their success through specialization, efficient grading and standardization of their produce, and bulk transport and handling. British agriculture was something of a jack-of-all-trades engaged in supplementing the more specialized efforts of overseas producers, and this was not conducive to an efficient marketing system.

British farmers plainly had an interest in remedying this state of affairs. The agricultural co-operative movement provided them with a business and sales organization for improving their position. The progress of the movement, however, depended upon the economic resources and efficiency of the co-operatives themselves and upon the willingness of farmers to join and support them. The co-operatives were a rather weak instrument for increasing the farmers' bargaining power directly, since they could neither control external competition nor compel their own members to buy and sell exclusively through their agency. Their contribution to agricultural betterment depended upon the improvements in production and marketing which they could effect to the profit of their own members.

The 'ingrained individualism of the British farmer'[1] is often blamed for the difficulties of agricultural co-operation in Britain. However, this individualism is largely the consequence of the social and economic heterogeneity of British farming. Co-operation flourishes best where farmers of similar education and outlook are practising the same general type of farming, as happens in Denmark or New Zealand. Agricultural co-operation developed slowly in Britain, and the movement was not strongly enough established to provide much defence against the economic blizzards which struck agriculture after the First World War. Moreover the onset of depression made the development of co-operation more difficult, since it intensified

[1] *Lucas Committee Report*, 1947, p. 5.

competition among farmers. In these circumstances the most pressing need appeared to be that of strengthening the farmers' bargaining power, and for this purpose some stronger machinery than voluntary co-operation seemed necessary. This machinery was found in the creation of statutory producer-controlled marketing monopolies.

These bodies were also intended to deal with the other aspect of the marketing problem, and it was hoped that they would use their powers to improve the general efficiency of marketing and distribution. However, there was no guarantee that they would do so, and some of the devices open to statutory monopolies are liable to impede this other objective of raising marketing efficiency. For example, controls over production may increase the average price received by farmers, but they may also restrict the opportunities available to the more progressive farmers or co-operatives for improving their products and increasing their sales. In any event, a statutory monopoly is under obvious temptation to rely upon its regulatory and bargaining powers for helping its members, rather than to face the difficulties and unpopularity which enforced improvements necessarily entail.

There are also limits on the ability of a producer-controlled board to bring about improvements in the distributive system. Farmers' leaders are fond of pointing out that they have the same interest as consumers in curtailing 'middlemen's' profits and in securing efficient utilization of their own output. So in principle they may have. But in practice it is very difficult for one sectional interest (producers) to control the functions of another sectional interest (distributors and processors). It is easier for the former to accept a 'business-man's' concordat of live and let live, and in some circumstances it may even pay a producers' board to co-operate with distributors at the consumers' expense.

The Agricultural Marketing Acts of 1931 and 1933 provided for the preparation of statutory marketing schemes, which would become law if approved by Parliament and a sufficient majority of affected producers.[1] Each scheme would provide for the creation of a producer-elected board and would specify the board's powers.[2] These could include powers to control (either by purchase or regulation) all sales of the product in question, to negotiate prices with distributors, and to specify terms of resale. It could also be empowered to provide services to farmers and to operate processing plants and other trading facilities. The 1933 Act added the power to regulate the volume of production through quotas or other devices.[3] The Minister of Agricul-

[1] See below, p. 102.
[2] The principal enabling powers are set out in Section 5 of the Agricultural Marketing Act, 1931.
[3] Section 10 of the Agricultural Marketing Act, 1933.

ture had power to deal with serious complaints by appointing a committee of investigation, on whose recommendation he might amend the marketing scheme.[1]

The purpose of the 1931 Act, according to the Labour Minister of Agriculture who introduced it, was 'to require the minority to play the game' and 'to equip the British farmer for the first time with a machine that will enable him to be the master of his own market'.[2] Farmers were not at first favourably disposed to this way of making them master. There was considerable dislike for the board's compulsory powers, which were of course essential to the whole concept. More particularly, the National Farmers' Union contended that there was little point or justice in compelling British farmers to co-operate if overseas competitors were still left free to undercut them, but this objection was met by Part I of the 1933 Act, which empowered the Government to restrict foreign imports where a marketing scheme was operating or in preparation. The Union then participated in the promotion of a number of marketing schemes, and among them schemes were successfully introduced for hops, potatoes, bacon pigs, and milk. Except for pigs none of these schemes dealt with products for which imports were in fact of much importance.[3]

The Hops and Potato Marketing Boards relied mainly upon controls over production to realize their aims. The Hops Board imposed production quotas based upon the output of producers in 1928–32, negotiated prices with the brewers, and destroyed any undesired surplus. The effect was to improve the profits of these producers already in the industry, but other farmers could only grow hops by purchasing the right from an existing producer. The Potato Marketing Board prohibited sales of tubers below a prescribed size during periods of plentiful supply. It also allocated acreage quotas, and excess of production was fined but not prohibited. Both methods did something to stabilize and increase producers' returns.

The Pigs Marketing Board was concerned only with bacon pigs. It negotiated prices with another board, the Bacon Marketing Board, which represented curers, and it fixed contracts with producers for the requisite supply of pigs. Its chief problem was to persuade pro-

[1] Section 9 of the 1931 Act. These powers were strengthened by the Agricultural Marketing Act, 1949. See below, p. 93.

[2] H. of C.O.R., 1930–31, Vol. 248, col. 67.

[3] British producers enjoyed virtually a monopoly in the liquid milk market, but not in respect of manufactured milk products. This problem was dealt with, not by restricting imports, but by the provision in the Milk Act of 1934 of a minimum guaranteed price for domestic milk sold for manufacturing into cheese and butter. Imports of potatoes were small in total, but they were occasionally enough to affect the market substantially; after 1934 licences were required for the importation of potatoes and this power was used to restrict imports when home supplies were plentiful. The proportion of hops imported was small, and was limited also by an agreement with the brewers.

ducers to supply suitable pigs on a regular basis and not to switch their supplies to the pork market when pork prices were favourable. The Board did not successfully control the pig market, or achieve any worthwhile results, but its existence provided grounds for the regulation of bacon imports by a system of quotas.

Much the most important marketing schemes were those concerned with milk. The Milk Marketing Boards' main concern was to insulate the profitable market for liquid milk from the largely unprofitable market for manufactured milk products. They did this by fixing differential prices for the two markets, prohibiting resale, controlling the retail price of liquid milk, and diverting any surplus to the manufactured market. Income from milk sales was pooled and standard prices were paid to producers on a regional basis. These methods replaced fierce competition for the more profitable markets with a system of assured markets for all milk producers, irrespective of location.

On several occasions the Boards tried to cut distributors' margins and became embroiled in disputes which were settled by arbitration. The unsuitability of the Boards for tackling problems of milk distribution led in 1938 to an abortive Government proposal to establish an independent regulatory Milk Commission.[1]

The Lucas Committee, no partisan of marketing boards, was impressed by 'the moderation and sense of responsibility which marketing boards, on the whole, displayed in pursuing the policies of price maintenance which their monopoly control of supply made possible'. It pointed out, however, that the pre-war conditions of a strong buyers' market imposed moderation, and that similar price maintenance policies in a sellers' market would not be defensible.[2] The boards performed a rescue operation for those sections of agriculture for which it was easiest to strengthen the position of the home producer. They achieved results by monopoly practices, and they did little to improve marketing efficiency even in those matters which most nearly concerned the farmer. However, the boards, and particularly the Milk Marketing Boards, became increasingly valued by farmers and by the Union for their contribution to economic stability. When war came in 1939 the pigs and potato schemes were suspended, and the Milk Marketing Boards were placed under the control of the Ministry of Food.

2

After the war the Labour Government appointed the Lucas Com-

[1] The Milk Industry Bill, 1938. The Bill was withdrawn under combined opposition from producers and distributors.
[2] *Lucas Committee Report*, p. 10.

mittee to consider the place of marketing schemes under new conditions. This Committee concluded that farmers now had adequate economic protection in the form of price guarantees, which left them with no need for the further protection of marketing monopolies. It thought that the value of producer-elected boards in the future would lie in their ability to improve the quality and presentation of farm output and to deal with marketing as far as the collecting centre, packing station, or other point of first purchase. In the Committee's view the boards had no qualifications for controlling or improving the distributive system beyond this point, and had shown no aptitude for the task. However, since horticultural prices were not guaranteed, horticulturists should be allowed to promote the pre-war type of marketing scheme, despite its drawbacks.

The second half of the Lucas Report's recommendations was rather less persuasive. It argued that the effect of guaranteed prices was to turn agricultural produce into 'the taxpayers' property', and from this doubtful premise drew the conclusion that all guaranteed products should be marketed by a series of Government-appointed commissions each of which would act as 'the business executive of the tax-payer'. These bodies would have all the regulatory and trading powers previously available to producer-controlled boards, and it was anticipated that they would be more energetic in improving the distributive system.[1] These general conclusions were reinforced by the report in the same year of the Williams Committee on milk distribution. This report not only confirmed the unsuitability of a producers' board for improving the efficiency of milk marketing, but produced more specific evidence in favour of the device of an independent commission.[2]

'Lucas logic' did not appeal in the slightest to the farmers' leaders, who clung hard to their marketing inheritance. Partly this was simply because producer boards, whatever their value in the new situation, had become an exemplar of solid and successful Union achievement, although the Union's early opposition to marketing legislation was an awkward skeleton in its closet. Partly it was because the boards were viewed as a kind of reinsurance policy: their prestige might be useful in putting pressure on governments over prices[3] and they would be vital in case of a 'political betrayal'. The combined Unions had insisted before the Lucas Committee that they saw no need for any amendments of the pre-war marketing legislation.[4]

[1] *Lucas Committee Report*, 1947, pp. 58–59.
[2] *Report of the Committee on Milk Distribution*, Cmd. 7414, 1947.
[3] For example, Mr E. C. Johnson, putting the Union's case for a fatstock marketing board, urged that it 'would be an extra string to the NFU bow in fighting the farmers' battles in the years to come'. *The Farmers' Weekly*, January 16, 1953, p. 25.
[4] *Lucas Committee Report*, 1947, pp. 53–57.

However, the Union's first reactions to the Lucas Report were extremely cautious and secretive. A resolution regretting the Report was withdrawn at the 1948 Annual General Meeting at the request of the President who mildly remarked, 'We have got to look at the Lucas Report as a contribution to the kitty of information and opinion on which we can draw for our constructive proposals for marketing.'[1] All that happened was a meeting of county branch chairmen, who formally approved a policy which was not disclosed. 'It can only be concluded that it is a definite policy on the part of Headquarters to keep secret from the general membership not only their agreed attitude in regard to agricultural marketing, but the views of the counties themselves.'[2]

The Milk Marketing Board was much less reticent and quickly declared its opposition to both the Lucas and Williams reports; this stand was strongly endorsed at a meeting of its regional committees and later at its annual general meeting. 'It looks,' said *The Farmers' Weekly*, 'as though the NFU verdict has already been decided for it by the MMB meeting. On the other hand, can you imagine the position where the Marketing Board decided one thing and the NFU another? Where would we poor individuals who subscribe to both be then?'[3] The danger was an unreal one. As their later records revealed, the Union leaders were quite as hostile as the Milk Board to Lucas, but they evidently judged it expedient to wait in silence. 'In this sphere of marketing,' said Mr Knowles at the end of 1948, 'there has existed for two years a balance so politically delicate that premature action had to be avoided at all costs.'[4] This was their justification for the long delay in announcing any marketing policy of their own.

The political atmosphere was indeed delicate. Both the Labour and Conservative parties had had a hand in the passage of the original marketing legislation. The Conservatives adhered in principle to their support of producer boards, the more freely because they were in opposition. The Co-operative wing of the Labour Party was strongly opposed to producer boards, and the party as a whole was sympathetic to the kind of public enterprise and control proposed by Lucas. Labour's interest in reducing the cost of living, its suspicion of 'middlemen', and its faith in planning drew it towards any plan for improving distribution by public action.

The Union was just finding its feet in price negotiations with the Labour Government, and it was understandably wary of precipitating any display of left-wing sentiment. But friendship with the

[1] *NFU Record*, February, 1948, p. 56.
[2] *The Farmers' Weekly* (editorial), May 14, 1948.
[3] *Ibid.*, December 24, 1947.
[4] *The British Farmer*, December 31, 1948.

farmers was also important to the Minister of Agriculture and his immediate associates, who did not wish to spoil Labour's record as the initiator of agricultural marketing. Since no immediate action was necessary, the Government took the easy course of remitting the Lucas Report for further study, while opening discussions with the Union on a more restiicted range of marketing topics.

The result of these consultations was a modest measure, the Agricultural Marketing Act of 1949. Its main purpose was to ensure that producer marketing boards, if and when established or revived, should be made more amenable to public supervision. The Minister of Agriculture was empowered to appoint up to one-fifth of the members of each board. This idea was not particularly significant, since the producers' representatives retained a large majority.[1] More to the point, any use by a board of its regulatory powers could be overruled in certain circumstances by the Minister of Agriculture. The board could appeal to a committee of investigation, although the Minister would be bound by the committee's recommendations only in the case of non-guaranteed products. The Minister's intervention also required Parliamentary approval, but he could give temporary directions to counter delaying tactics by a board.[2] By these provisions, it was hoped to bring the boards more into line with general post-war legislation for the control of monopolies.

The immediate effect of the Act was to set the Union free to advance schemes for the non-guaranteed horticultural products,[3] and the Government stressed that there was no intention of precluding further action upon the larger proposals of the Lucas report. However, by regularizing and encouraging the formation of producer boards and by providing an alternative and much milder device for safeguarding the public interest, the Act made action along Lucas lines much less probable. For this reason the measure was hailed with relief by Opposition spokesmen and bitterly assailed by some Co-operative Members of Parliament. Whilst not all of the Act's details were acceptable to the Union,[4] it too believed that the Lucas shadow

[1] A regular observer of the post-war proceedings of the Milk Marketing Boards has told us that it is not easy, from the Board's discussions, to tell which members are Ministerial appointees. The pre-war boards had each contained two members appointed by the producers' representatives after consultation with the Market Supply Committee (a Government advisory body concerned with the co-ordination of imports and home supplies).

[2] Agriculture Marketing Act, 1949, Sections 2–4.

[3] As the *Lucas Committee Report* had indeed envisaged. Some of the Act's provisions for making the boards more accountable were based on recommendations in this report.

[4] The Union could not really object to the new powers of Ministerial control, but it did criticize the Minister's power to give temporary directions, holding that this might involve boards in financial loss. The Conservative Opposition supported this criticism.

had been lifted; and according to the Vice-President, Mr H. Woolley, 'the NFU can claim credit if not for completely exterminating the Lucas Committee proposals—and I think it would be unwise to assume they are completely done with—at least for removing them out of the realm of serious politics at the present time.'[1]

3

The Union had for some time been under pressure from members to produce marketing schemes for horticultural products. The idea of covering the whole field with one comprehensive scheme was discussed by county branches of the Union in 1946 but was abandoned. A piecemeal approach revealed objections and difficulties which had been obscured by the general enthusiasm of producers for 'organized marketing'. Quite a number of schemes were prepared, and four of them (Peas, Herbage Seeds, Apple and Pear, Tomato and Cucumber) went to public inquiries, but the first two were subsequently abandoned and the third was defeated at the poll of producers.

Horticultural marketing is a complex business. Much of the produce is perishable; quality is important; mass standardization is difficult; and speed and flexibility in marketing are essential. Opposition from a minority of producers, a feature of most marketing schemes in their teething stage, was more effective in a field where the gains seemed less clear and the external opposition stronger. The promoters emphasized their intention to avoid compulsion and to interfere with growers and distributors as little as possible, but this weakened their case. For example, a principal aim was to establish grading standards, but producers were assured that grading would be voluntary and very leniently applied.[2] The various seeds schemes ran into the special problem that the consumers of seeds were farmers—a fact which necessitated 'an unusual amount of consideration'.[3] Opposition from processing and importing interests was relatively much stronger than with milk, potatoes, or eggs; the peas scheme withered under this opposition.

The Unions' response to these problems was to stress repeatedly the necessity for growers' and Union solidarity. Culinary-apple growers and cider-apple growers might have different requirements, but 'attempts to divide the apple growers were in effect attempts to

[1] *The Farmers' Weekly*, January 7, 1949.

[2] A sponsor of the Apple and Pear Scheme dealt with criticisms of the power to establish minimum grades by saying, 'I think this is largely due to a feeling that the standard will be high. In fact, the Provisional Board's intention is quite the reverse.' *The British Farmer*, April, 1953.

[3] *The British Farmer*, June 30, 1950. There was of course no intentional irony in the remark. Schemes were prepared originally for herbage and cereal seeds, and for root, vegetables and flower seeds. All were abandoned.

split the NFU'.[1] Such appeals were insufficient in themselves, and the Union sought to supplement them by emphasizing the value of marketing boards in pressing for import control. While the Apple and Pear Board was to have no direct power at all over imports, the Union argued that it could serve as 'a special avenue of approach to the Government',[2] and by 'strengthening the factual representation of the industry's case' would help the Government 'to stand up to pressure by outside bodies'.[3] These beliefs were a principal reason for the Union's enthusiasm for horticultural schemes, and they also help to explain the opposition from processors and traders and the Ministry's hesitation in approving them. Producers did not want the scheme 'for any of the purposes which appear in it', complained a Labour Member of Parliament (Mr Paget). 'The whole idea of this scheme has been to put pressure upon the Government to restrict imports.'[4] The practical difficulty was that only a strong and successful producers' board could hope to have much influence with the Government. In the event, it was pressure from the Union itself which persuaded the Conservative Government in 1953 to increase tariffs on horticultural products.

The domestic controversies which prevented all but one of the horticultural schemes from coming to fruition found expression also in the scheme that was established. Although the Tomato and Cucumber Board limited itself initially to modest and uncontentious activities and did not assume compulsory powers, it quickly fell foul of a group of abolitionists. This group secured representation upon the Board itself, whose annual general meeting became the scene of unruly disputations over its continued existence.[5] Some objectors harried the Board by refusing to make returns and by denying the authority of its disciplinary committee. Despite these difficulties the Board has had some modest success in improving grading standards and marketing intelligence upon a wholly voluntary basis.[6] This work is threatened by the tendency of many growers to judge the Board's value by its success in securing higher tariffs. After the rejection of a tariff application in 1959, a second attempt to secure the scheme's revocation by producers' poll showed that its supporters had

[1] Mr Tuker, chairman of the Provisional Apple and Pear Marketing Board, reported in *Ibid.*, April, 1953.
[2] Mr Tuker, *Ibid.*, July 31, 1951.
[3] Sir James Turner, *Ibid.*, March, 1953. The Union leaders are fond of assuming that the Government is an innocent victim of sinister pressures.
[4] H. of C.O.R., 1952–3, Vol. 510, col. 350.
[5] *The Farmers' Weekly*, reporting upon 'the verbal rough-house that nowadays passes for the annual meeting of the Tomato and Cucumber Board', stated that the abolitionists almost secured enough votes to reduce Board members' salaries to a penny each. The number present was not large. October 29, 1954.
[6] G. R. Allen, *Agricultural Marketing Policies* (Basil Blackwell, Oxford, 1959), pp. 295–302.

diminished. The next year a new tariff application was successful, but it is not clear that the Board added much to the Union's representations on either occasion.

Horticultural marketing, while important, was only incidental to the central issue of who should control the marketing of the guaranteed commodities. This issue was not fully joined until the Conservative Government started to unwind state control in 1953. The Union's credo was summarized in *The British Farmer*. 'Let there be no mistake about the vital importance of organized marketing to the industry and the nation. The Agriculture Act has not reduced the need, it has increased it. The Marketing Acts are the essential counterpart of the Agriculture Act and neither can render full service in the absence of the other.'[1] On the basis of this piinciple the Union sought the establishment of producer boards for all the principal commodities, which meant the revival of the pre-war boards and the creation of a new board for eggs, another—more tentatively requested—for cereals, and a third which would bring under one comprehensive roof all kinds of fatstock (cattle, sheep and pigs).

The Conservative Government's approach to marketing problems was highly pragmatic. It was sympathetic to the general principle of producer-controlled boards, which the party had supported in its *Agricultural Charter*.[2] Nor was it apparently worried by the volume of independent criticism which had been directed against the functioning of such boards. A not untypical Conservative viewpoint was that of Mr (later Sir Richard) Nugent who in a party pamphlet dismissed this criticism, undiscussed, by holding to the view that the producer board had proved itself 'a practical proposition', whereas alternative possibilities had not.[3] The Government therefore was quite prepared to restore the powers of the pre-war boards for milk, potatoes, and bacon pigs, subject to such adjustments as were necessary to enable these bodies to administer the Government price guarantees. This condition had seemed to the Lucas Committee impossible to fulfil, but Government and Union managed to make a mutually satisfactory arrangement without too much difficulty. The detailed arrangements were complex and included provision for sharing unanticipated profits or losses so as to encourage efficient administration, and powers of Governmental control over any determination of selling prices or distributors' margins. On these conditions the Milk Marketing Boards and the Potato Marketing Board resumed their

[1] *The British Farmer*, November 29, 1952.

[2] 'The basis of good marketing in the future should be producers' co-operation both through voluntary organizations and through statutory marketing boards.' *The Agricultural Charter*, Conservative Central Office, 1948, p. 20.

[3] *Agricultural Marketing*, Conservative Political Centre Discussion Series, 1951.

powers in 1954.[1] In addition, a Wool Marketing Board had been established in 1950 as part of the arrangements for adding wool to the schedule of guaranteed commodities.[2] In this case, the administration of the guarantee necessitated some type of central marketing agency, and there was not much external opposition to the creation of a producers' board.

When it came to a question of further boards, however, Tory pragmatism revealed its other face. One problem was that other established interests had to be considered. The National Association of British and Irish Millers was completely opposed to the formation of a producer-controlled cereals board, fearing that it might compel millers to accept more home-grown wheat of unsuitable quality. The millers were well-organized and launched a successful campaign to demonstrate the undesirability of a marketing board for cereals. Britain's heavy dependence upon imported cereals, particularly wheat, strengthened the millers' case and made the controversy a little unreal. The Union did not press its proposal, although the idea was revived from time to time when farmers experienced difficulties over cereal marketing.[3]

The major controversies concerned fatstock and eggs. The Unions' ambitious fatstock plan[4] represented a synthesis between technical and political objectives, with technical arguments helping out the case for complete monopoly control by a producers' board. It aimed to abolish the livestock auction markets where animals are bought 'on the hoof' and to direct all stock to abattoirs where they would be graded and paid for on a deadweight basis. The Union contended that deadweight grading is a more reliable test of quality than the liveweight method and that its proposed system would substantially reduce handling and transport charges. Both contentions are substantially correct, but they overlook the difficulties of devising a comprehensive grading system which would both satisfy farmers and meet the requirements of all buyers.[5] The Union admitted that its plan could not be quickly introduced, but it wanted a producer board with full powers to apply it as rapidly as possible. This board would

[1] The schemes under which these Boards operate were substantially revised, and financial agreements were entered into between Boards and Government. For details, see *Report on Agricultural Marketing Schemes for the Years 1938–55* (HMSO, 1957), pp. 19–24, 45–50.

[2] The wool marketing scheme was approved by 94.3 per cent of producers voting. *Ibid.*, pp. 38–41.

[3] For example, millers' renewed apprehensions were reported in the *Manchester Guardian*, March 16, 1955. The millers have consistently been a counterpoise to the Union's influence on such questions as whether Britain should participate in the international wheat agreement.

[4] *Marketing of Fat Stock*. Report and Recommendations of a Joint Working Party (National Farmers' Unions, 1952).

[5] See Allen, *op. cit.*, Chapter 9.

purchase all fat cattle, sheep, and pigs, allocate them to abattoirs, supervise their slaughter and grading, and itself purchase or build abattoirs if judged expedient.

Farmers were by no means unanimously in favour of this ambitious plan. It was well known that many preferred liveweight grading and would have to be educated in the virtues of the deadweight plan. Many certainly concurred in the Union's suspicions about the influence of dealers' 'rings' at the smaller livestock auctions before the war, but, as letters to the farming press revealed, others liked the opportunities for shrewd buying and selling which these auctions were believed to offer. However, as in all marketing issues, the bargaining strength of the proposed board was a strong factor in winning farmers' support. A farmers' organization which controlled all supplies of home-grown meat might exert considerable pressure in favour of controls over meat imports, and the Union's plan in fact assumed that imports would be closely regulated.

The Government rejected these proposals for two reasons. First, the Union's plan was opposed by numbers of livestock dealers, auctioneers, and butchers who organized themselves into a Livestock and Home Produced Meat Policy Committee and appealed to the Government's undertaking that private businesses commandeered during the war would eventually be returned. Second, the Government was evidently perturbed at the scale of the Union's proposals and feared that the existence of a large producer-run meat monopoly would contrast rather strangely with its other aim of maximizing 'consumers' freedom'. So perhaps it would; but when the Government observed that 'it would be essential to show how a trading Board with compulsory powers could be reconciled with consumers' choice' and added 'there would also be difficult problems of finance',[1] it seemed to forget that these objections had not been raised, as they might have been, against other Union schemes, although admittedly the argument about consumers' choice was particularly potent in this case. A much more serious objection, which the Government did not raise, was that if so comprehensive a regulation of fatstock marketing was indeed desirable, it was far from obvious that a producers' board was a suitable agency to provide it.

Presented with a deadlock, the Union suddenly resolved upon a new approach. It set up a commercial company, the Fatstock Marketing Corporation, for the marketing of pigs, cattle, and sheep on a grade-and-deadweight basis. An important preliminary had been to persuade the Government to agree to pay to this company subsidies equivalent to those which farmers selling at auction markets would receive. This done, the rapid financing and development of

[1] *Decontrol of Food and Marketing of Agricultural Produce*. Cmd. 8989, 1953. p. 5.

the company represented a considerable achievement. With an original capital of only £10,000, it handled in the first year a turnover of almost £100 million. 'Here is the answer to those critics of the industry who delight to insinuate that farmers have been so enervated by the years of control that they have forgotten how to be business men.'[1] FMC was described as 'a commercial, competitive version of a producers' board'.[2] All producers could become members of the Corporation for a nominal fee, and membership by 1961 was 100,000, but there is no share capital and financing and control of the Corporation are effectively in the hands of the Farmers' Unions and of a Union subsidiary (the NFU Development Co.).[3]

The Corporation's principal success was in the purchase of bacon pigs, over which it acquired at one time almost a monopoly, but it was less successful in persuading producers to market fat cattle and sheep through its agency. The Union did not give up its hope for a statutory marketing scheme, although it had suggested as a compromise that the compulsory powers of the board should be limited to pigs. The Government, supported by the Bosanquet Committee,[4] was quite prepared to accept a statutory board for bacon pigs only, but the Union, mindful of pre-war experience, insisted that all pigs must be included if the market was to be 'stabilized'. It was, however, just this stabilization of the various pig markets through administrative co-ordination which the Bosanquet Committee considered to be undesirable.

The Corporation had the advantage of commercial flexibility, and it was also instrumental in increasing the number of top-quality bacon pigs through the offer of higher premiums. The Union, however, could not make up its mind to substituting a commercial approach for the statutory schemes to which it was accustomed. Some Union members were also critical of their lack of control over the Corporation's policy, and of the absence of a fully democratic basis such as the marketing boards possessed.[5] These limitations were in a sense the Corporation's strength, but commercial experimentation was not easily reconciled with the Union's political and organizational concerns.

[1] *The British Farmer*, July, 1954.

[2] *Ibid.*, May, 1954.

[3] New articles of association in 1959 gave members restricted voting rights and introduced a system of electoral colleges, but the Unions retain powers of appointing some of the directors as well as ultimate control.

[4] *Report of the Advisory Committee on the Development of Pig Production in the UK* (Bosanquet Committee), Cmd. 9588, 1955.

[5] An example was the view of the chairman of the East Riding (Yorks.) Farmers' Union. 'I feel that we should be very careful not to sell off to the Corporation or any other body the power or authority vested in us as a Union by the thousands of members up and down the country.' *The Farmers' Weekly*, November 5, 1954.

The controversy over eggs took a very different form. Any close control over egg marketing was difficult because of the enormous number of small producers. By 1956 packing stations were handling about 75 per cent of home supplies, but there remained, however, a substantial demand for ungraded and unstamped but reputedly fresher eggs sold directly off the farms or by local retailers. The Union's technical case rested on the desirability of providing the packing-stations with a steady throughput, which in its view required the licensing and control of all producers with more than twenty-five birds. In addition, by developing egg products and advertising the virtues of the British egg, the proposed board might be able to widen the market for home-produced eggs.

After considerable delay the Government agreed to the promotion of a statutory scheme. It perhaps wanted to compensate the Union, by a placatory approach over eggs, for its refusal to accept the latter's fatstock plan. It was no doubt influenced too by an absence of organized opposition from distributive interests such as had occurred with fatstock and cereals. The reasons for this were rather curious. The egg packing stations had enjoyed an increased turnover and guaranteed profit margins under Ministry control,[1] and a continuation of close marketing control doubtless seemed more to their advantage than a return to competition. Producers' co-operatives controlled 40 per cent of the packing stations' output, and a third of the members of the Union's provisional marketing board, including the two principal promoters, had commercial interests in the stations. The position of the other large egg wholesalers was weakened by their dependence upon the packing stations for supplies and by the reduced flow of competitive imports. They were probably reluctant to risk antagonizing a prospective board with which they would later have to deal.

Yet opposition to the Union's plan did flare up from different quarters on an unexpected scale. The public inquiry into the scheme produced 901 objectors, occupied thirty-four days, and yielded many volumes of evidence. Many of the objectors were egg producers and producer-retailers who were indignant about the proposed restrictions on local and private egg sales. They included another producers' organization, the Poultry Association of Great Britain, which claimed 10,000 members including many specialist producers. The Association had submitted a marketing scheme of its own to the Ministry in 1953, but the Minister had ruled that this

---

[1] The comfortable profit margins of the packing stations under control had drawn the fire of the Comptroller and Auditor General, who suggested that £300,000 a year could have been saved by a different system of payment. *Trading Accounts and Balance Sheets*, 1954–55, HMSO.

organization did not substantially represent egg producers.[1] A mixed array of consumers' champions also entered the lists. They included some perennial objectors in principle to compulsory marketing like the Cheap Food League and the Liberal Party, which detected in this scheme a particularly obnoxious use of compulsion, as well as ex-Ministry officials, distinguished economists, and some forceful 'plain citizens'. A group of objectors organized themselves into a society with the cheerful title of SOCEM (Society of Objectors to Compulsory Egg Marketing).

At the inquiry the Union's technical case fared badly. The evidence showed clearly that many producers wanted to sell untested, ungraded, and unstamped eggs and that many customers and housewives wanted to buy them. The Union therefore had to show that control of this traffic was necessary in the interests of efficient marketing. Before 1939 the development of systematic egg marketing in Britain had possibly been impeded by the individualism of producers, but by 1956 the turnover of the packing stations had greatly increased, the seasonal flush in eggs had been reduced, and overseas competition had been almost eliminated as a result of Government guarantees. The fact that subsidies could in any case only be conveniently paid on eggs sold through packing stations meant that the requirements of 'orderly marketing' could easily be buttressed by some system of financial inducements. In these circumstances it might even have been supposed in the public interest that producers should be free to sell their eggs without subsidy.

In his report the Commissioner followed the Union in relying heavily on pre-war and largely irrelevant evidence about the weaknesses of voluntary marketing. He set aside the evidence of five economists on this question as inconsistent with 'the experience of the past and the evidence of practical men'.[2] He did, however, agree that the proposed controls over egg producers were excessive, and following his report the Government insisted that the exemption limit should be raised from twenty-five to fifty birds and that any producer should be entitled to a license for selling eggs free of stipulations about testing or grading. The Union complained grumpily that the Government's changes were 'neither necessary nor helpful',[3] but it accepted them rather than abandon its intentions, and the re-

[1] H. of C.O.R., 1953-4, Vol. 521, col. 1292. The Union claimed to represent over 200,000 egg producers. Including ordinary householders, there may be as many as a million egg producers in all. *Report on the Proposed British Egg Marketing Scheme*, Cmd. 9805, 1956, p. 10.

[2] *Ibid.*, p. 42. The Union did not call any economists to defend its scheme, but the Commissioner did not regard this as a defect. It is also worth noting that three of the objecting economists were 'practical men' in the sense that they had considerable administrative experience.

[3] *NFU News*, September 19, 1956.

vised scheme was then approved by a large majority of producers (94.2 per cent of those voting).

The achievement of an Egg Marketing Board was a mixed triumph for the Union. The Minister of Agriculture tried to justify the scheme to Parliament on technical grounds ('Hens, like Ministers, do not lay the same number of eggs each week'[1]), but Mr Amory's wit could not really conceal the thinness of the Union's case. Two of the Commissioner's three reasons for recommending a modified scheme were concerned with the need for some agency to administer the egg subsidy, but that agency need not have been a producer-controlled board. However the Union's view that any alternative subsidy arrangement would be less favourable to producers was doubtless an important factor in securing the high poll in favour of the scheme.

4

Schemes under the Agricultural Marketing Acts require the approval of the Minister of Agriculture, Parliament, and sufficient producers. If there are objections (as there almost always are) the Government must authorize a public inquiry to consider them, and it often requires some modifications of the scheme in the light of its Commissioner's report. If these are accepted by the promoters, the scheme is submitted for Parliamentary approval. At the ensuing poll the scheme requires the support of two-thirds of the registered producers voting, who must also control two-thirds of the voters' combined productive capacity. A scheme can be revoked if a majority of registered producers so decides. The scheme is administered by a periodically elected board, usually consisting mainly of producers elected on a regional basis, together with a small number of special members elected for the whole industry and a sprinkling of Ministerial appointees. Much of a board's work is carried on by a small executive committee of up to seven members, one of whom is a Ministerial appointee. Offences against its regulations are dealt with by a small disciplinary committee with power to impose substantial fines.

Before the war the disciplinary powers of the boards were frequently attacked as wrong in principle and unfairly administered in practice. These charges were investigated by the Falmouth Committee, and both the principle and the boards' administration were vindicated, though certain changes were recommended.[2] The most important of these was that the jurisdiction of the whole board should be replaced by that of a disciplinary committee headed by an

[1] H. of C.O.R., 1956-7, Vol. 562, col. 329.
[2] *Report of the Departmental Committee on the Imposition of Penalties by Marketing Boards and Other Similar Bodies*, Cmd. 5980, 1939.

independent legally trained chairman, and this was provided for under the Agricultural Marketing Act of 1949. (Section 5.) The change has certainly made the boards less vulnerable to accusations of procedural injustice, although attacks on the principle of their disciplinary authority have continued to occur.

Formally the arrangements for establishing and operating the marketing boards are tolerably democratic, but it is often alleged that they are vitiated in practice by the dominant position of the Union. To start with, no other organization save the Union seems likely to get the Government endorsement without which a scheme cannot proceed. Other bodies are likely to be told that they are not 'sufficiently representative of producers' or else that their proposals are impracticable. The case of the Poultry Association has already been mentioned. Another example of an unsuccessful marketing proposal was that of the Accredited Poultry Breeders' Federation, which contained 1,500 of the 3,500 accredited breeders. The Federation realized that Union support was essential for success, and this support was not forthcoming.[1]

Moreover, once Government backing has been obtained, the Union is in a very powerful position. None of the public inquiries have caused the Government to withdraw its support, and only the egg marketing inquiry produced major modifications. The leading lights of the appropriate Union commodity committee or 'working party' become the members of the provisional marketing board which officially promotes the scheme. The Union puts the full weight of its organization and propaganda behind the scheme, and is not reluctant to represent the issue as a matter of 'loyalty' to the Union itself. By contrast, any opposition to the scheme has to be hastily improvised and to contend with difficult problems of organization and publicity. For example, objectors have often had to secure voting lists at considerable expense from the provisional register of producers possessed by the promoters.

Once a scheme is in force, none but Union-approved candidates usually seek or secure election to the boards.[2] According to the chairman of the Milk Marketing Board, Sir Thomas Peacock, 'With the nationwide organization they (the Union) have got nobody would have a chance against them'.[3] Occasionally, rivalry between Union county branches or disagreement over some technical issue of policy has produced a mild electoral contest for regional members;

[1] *The Farmers' Weekly*, February 23, 1951.

[2] Candidates require the nomination of a variable number of sponsors or, under some schemes, of the Union itself. They generally have to arrange for their own meetings and publicity unless, as has been known, the Board is willing to circulate their addresses with its other material.

[3] Report (unpublished) of the milk marketing scheme inquiry held in November 1954; second day, p. 124.

for example, a few contests have occurred in the Milk Marketing Board over the merits of different breeds of dairy cattle. Stronger opposition has generally been confined to those boards weak enough to be susceptible to the attacks of outright 'abolitionists'. Only the minor Tomato and Cucumber Board has consistently been in this position. However, in 1958 a convinced opponent of the boards, Mr Jack Merricks, broke all precedent by being elected to the Potato Marketing Board as a special member, displacing the Board's chairman in the process. His success probably reflected farmers' dissatisfaction less with the Board's existence than with its actual functioning, which Mr Merricks, himself an able farmer, had potently criticized in appropriately bucolic terms.[1]

Some of the criticism of the Union's dominant position in the sphere of marketing schemes is patently unfair and irrelevant. After all the Union is a comprehensive organization with no real rival. It is natural that it should take the lead in presenting marketing schemes, and inasmuch as its leaders have genuinely been under pressure from county branches and commodity committees to put forward schemes for almost every branch of agriculture, they cannot easily be condemned for 'empire-building'. It is equally natural no doubt that the elected members of the boards should be Union members carrying the backing of its county branches. Moreover the Union does not *always* have its way, as is sufficiently shown by its failure to proceed with some schemes, its defeat at the poll for the Apple and Pear Scheme, and its reluctant acceptance of rather considerable modifications of the Egg Scheme.

Nevertheless the Union's powerful advantages make its heavy-handed promotion of some schemes especially unfortunate. Once the Government has agreed to the promotion of a scheme, the Union seems sometimes to have displayed indecent haste to secure its members' confirmation and to have shown little tolerance of criticism. Both the revised potato scheme and the egg scheme were dispatched to the counties at the height of the harvest season; little time was allowed for consideration of criticism; and the egg scheme was circulated originally in a truncated form.[2] These methods are partly a reflection of the Union-Government partnership. In the Union's eyes

[1] 'I kill my thistles, weed out docks, and spray for potato blight. Whenever I find a pest I fight against it, and that applies to the Potato Marketing Board.' (*The Economist*, November 8, 1958, p. 497). Mr Merricks's main criticism was that the acreage quotas imposed by the Board discouraged efficient production and made farming systems inflexible. He lost his seat in 1961.

[2] In some branches, at least, members were asked to endorse the egg scheme without being shown a full draft. Under protest, this was rectified, and an extra week allowed for the scheme's consideration. It is fair to add that only eleven of the 1,200 local Union branches registered formal objection to the egg marketing scheme. See Cmd. 9805, 1956.

the difficult task is always to 'do a deal' with the Government; once this is done, any idea of the deal being spoilt for lack of support among its own membership seems intolerable. And the same reason —the need to endorse a scheme on which Union and Government have agreed for fear that the alternative would be no scheme at all— equally helps to explain the willingness of producers to vote for schemes, in spite of doubts about their details or presentation.

Once in existence, the marketing boards cease to be beholden to the Union in any formal way, and the more successful ones build up a distinctive *esprit de corps*. They retain close contacts with the Union, and even the powerful Milk Marketing Board is fairly deferential to Union opinion. According to its chairman in 1954, who was previously president of the Union, 'if the Board do anything wrong, the NFU are the first people to come down on them'.[1] The boards and the Union view problems of common concern from somewhat different vantage points, and this sometimes gives rise to conflict and mutual checks. Although the boards are typically much concerned with the problems of weak producers, they must necessarily adopt a somewhat more commercial approach than the Union to methods of production and marketing. When, for example, the Milk Marketing Board proposed to end the price bonus on the first 400 to 500 gallons of a producer's monthly sales (a wartime innovation designed to help small producers), opposition was funnelled through the Union's machinery much more than through the Board. The Board eventually won its point, but this was less a defeat for the Union than a kind of division of labour between it and the Board. The latter made the necessary commercial decision and the former ventilated producers' dislike of it.[2] While Union and boards sometimes have their differences, they are too much part of the same farmers' movement for their basic solidarity to be easily shaken.

5

As already noted, the weak 'marketing sense' of British farmers has often been deplored by committees of inquiry. One of the original purposes of the Agricultural Marketing Acts was to help farmers to overcome this weakness, by establishing producer-controlled boards which could bring home to their members the requirements of the

[1] *Milk Marketing Scheme Inquiry*, 1954, Second Day, p. 108, Mr T. Peacock.
[2] A speaker at the Union's 1957 annual general meeting actually proposed a vote of censure on the Milk Marketing Board, on the grounds that its methods for enforcing milk standards were 'undemocratic and high-handed'. The chairman of the Union's Milk and Dairy Produce Committee (Mr Vincent) opposed the motion, which was not voted on, but said that he would express his views to the Board 'in no uncertain terms at the appropriate moment'. *The Farmers' Weekly*, January 25, 1957.

market, and which could improve the quality, presentation, and marketing of their products. However, in the pre-war period 'the "farmer in the field" was too prone to regard a marketing board merely as an instrument of price negotiation and not at all as an instrument for the improvement of his own productive and marketing technique'.[1] Since the 1947 Agricultural Act, the price maintenance function has become less important, and a development of the other functions of the Boards might therefore be expected.

That this has not occurred on any significant scale is probably due to the fact that statutory marketing boards are not the only, nor necessarily the best, instruments for improving the 'marketing sense' of farmers. Their advantages are plainly largest where action needs to be on a comprehensive scale or to be effectively enforced. Examples of such action by some of the boards are the provision of market intelligence, the inspection of wholesalers' accounts, and the determination of grading standards. Improvements in grading and packaging, however, can be achieved more quickly and to higher standards by farmers' co-operatives or private companies, although such progress is necessarily piecemeal. The Milk Marketing Board has developed a number of technical services to producers, including milk recording, artificial insemination, and the provision of grass drying centres. In each case, however, the Government stimulated the development of the service and provided substantial financial support.[2]

Any farmer-controlled organization has to reckon with the difficulty of educating its members to adopt new methods and to accept higher standards. Even the Fatstock Marketing Corporation, which is a commercial organization, has been faced with this difficulty, and the statutory marketing boards have been more closely tied by their democratic basis and their accountability to all producers, both progressive and backward. The Milk Marketing Board has risked temporary unpopularity on minor matters, but it has not taken the initiative on such major matters as the quality of milk supplies. Improvements have mainly been left to Government regulation, supported by Government financial aid. For example, in many countries (e.g., Denmark, Holland, USA), milk is graded and priced according to its content of butter fat and solids-not-fat. In Britain it is not, with the consequence that producers have concentrated upon increasing output through the use of high-yielding breeds of cow, irrespective of the nutritional or conversion value of the milk being produced. The Board has acquiesced in a trend which

[1] *Lucas Committee Report*, 1947, p. 13.
[2] Ministry of Agriculture, *Report on Agricultural Marketing Schemes for the Years 1938–1955*, HMSO, 1957.

is temporarily profitable to a majority of its members, but which is probably short-sighted.[1]

Government controls have limited the scope for the boards to intervene in the distributive system in recent years. If it had been adopted, the Union's fatstock plan would have cleared the ground for a reorganization of abattoirs for the purpose of reducing their number and increasing their efficiency.[2] It is most unlikely, however, that any producer-controlled board either would or could have carried out a comprehensive regulation of this kind; certainly none of the existing ones has ever attempted to do so. If such regulation is indeed desirable (a question which goes beyond the scope of this book), it clearly should be a matter for some independent and publicly accountable agency. On the other hand, there should be increasing opportunities for farmers' organizations to participate in processing and distribution on a competitive basis. Statutory marketing boards, however, are rather rigid organizations to engage successfully in trading activities. Agricultural co-operatives and such bodies as the Fatstock Marketing Corporation are more likely, because of their greater freedom and flexibility, to enter this field successfully.

We may conclude that the principal function of statutory marketing boards does not consist now, any more than it did before the war, in the improvement of production and distribution. The boards' activities in these spheres are rather limited, and many of them might be done better by a different type of organization without compulsory powers. The Pig Industry Development Authority and the Horticultural Marketing Council are examples of organizations which have been set up specifically to improve the efficiency of their industries.[3] The agricultural co-operative movement has grown since the war, and the greater stability of British agriculture should provide ground for further growth.[4] The marketing boards themselves must

---

[1] It is only fair to note that the Board has imposed severe penalties upon producers whose butter-fat content is below the statutory minimum. The desirability of a higher butter-fat content in liquid milk can also be questioned on medical grounds, but a higher content of solids-not-fat is certainly desirable, but has not been attained. See *Milk Composition in the UK* (Cook Committee Report), Cmnd. 1147, 1960.

[2] The case for such measures was favourably regarded by the Lucas Committee and is well set out by T. J. Shaw, 'The Future of Agricultural Marketing', *Journal of Proceedings of the Agricultural Economics Society*, January, 1952.

[3] The Pig Industry Development Authority was created under Part 3 of the Agriculture Act (1957), and was financed by a levy on any subsidy paid on pigs slaughtered. The Horticultural Marketing Council was financed initially by a small Government grant, prior to the introduction of a producers' levy, and had a more limited scope. *Horticulture*, Cmd. 61, 1957. The governing bodies of both organizations consist mainly of representatives of producers and distributors.

[4] The annual turnover of the English societies increased from £25 millions in 1946 to £108 millions in 1955. Probably two-thirds of British farmers belong to

still be principally regarded as instruments for strengthening the economic position of farmers. The Union has pressed for their revival and extension in this belief, but as yet this expectation has hardly been justified.

Milk provides the most important test of this question. Between 1953–4 and 1959–60, the Government was able to reduce the milk subsidy (excluding special welfare schemes) from £46 million to £8·5 million.[1] This was achieved through limitation of the quantity guaranteed and through a series of increases in the retail price of liquid milk. The Government agreed to increase the quantity if liquid sales expanded, but the increases in the retail price of milk naturally made this harder to achieve.[2] As production increased, the Board had to sell a rising surplus for manufacturing uses and deduct its large losses from the average prices paid to producers. The Government, on the other hand, was able to effect considerable savings during a period of rising milk output and falling milk profits.

It is true that a programme of retrenchment was probably necessary, although the reduction of the milk subsidy was hardly consistent with the nutritional aims which the Government had pursued previously. In any case, the Government's case was made much easier by the existence of a producer-elected board which had to shoulder some of the blame and which could mollify some part of producers' indignation. The Union had hoped in 1952 that the restoration of the board's powers would have the effect of 'insulating the (milk) industry from some of the consequences of wrongful administration of the Agriculture Act'.[3] The actual effect was rather a return to pre-war Marketing Act methods of price discrimination as the principal means for maintaining producers' prices.

A further development occurred in 1961, when the Government made an increase in the guaranteed milk price conditional upon the adoption of a system of production quotas by the industry.[4] The idea of penalizing excess production by paying a much lower price for any surplus had already of course been applied to the industry as a whole, but it was now the Government's intention to bring this point home to the individual producer. Individual quotas would

co-operatives, although most members do much of their buying and selling through other channels. Margaret Digby and Sheila Goret, *Agricultural Co-operation in the United Kingdom* (Basil Blackwell, 1957), pp. 36–7.

[1] In the latter year milk was not subsidised at all in England and Wales. It should be noted, however, that milk producers secured a large share of the benefits from the £95 million expended in the latter year on direct grants.

[2] Following small increases in liquid milk consumption guaranteed output for England and Wales was raised by stages from 1,651 million gallons (1954) to 1,698 million gallons (1961).

[3] Sir James Turner reported in *The British Farmer*, January 31, 1952.

[4] Cmnd. 1311, p. 6.

protect weaker producers, but would be a severe handicap to the many producers who could profitably and efficiently expand their output at rather lower prices. The Union and the Milk Marketing Board had both considered and rejected this quota plan, but they agreed to try to find an acceptable scheme.[1] In this case, it was the Government which appeared to insist on production controls as a means of protecting weak producers, although the effect would inevitably be to make consumers pay higher prices for their liquid milk than would otherwise be necessary.

The Potato Marketing Board does not trade extensively in potatoes, but buys them if the market price falls below a certain level. Initially this support price was guaranteed by the Government which paid 95 per cent of the Board's losses. Under revised arrangements introduced in 1958, support was restricted to potatoes sold for human consumption and any subsidy due was paid to the Board to use as it saw fit.[2] In effect these changes encourage the Board to use its strengthened powers to regulate production so as to maintain market prices. It can now exercise a closer control over the acreage planted, as well as specify the size of potatoes which may be sold. Given the greatly fluctuating supply of potatoes, the use of production controls may not be unreasonable, and there are obvious advantages to the Government in allocating this function to a producers' board. However, it is questionable whether the Board has discharged this task with sufficient skill to stabilize prices effectively and to compensate for the inevitable restrictions on efficient producers.[3]

The Wool Marketing Board has been uniquely successful in using its bargaining powers to reduce distributors' margins, and its operations have certainly helped to keep down the cost of the wool subsidy.[4] The Hop Marketing Board provides price support for a commodity which is not guaranteed. The Egg Marketing Board initially followed much the same policies as the Government trading company which preceded it, and it has no clear ways open to it for raising prices or reducing the cost of support.

In general then it may be said that several of the marketing boards have helped to reduce the direct cost of agricultural subsidies by reintroducing pre-war techniques of price regulation and production control. These effects have not resulted from any very far-sighted deliberation on the part of either Union or Government. The Union

[1] The Union had rejected a quota plan at its 1961 Annual General Meeting. Later, it failed to find an acceptable scheme.

[2] A further development came in 1961 when the Government proposed the creation of a market support fund, to be financed two-thirds by the Government and one-third by the Board, which would be used to buy potatoes when market prices were low. Cmd. 1311, 1961, p. 9.

[3] See the interesting analysis in Allen, *op. cit.*, pp. 284–295.

[4] *Ibid.*, p. 303–308.

gave too little thought to whether its addiction to marketing boards was appropriate under post-war conditions, while the Conservative Government pursued a highly pragmatic search for arrangements which would yield maximum satisfaction to the farmers at minimum charge to the Exchequer. In the narrow context of political bargaining, the Government's policy appears as the more successful, but the consequent diversion of attention from the important economic and technical problems of marketing has done a grave disservice to British Agriculture.

CHAPTER V

THE BIRCH IN THE CUPBOARD

1

IN return for a guarantee of economic security the representatives of British agriculture accepted on behalf of their industry an obligation to satisfy certain minimum standards of husbandry and estate management. These standards were to be enforced not by indirect economic pressures but by the direct might of the state. Under Part II of the 1947 Agriculture Act all farms and estates were declared liable to periodic inspection, and their occupiers and owners were required to comply respectively with the 'rules of good husbandry' and the 'rules of good estate management'.[1] Where the farmer was also the owner he was obliged to satisfy both sets of standards. If a farmer or owner failed to comply with these standards he could be placed under 'supervision' and required to comply with any directions issued to him. If his performance remained unsatisfactory after a period of time, he could be made to vacate his tenancy or quit his holding. An owner was not of course deprived of his property without compensation, being entitled to sell his land or to let it to an approved tenant. But he could be required to farm as others thought best and, failing satisfaction, be made to vacate simultaneously his farm and his home. Many farmers were so treated.[2]

Such powers may seem to reflect a harsh attitude toward individual rights which is inconsistent with Britain's long tradition of freedom. Townsmen in particular are inclined to wonder that they were ever granted. It is therefore well to recall their actual context. First, they were originally war powers, and for a time at least they appeared equally necessary under peacetime conditions of economic stress. Second, Britain has become increasingly conscious of her small area in relation to all the competing pressures on land. The fear of a 'land famine' together with the much older view of land as a 'sacred trust' combined to suggest that the nation could no longer tolerate idle or ill-farmed acres. Third, most farmers believed that the coupling of sanctions against inefficiency with the guarantee of economic support was reasonable and necessary. Finally, the sanctions were part of a system of 'self discipline'. Even in wartime there had been no question of entrusting coercive powers to public officials. They were in the

[1] Agriculture Act, 1947, Secs. 10 and 11.
[2] The relations between landlords and tenants were governed according to similar principles. See Chapter VIII.

hands of farmers and other members of the farming community sitting on the War Agricultural Executive Committees. The 'War Ags' were selected by the Minister of Agriculture and acted exclusively as his agents, but care was taken to make their membership tolerably representative. Under the Agriculture Act these committees were reconstituted, and a majority of their members had to be drawn from lists submitted by the main agricultural organizations.[1]

The new law was based in part on the committees' war powers to give directions regarding the use of agricultural land and (with the consent of the Minister) to take possession of land or to terminate tenancies. These powers were used mainly in connection with odd pieces of land and occasional intractable individuals, but their presence in the background stiffened the whole programme of informal advice and voluntary compliance. Between 1940 and 1947 there were some 10,000 cases of dispossession, but the great majority involved non-resident owners, parts of holdings, derelict land, etc. During the same period nearly 3,000 tenancies were terminated, but again about half involved only accommodation land.[2]

The main work of the 'war ags' was not the exercise of compulsion but the administration of cropping programmes and the provision of services. National production targets were distributed among the counties, and the committees then allocated quotas to each district, leaving their local district committees to work out the details with individual farmers. Each member of a district committee was usually responsible for certain farms, and he often gave detailed instructions about their management. During these times of crisis his decisions were normally upheld by the committee and by the Ministry, and indeed they were rarely challenged.[3] That this authority was sometimes exercised with an unnecessarily heavy hand and that there were individual cases of injustice was inevitable, but on balance the work of the 'war ags' was creditably done. There is little exaggeration in the evaluation of the official historian of the wartime agricultural programme.

It is impossible adequately to describe the devotion behind the long

---

[1] See Chapter VI for a discussion of the constitution and other activities of the county committees.

[2] These war powers were exercised under the Cultivation of Lands Order, 1939, S. R. & O., No. 1078. They continued to be exercised during the hiatus between the end of the war and the enactment of new legislation but at a declining rate. See Murray, *Agriculture*, pp. 302-3.

[3] Murray points out that it is impossible to ascertain the extent to which compulsion had to be used to implement cropping directions, since formal orders were often issued even where compliance was voluntary in order to make the farmer eligible for certain grants or to protect him from legal action by his landlord. *Ibid.*, pp. 301-2.

hours spent in visiting farms, field by field, by day and by night, in all seasons of the year; the infinite patience required in cajoling reluctant farmers to change their systems, and, often, in surmounting the suspicions and criticisms with which some farmers greeted the advice of their neighbours; the determination required to overcome the tedium of committee work and the weariness of form-filling and report-writing added to the continuous labour of running their own business. The reward to these men, who persisted in their work over so many years, was often only the sense of having fulfilled their duty and the knowledge that the ordinary farmer in the early years of the war would never have accepted directions or advice from anyone who was not himself facing the new problems and who had not himself made a success of farming.[1]

Shortly after the reconstitution of the committees in 1948 the Minister announced a new production drive. Another farm survey, like that conducted during the war, was initiated which was intended to be the beginning of a continuous programme of tri-annual visits. The farm survey was the basis of the committees' whole discipline-advice programme. Normally visits were made by two district committee members (accompanied by one or more officials) who walked around the farm, talked with the farmer, and filled in survey forms issued by the Ministry. Based on the broad rules of good husbandry set out in the Agriculture Act, these forms provided for an assessment of such features as suitability of crop rotation, efficiency of grassland management, use of fertilizers, adequacy of machinery and labour force, yields, and output. As during wartime, each farm was graded 'A' (good), 'B' (fair), or 'C' (poor). Where a survey revealed poor farming the district committee first attempted to persuade the farmer to improve, and a member living nearby might undertake to give him periodic advice. It was not unusual for committee members to lend machinery or other assistance to a farmer 'in trouble'. The district advisory officer would be asked to give special attention to this farmer if he was not already doing so. In most cases this was sufficient, though many farmers needed periodic prodding. Where it was not, the district committee reported the case to the county committee's husbandry sub-committee for further action.

Again the farmer received a series of visits, this time from a panel of the sub-committee. Again he was urged to avail himself of the assistance of the advisory officers, and he might be given advice by the panel members themselves. Again he was impressed—and at this stage more strongly—with the fact that drastic action might become necessary. The panel then reported back to the next meeting of the sub-committee where a proposal might be made to put the farmer

[1] *Ibid.*, p. 339.

under supervision. The sub-committee might, however, decide to try more persuasion, postponing its own decision or returning the case to the district committee where the whole process began again. Before a supervision order could be made, the farmer had to be notified and given an opportunity to make representations which were heard by the sub-committee.

Supervision orders were reviewed annually. If the farmer showed little or no improvement the sub-committee would usually recommend a second year of supervision, after which dispossession might be proposed. The county committee normally reviewed these decisions at length, sometimes sending out still another panel to inspect the farm.[1] Committee recommendations for dispossession were examined at the Ministry's provincial and headquarters offices, primarily to ensure that all procedural requirements had been fulfilled, which was by no means always the case. Though the final decision to proceed with dispossession was formally the Minister's, the substantive content of a committee's decision was rarely questioned.

This task of defining and applying broad standards of husbandry and estate management was of course neither easy nor popular. A farmer's whole future might hinge on a judgment whether or not he had maintained 'a reasonable standard of efficient production, as respects both the kind of produce and the quality and quantity thereof, while keeping the unit in a condition to enable such a standard to be maintained in the future'.[2] But at least these judgments were made by practical local people who could be expected to appreciate the farmer's problems and to apply their powers with sympathy and moderation.

The continued co-operation of the committees was vital to the success of the programme, and this introduced an unusual and delicate set of considerations into the questions of administrative reform which inevitably arose with the accumulation of peacetime experience and criticism. The first thoroughgoing examination of the workings of the committees was made by the Ryan Committee which reported in 1951.[3] It suggested that the system of alphabetical grading be abolished on the ground that it conveyed a false impression of ob-

---

[1] In 1955, as a result of a remark by Lord Justice Denning in the *Graham and Benney* case (see below, pp. 122-3), committees were instructed that one body should deal with the case from beginning to end, and most of them delegated the authority to decide all questions relating to sanctions to a single husbandry and estate management sub-committee. By this time sanctions were moribund and the question was almost entirely academic.

[2] Agriculture Act, 1947, Sec. 11 (1).

[3] Ministry of Agriculture and Fisheries, *Report of the Committee to Review the Organization of the Ministry of Agriculture and Fisheries* (London: HMSO, 1951). Cited henceforth as *Ryan Committee Report*, 1951.

jectivity and national uniformity,[1] and that farmers be given more information about the opinions of visiting panels. It recommended dissociating the professional advisory service from the committees' farm survey and sanctions work. And it recommended that the committees be denuded of most of their administrative functions. The Ministry accepted most of the Ryan recommendations, but the committees decidedly did not. As they saw it, they were to be deprived of the administrative work which they rather liked, while at the same time being asked to perform unaided the difficult and often disagreeable task of disciplining their fellow farmers.

When the vehemence of the committees' opposition was discovered, the Ministry had to lay aside its plans for full reform and try to heal a breach with the committees which threatened the entire local administration. It was doubtless with some considerable relief that the Minister, Mr Thomas Williams, turned the problem over to his Conservative successor in the autumn of 1951. Williams could, however, look back on a period during which the sanctions had been administered with considerable energy. Between March, 1948, when the Agriculture Act came into force, and the end of 1951 more than 3,000 supervision orders had been issued and 157 farmers and ten landowners dispossessed.[2]

The Conservative Minister of Agriculture, Sir Thomas Dugdale, was no more ready than Williams had been to antagonize the committees over the Ryan report. He gently suggested that they adopt the farm survey procedures recommended by Ryan, but most of them failed to do so. In more and more counties the survey was all but abandoned, but the effects were not immediately felt. Indeed, Dugdale took at first a curiously strong position on sanctions. Committees were told in the customary spring circular in 1952 that they had not been vigorous enough in imposing sanctions during the previous four years, that there had been too few supervision orders and too few dispossessions. In a personal letter to them Dugdale wrote:

I rely on you, the man on the spot, to persuade the half-hearted farmer to mend his ways, to give your personal advice when and where it can help and to recommend really inefficient farmers for supervision. I know that this is not always a pleasant task, but I am sure you realize that guaranteed prices and assured markets must be matched by good husbandry.[3]

[1] The absence of uniformity was a common ground of criticism during the war. One district committee, for example, graded 98 per cent of its farmers 'A'. Murray, *Agriculture*, p. 329.

[2] See Appendix B.

[3] *The Farmers' Weekly*, June 13, 1952. This journal criticized Sir Thomas for laying too much emphasis on 'the big stick and . . . on threats rather than on positive offers of friendly help'. August 1, 1952.

The new Parliamentary Secretary, Lord Carrington, was even more explicit: 'There is no room for the inefficient farmer, and the county agricultural executive committees will have to take stern action in future to keep up a higher standard of husbandry.'[1]

In 1952 supervision orders (998) and dispossessions (113) reached their highest peacetime figures. To some extent this was the result of a momentum built up over several years; but it was no coincidence that the Dugdale policy was linked with a new (though more modest) drive to increase food production. The morale of the committees and their willingness to wield the stick was always most pronounced at such times. This was understandable enough, but the connection naturally militated against the development of a code of good husbandry suitable to normal conditions. The Ryan Committee complained with reason that supervision orders were often directed towards increasing production rather than improving farming standards.[2] This view was given formal endorsement by the Ministry, but in practice the committees' disciplinary powers were associated with the need for more home produced food. Especially at the political level, 'more efficiency' and 'more food' were used almost synonymously. Thus when in 1953 the food shortage had been largely overcome, Dugdale's statements on sanctions took on a much different emphasis. He stressed that the purpose of the farm survey was mainly advisory and that sanctions should only be imposed when it was perfectly clear that a farmer would not take advice. This softer line seemed to confirm what many of the committees had suspected all along, that they could not expect any real backing from London in the imposition of sanctions. Their response is indicated by the fact that the number of supervision orders in 1953 dropped to 543, little more than half of the previous year's total.

2

One inevitable but awkward consequence of the 1947 'partnership' was that farmers and landlords affected by sanctions could not count on the unqualified support of their own representative organizations. One farmer, for example, on being served with a supervision proposal, appealed to the National Farmers' Union, of which he had been a member for fifteen years, 'and to his consternation and bewilderment discovered that the man leading the attack for the A[gricultural] E[xecutive] C[ommittee] was the chairman of the NFU and a magistrate as well. What can he, and does he now think of the

---

[1] *Manchester Guardian*, January 14, 1952.
[2] *Ryan Committee Report*, 1951, p. 10. Yet throughout its report the Ryan Committee itself saw sanctions and the production drive as closely intertwined.

NFU?'[1] Another was advised by his solicitor that 'we might as well have put our heads in a lion's mouth as to go to the NFU for help'.[2] Even where Farmers' Union-County Committee cliques were avoided (and they were not always easy to avoid), a farmer threatened with sanctions knew that his Union's support would be qualified by the 1947 agreement. Both the farmers' and the landowners' organizations ordinarily limited their assistance to a member threatened with sanctions to what could be given 'across the table': a full explanation of his rights and the correct procedure, a frank appraisal of the merits of his case, and broad advice on how to proceed.[3] Some Farmers' Union branches did give active support in what they considered to be especially deserving cases, sometimes sending out inspecting panels of their own. To try to avoid giving the impression of condemning those farmers who did not get such support, it was the practice of local Union leaders to speak ostensibly as private individuals.[4]

Partly because the major organizations could not take the view, 'our members, right or wrong', there grew up an organization which was not a participant in the 1947 agreement. The Farmers and Smallholders Association, like its partner, the Cheap Food League, opposed the whole conception of state subsidies and controls. Just because its main concern was with general principles, the Association would support almost any farmer in trouble. If he was plainly a poor farmer some other defence was found—that he was an ex-serviceman, that his family had been on the farm for generations, that he was being turned out of his home, that he was a lover of liberty. The Association not only made full use of the procedural protections for individuals but it organized petitions, got letters sent to Ministers and questions put in Parliament, and publicized individual cases of alleged stupidity and injustice.

Ostensibly the Association aimed at becoming a second general

[1] Letter to *The Farmers Weekly*, July 11, 1952, p. 28. See also June 6, 1952, p. 28. For earlier criticism of this kind see *Living Casualties* (Church Stratton, Salop: The Farmers' Rights Asscoiation, n.d.); F. D. Smith and Barbara Wilcox, *Farming Is Still a Gamble* (London: People's Universities Press, 1948), pp. 45–46
[2] From the files of the Farmers and Smallholders Association.
[3] See *The British Farmer*, October, 1953, p. 7; *Country Landowner* (Official Journal of the Country Landowners' Association), October, 1952, p. 156.
[4] See for example, National Farmers' Union Shropshire County Branch, *Forty-Sixth Annual Report for the Year Ended November 30, 1953*, p. 61, where members of the branch parliamentary committee are reported as making representations on a member's behalf 'in their capacity as practical men'. Many county branches distinguished between Committee-initiated action and landlord-initiated action, giving more extensive support to members in the latter cases. Union headquarters occasionally supported members in landlord-tenant cases before the Agricultural Land Tribunals and in the courts where questions of broad principle were at stake. See *The British Farmer*, August, 1953, 'Work in Progress'.

farmers' organization, but there was never any serious prospect of that. With a membership numbered in the hundreds, it was a head with almost no body; or rather it was a head that might attach itself to one of several bodies according to the needs of the moment—the Farmers and Smallholders Association, the Cheap Food League, the Council for the Reduction of Taxation, the Independent Livestock Producers Association, and others. These phantom organizations provided the several platforms from which a small staff in two or three rooms in Austin Friars directed their propaganda against subsidies and controls. 'We don't want too many members', one of them said, 'They take up too much time.'

The Farmers and Smallholders Association carried on a remarkably tenacious and not unsuccessful harassment of the Ministry of Agriculture and the 1947 Act. The organization never had any real agricultural roots, but it had in its favour the latent hostility to disciplinary powers, the co-operation of a section of the press, a friendly Member of Parliament (the late Sir Waldron Smithers), and its own perseverance in seeking out and attaching itself to cases that could be used in its campaign. When finally a Conservative Government repealed the disciplinary provisions of the Agriculture Act, its spokesman had to admit that the only agricultural organization favouring repeal was the Farmers and Smallholders Association.[1]

The Farmers and Smallholders Association was not the only or even the major force which eventually brought down the disciplinary provisions of the Agriculture Act. While Sir Thomas Dugdale and the Conservative Government were trying to pour oil on waters troubled by Ryan, and to decide what to do about sanctions, the Ministry suffered the first of a series of blows which in the end made up their minds for them. The Crichel Down investigation in the summer of 1954 had nothing to do with sanctions; but it revealed serious blunders and inequities in the disposition of land taken over during the war,[2] and sanctions and the Committees were included with the rest of the wartime legacies in an orgy of shocked disapproval. The behaviour of some of the civil servants involved in the Crichel Down case was certainly indefensible. Behind it, however, lay the uncertainty of the Conservative Government about its policy with respect to state agricultural holdings, an uncertainty which extended also to the sanctions against inefficiency. As a result of Crichel Down, the Conservatives decided to take the State out of the

[1] H. of C. O. R., 1957/58, Vol. 579, col. 11. By this time the Farmers and Smallholders Association had lost interest in the Agriculture Act and turned its attention to statutory marketing schemes which provided, from its point of view, a more profitable object of attack.

[2] Ministry of Agriculture and Fisheries, *Public Inquiry Ordered by the Minister of Agriculture into the Disposal of Land at Crichel Down*, Cmd. 9176/1954.

business of farming as quickly as possible, while sacrificing the amiable Sir Thomas Dugdale according to the customary constitutional rites. The change of Minister was symptomatic. Sir Thomas, a bluff Yorkshire squire, had seemingly been ready to apply the Agriculture Act in much the same spirit as his Labour predecessor, though he revealed some doubts about whether the Labour-manufactured bottle could properly contain the old-style Tory paternalism which he represented so well. His successor, Mr Heathcoat Amory, had a liberal's scepticism of direct state controls and stronger trust in economic forces.

On the very day that Dugdale announced his resignation a High Court decision cast a further shadow over the disciplinary provisions of the Agriculture Act, though once again those provisions were not directly involved.[1] The Act provided that any farmer or landowner faced with dispossession could appeal to an agricultural land tribunal whose decision was final.[2] These tribunals consist of a permanent legally qualified chairman appointed by the Lord Chancellor sitting with two members appointed (until 1954) by the Minister from panels nominated by the farmers' and landowners' organizations. The tribunal reheard the whole case, revisiting the farm in question and taking account (if it chose) of improvements effected while the appeal was pending. The Agriculture Act also allowed an appeal in other cases, including those in which the Minister decided to retain land requisitioned during the war in order to secure its more efficient use, and it was under this provision that the *Woollett* case arose.[3]

In 1947 Mrs Woollett and her husband purchased a small plot of land in Essex, amounting to about four acres, which was at that time being farmed by the Essex war agricultural executive committee. In 1949 the Ministry released part of the land to Mrs Woollett and indicated that the rest would probably be relinquished the next year. The Woolletts then prepared to work the land as a smallholding, but six months later they received notice that the Minister had changed his mind and proposed to retain it. Mrs Woollett appealed to an agricultural land tribunal which upheld the Minister, giving no reasons. This decision was challenged in the High Court, principally on the ground that the nominated members had been improperly appointed. The actual selections had been made in a very informal fashion, and without explicit authorization, by the secretary of the tribunal, an officer of the Ministry's agricultural land service. This method of selecting the lay members of the tribunals had grown up without much thought, and there was considerable confusion, even

[1] *Woollett* v *Minister of Agriculture and Fisheries* [1954] 2 All E. R. 776.
[2] Agriculture Act, 1947, Secs. 16(5), 17(3) and 9th Schedule. See 'Agricultural Land Tribunals,' *The British Journal of Administrative Law*, May, 1954.
[3] Agriculture Act, 1947, Sec. 85. See Secs. 15(2), 31(6), and 5th schedule.

among those immediately involved, about who was actually responsible.[1]

The Agriculture Act provides that the acts of an agricultural land tribunal shall be valid even where there has been a defect in the appointment of its members and that a compulsory purchase order must be challenged within six weeks of its issuance,[2] which Mrs Woollett had failed to do. But Mr Justice Stable swept these obstacles aside by holding that there had not been a *defect* in appointment, but no appointment at all. Having been no appointment, there was no tribunal; and having been no tribunal, there was no certificate of compulsory purchase. Therefore neither the saving provision nor the time limitation had any application. The ingenious chain of reasoning by which this conclusion was reached is less important than the judge's emphasis on the fact that the tribunal 'is literally the only protection that the subject has against the encroachment of the executive'.[3] and his determination to impose an even stricter standard of regularity than the Act itself seemed to require.

The Court of Appeals could not accept the judge's legal reasoning, though it did not disagree with his assessment of the merits of the case. Lord Justice Denning thought that the appointment of the nominated members was a regrettable irregularity but one covered by the saving provisions of the Act.

It is no doubt hard on Mrs Woollett to have her little piece of land taken from her. She spent much money in the reasonable expectation that it would be released to her, only to find afterwards that the Minister decided to retain it. But there is nothing that can be done about it. The Minister has certified that it is necessary for him to retain the land and no one can say him nay. In my opinion the appeal should be allowed and judgment entered for the Ministry.[4]

The Appeals judges did not conceal their opinion that justice was on the side of Mrs Woollett, though the law was not. The Minister won the argument over technicalities, but the saving provisions of the Act on which he relied seemed dangerous in their wide scope.

---

[1] At the Tribunal hearing it had been claimed that since the lay members were appointed by the Minister, the Tribunals were not independent, and the chairman had countered with the assertion that the Minister had nothing to do with it because the selections were made by himself. [1954] 2 All E.R. 780.

[2] Agriculture Act, 1947, Ninth Schedule, para. 20 (2); Sec. 92.

[3] [1954] 2 All E.R. 781.

[4] *Woollett* v *Minister of Agriculture and Fisheries* [1955] 1 Q.B. 123. Lord Justice Morris thought that at most there was a defect in the method of making the appointments and that this was covered by the saving clause. Lord Justice Jenkins thought that, in spite of the lack of formality, the appointments were not defective.

Also the case disclosed a lack of care in the constitution of these vital appeals tribunals and of consideration in dealing with private citizens; and the Minister himself lent weight to the widespread feeling that an injustice had been done when he decided in the end to let Mrs Woollett keep her bit of land.

Part of the damage done to the prestige of the Ministry and the agricultural land tribunals was repaired by amendments to the Agriculture Act passed in 1954, but initiated prior to the first *Woollett* decision.[1] The keeping of the farmer and landowner panels was transferred to the Lord Chancellor, and the selection of members for each sitting was vested in the chairman. Although this was applauded as likely to give the tribunals 'a greater weight of independence of mind',[2] it made no real difference. The tribunals were no less independent under the old system than under the new, and in practice the *ad hoc* members continued to be selected by the tribunal secretary.

This formal change was not enough for the more vocal critics of the Act. Sir Waldron Smithers told the House of Commons that the 1954 amendments were 'only a very small and a timid step' in the right direction, and that in establishing the tribunals Parliament had 'put back the clock 300 years'. Later he warned that 'we shall continue to fight until dispossessed farmers have a right of appeal in open court on the facts and merits of their complaints'.[3] Such a desire was never widespread among farmers, and Sir Anthony Hurd expressed the much more common view when he told the House of Commons:

If I were a farmer or landowner in trouble, I would ten times rather be judged by my peers who have practical knowledge of the matters at issue than be dragged up to London into the High Court. I would know where I stood because I would be talking the same language as the men who were to pass judgment on me.[4]

The fact is that most of the critics were not primarily interested in reforming the existing system but in discrediting the tribunals, and through them the Ministry, and in stifling the Agriculture Act by transferring its administration to the courts.

Though neither Crichel Down nor the *Woollett* case concerned sanctions, the furore over them influenced the new Minister of Agriculture to attempt to clarify his policy. In the autumn of 1954 Mr Heathcoat Amory reaffirmed that farmers were under an obliga-

---

[1] Agriculture (Miscellaneous Provisions) Act, 1954, Secs. 4–6; First Schedule.
[2] *The Economist*, September 4, 1954, pp. 724–27.
[3] H. of C.O.R., 1953–54, Vol. 522, cols. 860–61, 1561.
[4] *Ibid.*, cols. 873–74. See also cols. 842, 1571.

tion to make the most efficient use of the land, but he emphasized that sanctions were to be used only as the very last resort. By this time the farm survey was referred to in the past tense. The committees were advised to ignore small holdings of land altogether and warned to be very sure, before imposing a supervision order, that they would be willing to go ahead with dispossession if there were no improvement.[1]

It proved impossible for the Minister to hold even this limited position, for no sooner had his Department won its somewhat less than glorious victory in the *Woollett* case than it was embroiled in further litigation. At each step in the supervision-dispossession procedure the affected farmer or landowner had the right to make representations before a person appointed for that purpose by the Minister. The Minister delegated his power to the committees, and they ordinarily appointed their husbandry and estate management sub-committees. This practice was challenged by two farmers, Thomas Graham who had been put under supervision, and George Benney who had been ordered to vacate his farm and let it to an approved tenant. Graham and Benney argued that the Agriculture Act contemplated a hearing by some independent person, which the sub-committee dealing with the case clearly was not, and this argument was accepted by the High Court. The Chief Justice purported to rest his opinion 'entirely upon a question of construction', but he added that if the sub-committee heard the representations a farmer might reasonably say:

What is the good of my going before these people who have already decided that they are going to make this dispossession order? If I go before some independent person I may be able to satisfy him that he ought not to make the order and he will tell them so.[2]

Mr Justice Devlin agreed and chided the Solicitor-General for his argument that the provision for representations was merely executive machinery, an ear trumpet for whoever was making the decision, 'because I think that it shows a failure to appreciate the spirit of the

---

[1] See *The Farmer's Weekly*, October 15, 1954, p. 45.

[2] *Regina* v. *Minister of Agriculture and Fisheries*, Ex parte *Graham* and *Regina* v. *Agricultural Land Tribunal* (*South Western Province*) Ex parte *Benney* [1955] 2 Q.B. 151. The provision being construed was section 104(5) of the 1947 Agriculture Act which reads that 'no officer or servant of a County Agricultural Executive Committee, or any sub-committee or district committee thereof shall be appointed . . . to receive representations relating to land in the area of the Committee'. The Ministry had interpreted this to mean that no officer of a county committee or *of* a subordinate committee could hear the representations, but the Lord Justice read it to mean that neither committee officers nor the subordinate committees themselves could hear them.

Act as well as the letter of it'. Had the judges been free to examine the Parliamentary debates, where this point was discussed, they would have discovered that their understanding of Parliamentary intent was in error and that the Solicitor-General was correct.[1]

Again the Ministry's interpretation of the provision was upheld on appeal, but at the cost of another tongue-lashing from the court. Indeed although the representations had been properly heard, a technicality was found in the *Benney* case sufficient to upset the Minister's decision. The Tribunal had inadvertently and without authority eliminated four acres of land from the Minister's order. Again it was Lord Justice Denning who best expressed the judicial attitude. Speaking of Mr Benney he said:

He is the owner for life of Tucoyse Farm, Constantine, Cornwall. There is a farmhouse, a cottage and 155 acres of land. He is fifty-seven years of age now. He has farmed the land himself for the last twenty-four years. His father before him farmed it for forty-eight years, and his grandfather for many years before that. The farmhouse is seventy-two years old and was built for his father on his marriage. The farm is his sole means of livelihood and he has no other place to live. Yet a dispossession order has been made against him, turning him out of the land of which he is the owner and out of the house where he has lived all his life, with no provision made for alternative accommodation or other work. His only offence, if it is an offence, is that he has not maintained a reasonable standard of production on the holding.

It may be said that those facts are not relevant to the cold points of law which have been brought before us, and in a sense this is true. All I say is that if an English farmer is to be turned out of his farm, which he and his family have worked for generations, it should not be done except with the full authority of Parliament and in strict accordance with all the safeguards and provisions laid down by Parliament. . . . Benney had no right of appeal from the decision of the tribunal to anyone. He had no right of appeal to the Queen's courts on the merits of the case. He was bound to leave his home and his land unless he could find some technicality on which to upset the proceedings. That is why the Queen's courts have of late been asked to consider the technicalities of these cases.

The Lord Justice admitted that the point here was a very technical one indeed, since the four acres omitted from the tribunal's order were narrow strips on the edge of the farm: 'but technical though it is, I think that Benney is entitled to take advantage of it.'[2]

[1] H. of C.O.R., Standing Committees, 1946/47, Vol. II, col. 973.
[2] [1955] 2 Q.B. 165–67.

All proceedings under the Act had been halted pending the final decision in these cases, and in the light of the decisions new regulations were drawn up and some effort made to get the ponderous machine into action again. But most of the committees had given up entirely the idea of exercising sanctions by this time, and the rest determined to take action only rarely and in the very worst cases. Then came the report in 1956 of the Arton Wilson Committee which recommended that the administration of sanctions be shunted off to a small executive panel, while the committees concentrated on advisory work.[1] Though most of the committees knew better, the report encouraged the view that the birch could exercise its influence even if it were scarcely ever taken out of the cupboard. Thus the Government might be saved the trouble of either repealing the disciplinary provisions or enforcing them.

Later in 1956 the slight momentum still remaining in the sanctions programme brought to culmination a case begun six years earlier. In 1950 Lady Garbett, farming the 160 acre Horeham Manor, had been put under supervision by the East Sussex county committee. After three years a proposal was made to dispossess her, but the Agricultural Land Tribunal held against the Ministry on technical grounds. The standard of husbandry remained unsatisfactory, and steps were again taken to dispossess, this time successfully. In 1956 the Ministry took possession of the farm, turning its management over to the county committee. On its merits the Ministry could hardly have had a better case, and no one who knew the history of more than five years under supervision took seriously Lady Garbett's claim that the farm had been taken 'just at the time when we were likely to do well'.[2] Politically it could hardly have had a worse one. Already under heavy criticism, the Ministry was now put in the position of seeming to harass a defenceless, widowed gentlewoman, the niece of an archbishop. 'Mr. Heathcoat Amory should resign rather than take the responsibility for bundling poor Lady Garbett out of her own freehold house.'[3] That the whole affair had a farcical air—the Minister of Agriculture was by this time a rather tattered villain—

[1] Ministry of Agriculture, Fisheries and Food, *Report of the Committee Appointed to Review the Provincial and Local Organization and Procedures of the Ministry of Agriculture, Fisheries and Food*, Cmd. 9732, 1956. Henceforth cited as *Arton Wilson Committee Report*.

[2] *The Times*, May 29, 1956.

[3] Farmers and Smallholders Association, 'Statement Issued by Mr Oliver Smedley . . . in regard to the case of Lady Garbett,' October 5, 1956. (Mimeo) The Ministry was careful to emphasize that 'in considering any dispossession proposal, care is always taken to limit personal hardship, particularly as regards accommodation, as far as possible. In Lady Garbett's case it was understood that Horeham Manor Farm was not her only home.' Ministry of Agriculture, Fisheries and Food, 'Press Notice' MAFF 184/56, May 31, 1956.

made it no less damaging. Lady Garbett refused to make the Ministry's task any easier by selling the farm herself or letting it to an approved tenant. Many newspapers had a field day with the alleged bureaucratic oppressions, seldom bothering to point out that the decision had been made not by officials but by fellow-farmers. On this occasion the courts came to the Ministry's defence and no less a person than Lord Chief Justice Goddard remarked upon the fairness and patience of the dispossession proceedings.[1]

The final blow to Part II of the Agriculture Act was dealt by the report in 1957 of the Franks Committee on Administrative Tribunals and Enquiries. It deplored the combination of executive and adjudicatory activities in the hands of the county committees and urged that if the 'present policy of control over agriculture' were to continue, separate bodies should be established to assume the adjudicatory functions.[2] Under the proposed system the county committee would prosecute its case before the new tribunal which would be required to give reasons for its decisions. Appeal would lie (as before) to the agricultural land tribunals, and the Franks Committee thought that supervision as well as dispossession orders should be reviewable.

These recommendations would have allocated to the county committees an exceedingly difficult and unpleasant function, which they would hardly have contemplated accepting even with firm Ministerial backing. Since the Government had little inclination to provide such support, the alternative of complete repeal (at which the Franks Committee broadly hinted) appeared easier.[3] Both Government and committees were now tired of hostile criticism from the press and from judicial or judicially-disposed bodies. Ironically, the one obstacle to repeal was the continued support of sanctions by all the principal agricultural organizations. That the Government nevertheless took that course was, so far as major policy is concerned, unprecedented in the post-war period.

Part of the reason for this was Mr Heathcoat Amory's unusually

---

[1] R. v. Hailsham Justices, ex parte Garbett. See The Times, January 31, 1957.

[2] Report of the Committee on Administrative Tribunals and Enquiries, Cmd. 218, 1957, pp. 34–36. It was suggested that, although the new bodies would have to include local agriculturists, they should be under the chairmanship of someone with legal qualifications who was independent of the area concerned. Though the Franks Committee did not of course give an opinion on the wisdom of continuing the policy of 'control', the tone of its remarks did not indicate a sympathetic attitude.

[3] 'Bluntly, these provisions have been dead for a long time, and I do not want to spend too long on their funeral oration. If there had been doubt about the need to bury them, then the conclusions of the Franks Committee should have clinched the matter.' Mr Hare, Minister of Agriculture, on Second Reading of Agriculture Bill, 1958. H. of C. O. R., 1957/58, Vol. 584, col. 1110.

independent attitude toward the National Farmers' Union,[1] but it was also true that the Union's support of sanctions had become equivocal. It is one of the curious facts of this history that farmers, even as late as the mid-1950's, did not share what was by then a very widespread hostility to sanctions. Generally speaking they were aware that dispossessions were few and mostly well deserved, and they rarely took the view that a man's land is his to do with as he likes. Moreover some landlords and farmers strongly held the view that the 'birch in the cupboard' (even if never used) served as a useful public testimonial to the value of agriculture and of agricultural land. Above all there was the National Farmers' Union's strong commitment to the idea that sanctions and economic support would stand or fall together. Hertfordshire farmers were told, for example, at the time of the publication of the Arton Wilson Report, that the Union saw it as the 'thin end of the wedge' for doing away with the Agricultural Act altogether. 'It simply means this—bring about a breakdown in the working of Part II of the Act and the Government can then throw the whole thing overboard—guarantees and all!'[2]

Yet the Government may have thought, with reason, that the Union's support of Part II, as well as that of the Country's Landowners' Association, was by this time mainly a matter of building a record in case of a future 'betrayal'. It could point to the fact that the new and more definitive guarantees of the 1957 Act had not been tied to sanctions, and it was convinced that when the Union saw that the new guarantees were to be maintained, even when sanctions were dropped, opposition would evaporate.[3] That the Conservatives correctly assessed agricultural opinion is indicated by the fact that the Farmers' Union did not really press its opposition, and the apparent flouting of the Union cost the Government nothing beyond a minor Parliamentary embarrassment. In 1958 the sanctions provisions of the 1947 Agriculture Act were repealed.[4]

---

[1] See above, p. 69. The difference from his predecessors is indicated by an exchange in the House of Commons in May, 1957, before the Conservatives had decided to repeal the sanctions provisions. Mr Tom Williams asked, 'Is the Minister aware that the National Farmers' Union is quite happy that Part II should be administered as well as Part I?' To which Mr Heathcoat Amory replied dryly, 'I am always glad when the National Farmers' Union is happy.' H. of C. O. R., 1956/57, Vol. 570, cols. 4–5.

[2] *The Hertfordshire Farmer*, Journal of the Hertfordshire County Branch of the National Farmers' Union, June 14, 1956, p. 211.

[3] See H. of C. O. R., 1957/58, Vol. 579, col. 12. The agricultural workers' opposition to the repeal of sanctions had a different basis, a continued but vague attachment to the idea of state supervision of agriculture; but on broad questions of this kind the Conservatives gave no more weight to worker opinion than had Labour in its day.

[4] Agriculture Act, 1958, Sec. 1.

3

Though the system of sanctions against inefficient farmers and owners has now been repealed, we believe that it has been worth considering its history at some length. The system was central to the 1947 Act; it represented one way of trying to relate state support to improved efficiency; and it called for close co-operation between Government and agricultural interests, providing a striking example of the principle of 'partnership' in action.

In spite of a great deal of discussion of the subject, the materials on which to base a balanced evaluation of the Committees' discharge of their disciplinary responsibilities remain extremely elusive. On the one hand there was a steady fire of criticism, much of it ill informed or deliberately distorted. On the other hand there was the wall of official defence which is no more revealing. The reports of the Ryan Committee and the Arton Wilson Committee contain helpful clues, but most of their observations are too general to provide the materials for an adequate evaluation.[1] In an attempt to fill this gap we have conducted extensive interviews with committee members and their officers, with local representatives of the agricultural organizations and other members of the agricultural community, and with many of the commitees' most vehement critics. We have attended meetings of the committees, of their subordinate bodies, and of the agricultural land tribunals; and we have examined, in addition to published material, unpublished letters and files relating to a large number of cases where injustice was alleged.

The first and perhaps the most important characteristic of the committees' most articulate critics is that they seldom distinguished between charges of injustice in the administration of the Agriculture Act and criticisms of the Act itself. Obviously this was often an intentional confusion, but many people were simply unable to understand the conception of justice on which the sanctions were based. One landlord who tried unsuccessfully to turn out his tenant wrote to the Farmers and Smallholders' Association, 'What I cannot understand is why when one has bought a thing it is not his.'[2] These sentiments were echoed in an article in *Picture Post* called 'Is This Justice?' 'It is clear that Mr Trechman has been acting under the assumption that, just because the property was bought for him, it was his to do with as he liked.'[3] It is significant that in this article three cases of 'injustice' were described, and in only one of them is it

---

[1] We have, however, had the opportunity of examining much of the valuable unpublished evidence given to these committees.

[2] From the files of the Farmers and Smallholders Association.

[3] July 24, 1954, p. 34.

even claimed that the 'victim' had fulfilled his obligations under the Agriculture Act.

In spite of a now widespread impression to the contrary, the sanctions were not manifestly wrong in principle. In the first place, the view of sanctions as a *quid pro quo* is not unreasonable, although it had less practical effect on public opinion and Government policy than the National Farmers' Union had expected. The state assumed coercive powers only because it was also providing economic support. It is true that the agricultural organizations might (and in later years sometimes did) argue that the state's treatment of other industries entitled agriculture to some degree of unconditional support. But their hearty assent to the linking of moderate obligations to considerable benefits strengthened the case for sanctions. Those who objected to *both* Parts I and II of the Agriculture Act were on better ground.

Broader attacks upon the principle of sanctions rested on the assumption that comprehensive state intervention in the affairs of an industry is intrinsically less satisfactory or desirable than a more 'automatic' system of market reactions. This contention raises issues which are much too broad and intricate to explore here. It should be noted, however, that once the state had embarked upon intervention in agricultural affairs, it became inevitably drawn into establishing some criteria by which to regulate its distribution of aid. It is true that the chosen criteria might have been those associated with business efficiency, with the state simply utilizing the market mechanism. In the case of agriculture, though, good business is far from being equivalent to good husbandry. If the land is to be treated as a 'sacred trust', whose condition and upkeep ought to be maintained at a satisfactory level irrespective of immediate financial profit, some more direct system of state control becomes necessary. In accepting this conception, the framers of the Agricultural Act may have taken a wise view of the state's agricultural objectives.

The state-directed, farmer-operated disciplinary system was not unreasonable on its face or necessarily wrong in principle. In our view, it cannot be judged without a careful examination of how it actually worked. Three questions need to be considered. First, how fair was the procedure for supervision and dispossession, and how much substance was there in the many accusations of partiality and injustice? Second, what was the value of a sanctions programme in peacetime? Third, why did the system fail, and was its failure inevitable? We shall treat these three questions in turn.

(a) The procedure for applying sanctions does not appear to have been inequitable; indeed, it is doubtful if further procedural safeguards would have allowed the system to work at all. The criticisms of the Franks Committee and the hostile comments of many judges overlooked this point. The Franks Committee condemned the county committees on the grounds that their mixture of executive and adjudicatory functions was 'wholly undesirable'. 'Given such a combination the parties cannot feel that their case will receive a fair hearing and be impartially decided.'[1] But this was a false reading of the committees' function.[2] Their task was not to sit as independent judges but to use a mixture of advice and (where necessary) coercion in order to uphold certain minimum standards of husbandry and estate management. The farmers' judicial protection lay elsewhere, in the right of appeal to an independent tribunal.

Two examples may be given of this point. The Franks Committee considered the provision for making representations to be a judicial protection and asserted that it did not meet the elementary requirement 'that citizens should know in good time the case which they will have to meet. . . '.[3] The hearing was intended, however, to allow the committee and the farmer concerned to discuss whether there *was* a 'case' for disciplinary action and to enable the committee to form some judgment about the man with whom it was dealing. Was there some member of the committee whose advice he might take? Did he need to be threatened, or was he now genuinely desirous of improving so that no further formal action was necessary? No doubt the farmer was entitled to be told before the hearing why the committee was considering disciplinary action, but this was not intended as an indictment carrying a series of allegations which had to be found true or false. An unco-operative farmer might be asked what he would do in the committee's place, and though a judge does not ask such a question, it was reasonable for the committee to do so.

Similar considerations apply to the supervision order itself. The Franks Committee viewed it as a form of punishment and therefore recommended that an appeal should lie to the agricultural land tribunal. Of course it was true that the imposition of a supervision order 'must affect reputation and standing',[4] but the error lay in the strict dichotomy between measures that are 'penal' and those that

---

[1] *Report of the Committee on Administrative Tribunals and Enquiries*, Cmd. 218/1957, p. 35.

[2] See R. M. Jackson, 'County Agricultural Executive Committees,' *The Law Quarterly Review*, July, 1952, pp. 374–75. It is true that in settling disputes between landowners and tenants, the committees acted as adjudicatory bodies. See Chapter VIII.

[3] *Report of the Committee on Administrative Tribunals and Enquiries*, 1957, p. 17,

[4] *Ibid.*, p. 36. The Franks Committee asserted that 'a substantial part of the agricultural community' regarded supervision orders as penal measures, but it had at the same time to record the opposition of the National Farmers' Union and the Country Landowners' Association (as well as the Arton Wilson Committee) to an appeal from these orders.

I

are not. The supervision order was actually a little of both. The Franks Committee recommendations would have imposed such a procedural burden on the committees that no farmer could reasonably have been expected to serve on them, and it would have thoroughly judicialized a programme of advice and discipline which was most effective when its judicial and penal aspects remained in the background. The Committees' first task was to rehabilitate inefficient farmers, formulating a 'case' for dispossession only as a last resort.

The Agriculture Act attempted to substitute practical and representative administration for a portion of the traditional judicial protections. Obviously this left some room for error and injustice, but there was no sure procedural or judicial safeguard that would not have strangled the advice-discipline programme. Moreover, the number of cases where committees treated individuals less fairly than courts or other judicial bodies would have done was remarkably small. Perhaps the most serious criticism that could be levelled at the committees was their tendency to confuse informality with secretiveness. Once they decided to take disciplinary action, they sometimes took the view that all that mattered was getting on with it. Having stretched their patience so far, they were naturally irritated by further delays, and they sometimes deliberately kept the formal record scanty in an attempt to reduce the chances of their being reversed. As a consequence, a farmer sometimes received no clear idea of what the committee thought was a reasonable standard to aim at, beyond the informal, oral, and not always consistent remarks of visiting panels and advisory officers.[1] This defect was gradually being removed by Ministerial direction which, although less forceful than it ought to have been, was certainly preferable to a rigid judicializing of committee procedure.

More dramatic, though in fact much less significant, were the sinister possibilities inherent in control by fellow farmers who were also business competitors; and these were eagerly exploited by the committees' critics. The Farmers' Rights Association (an organization disbanded shortly after the war) protested:

The farmer once evicted, the Agricultural Executive Committee may then force the sale or the letting of the farm to one of its own nominees who may be, and often has been, a member of the very

---

[1] See for example *The Times*, May 23, 1956, where a farmer is reported as alleging that he was given no reasons for the committee's issuing a certificate of bad husbandry against him until he had lodged his appeal to an agricultural land tribunal. Several cases of failure to provide timely and reasonably full information to farmers in dispossession cases have been found in the files of the Farmers and Smallholders Association.

Agricultural Executive Committee which ordered the dispossession, or of another Committee, or he may be a son or relative of a member, or a friend or business associate.[1]

There is little doubt that there were some such cases during the war, and in 1947 the Minister reported that his approval was required for any transfer of compulsorily acquired land to a committee member.[2] It is extremely difficult, however, to find concrete charges relating to the post-war period which have even the colour of probability. In April, 1953, Sir Waldron Smithers, the committees' chief Parliamentary critic, asked the Minister of Agriculture 'if he is aware that a number of farms which have been taken over by him under the Agriculture Act, 1947, have been allocated to members of the county agricultural executive committee and to their relatives?' Sir Thomas Dugdale replied that he was not aware of any such cases, and he challenged Smithers to give names, which the latter was unable to do.[3] A year later a specific instance was at last revealed but it was perfectly innocuous.[4] If there were such cases they were certainly outnumbered by those where committee members refrained, even at some cost to themselves, from the appearance of private gain as a consequence of their public duties.

Moreover, the agricultural land tribunals were in practice a strong safeguard. Of 1,926 appeals from decisions of the Minister heard between March 1, 1948 and February 28, 1958, 544 were allowed. The majority of these cases were concerned with landlord-tenant disputes and other actions taken under the Agriculture Act, and the record over dispossession cases initiated by the state was slightly less favourable to appellants; 42 out of 177 appeals were allowed.[5] Nevertheless, this does not look like a record of Ministerial domination, and despite certain vagaries over their appointment, the tribunals always behaved as completely independent bodies. They

[1] *The New Morality* (Church Stretton, Salop.: The Farmers' Rights Association, n.d.), p. 3. In this pamphlet three cases are described where, after dispossession, farms were let to a member or relative of a member of the Committee but all cases relate to War Agricultural Executive Committees.

[2] H. of C.O.R., 1947/48, Vol. 445, col. 437.

[3] *Ibid.*, 1952/53, Vol. 514, cols. 2320–21. Smithers' retort, 'What about the *Odlum* v *Stratton* case?' only revealed the groundlessness of his charge. The *Odlum* case (1946) reflected no credit on the County Committees involved nor on the then Minister; but it arose during the war and it had no bearing on the point at issue.

[4] In reply to a question the Minister of Agriculture reported that certain requisitioned land held by the East Sussex county committee was let to a man who became a member of a sub-committee three years later, and other land to a Committee member whose farm adjoined it. H. of C. O. R., 1953/54, Vol. 531, cols. 1369–70.

[5] Information from Ministry of Agriculture, Fisheries and Food.

reheard each case on its merits and their decisions were final.[1] The impression stimulated by the Woollett case and fostered by the Ministry's critics that the tribunals were somehow tainted never had any foundation in fact. As we have seen, the law courts have itched to review dispossession cases 'on their merits', but the crux of these agricultural cases was the particular application of general rules of good husbandry and estate management. There can be no doubt that the practical judgment of the committees and the tribunals on this point was far superior to any that could have been expected from the ordinary courts.

All this is not to deny that cases of genuine hardship did arise in the administration of sanctions. How could it have been otherwise? Even though dispossession was rare and generally well-deserved, it still entailed a severe blow, particularly in the light of farmers' traditional attachment to their own holdings. The opposition of 'human facts' and public policy did indeed raise hard questions, as may be seen from these two comments on a dispossession case, one by the Minister and the other by the farmer himself.[2]

Mr **** is an owner-occupier who has been under supervision for both his farming and his estate management. The conditions on his farm were first brought to the notice of the **** Agricultural Executive Committee . . . twelve months after he took possession of the farm. At that time the Committee found that the cattle were suffering from malnutrition and that no hay, straw or other feeding-stuffs were available for them. The pasture land was poor and the arable dirty. The farmhouse and buildings were in a very poor state.

. . . .

I am sure that Mr **** was given every opportunity both to improve the farm and to put his views on the matter to the Committee during the period of supervision. The action which has been taken was necessary in the interests of good husbandry.

In contrast to the Minister's cool reasoning is the farmer's heartfelt outburst. He claimed that his wife had died as a result of harassment from 'this lot' at the County Committee.

---

[1] Thus unlike most administrative tribunals they complied with the Franks Committee dictum that all such tribunals should not be 'part of the machinery of administration' but 'independent of the Department concerned'. *Report of the Committee on Administrative Tribunals and Enquiries*, 1957, p. 9. This view may have been mistaken (see, for example, the criticisms in J. A. G. Griffith, 'Tribunals and Enquiries' in *Modern Law Review*, March, 1959), but it is curious that the Franks Committee which was otherwise so critical of the administration of sanctions did not give weight to this point.

[2] From the files of the Farmers and Smallholders Association.

I feel very much the Coronation year when there will be plenty of joy, and the like's of us that have led a fair straight life all along, we can be turned on the road as the law stands now, if we had not tried it would be different, but we have tried, and tried hard, and the place has improved, but we are high up and one of those out of the way places.

One friend of the Farmers and Smallholders Association wrote privately, with respect to a case he had been asked to investigate, that dispossession was probably justified under the Agriculture Act. 'But the human fact remains that a man with eleven children is being turned out of his house and home because a variety of officials do not like the way he farms his land.'[1] The committees were inevitably instrumental in causing hardship of this kind, but they could not justly be accused of callously disregarding it. It is very doubtful if 'judicializing' their procedure would have made the committees any more sympathetic or lenient, but it would certainly have made them more rigid and considerably less effective.

As representative local bodies, the committees' strength lay in their capacity to administer an acceptable programme of advice, aid, and coercion. It was not easy to push such a locally-sensitive machine into effective action; it would have been quite impossible to have done so if its proceedings had been subordinated to strict judicial methods. Still less realistic was the Franks Committee remedy of requiring the committees to act as prosecutors before some separate tribunal. The Conservative Government admitted that the committees neither would, nor could be expected, to function in this way.[2] The only real alternative to administration by representative lay bodies (with provision for appeal) would have been to entrust enforcement to government officials and to make them prove their case, with full judicial safeguards, before some independent body. It is most improbable that farmers would have preferred the juridical charms of the latter course to the practical advantages of the former. On balance too their preference would have been justified. Whether or not the committees were effective administrators, they were reasonably humane ones. Far from being insensitive to personal hardship and anxious to throw their neighbours off their farms, they

[1] *Ibid.* Two cases which have become classics in the anti-Committee literature are those of a Mr Bell who shot himself when ordered to quit his farm by the Northumberland 'War Ag' and Mr George Waldon who was killed in 1940 resisting the efforts of police officers to evict him after he had been dispossessed by the Hampshire committee. These were, of course, wartime cases when action was speedier and safeguards far less. A. G. Street, one of the most articulate opponents of sanctions, took the latter case as the inspiration for a novel, *Shameful Harvest* (London: Faber and Faber, 1952).

[2] H. of C. O. R., 1957/58, Vol. 584, col. 1111.

were all too willing to find reasons for avoiding the imposition of sanctions—the farmer's illness, his financial difficulties, his family responsibilities, or his advanced age. They resembled over-indulgent parents, saving the rod and spoiling the child, far more than some stone-hearted rural gestapo trampling down the rights of British yeomen.

(b) The practical value of the sanctions policy under peacetime conditions is much more difficult to judge than the question of administrative justice. Despite all the controversy, the committees' use of their disciplinary powers was not numerically very considerable. During the ten-year existence of Part II of the Agriculture Act only 377 farmers and twenty-three landowners were dispossessed, though the numbers placed under supervision—4,200 farmers and 811 owners—were more considerable.[1] While it cannot really be inferred that supervision on its own caused all but a few of these latter to 'reform',[2] it is true that the use of supervision orders, and the considerable patience with which they were administered, did have some direct effect upon the practices of about one and one-half per cent of all farmers. That is still a very small proportion, but fear of committee action spread its influence over a wider circle. Moreover, sanctions provided, as we have seen, the occasion for much of the committees' advisory work. They served as a specific job of work to do, holding the committees together and giving unity and force to their other activities. There is little doubt that if the programme of sanctions had not come under such heavy fire from 1953 onwards its total impact would have increased substantially.

On the other hand, was it worth while trying to define and enforce standards of farming efficiency once the urgency of increasing home food production had disappeared? The link with national production objectives, however awkward in the long run, did furnish a definite yardstick. A farmer could reasonably be said to be inefficient if his land was plainly underfarmed and his output was low; but such verdicts were much less easy and also, it seemed, less necessary once the emphasis had shifted from increased production to economic efficiency. Particularly when the degree of economic security was lessened, the farmer's own judgment of his economic interest became entitled to at least *prima facie* respect. Nevertheless the continued use of Part II powers would have had two real advantages. First it would have helped to ensure that the condition of farms was such that they could expand output rapidly and without too much diffi-

---

[1] See Appendix B.

[2] This was the view of the ex-Minister of Agriculture, Mr Williams, H. of C. O. R., 1957/58, Vol. 584, cols. 1126–29. But of course many supervision orders lapsed, particularly after 1953, because the difficulties of dispossession seemed too great to warrant further action.

culty or expense whenever the need to do so returned. This seems a not unreasonable condition to attach to a system of state support that is partly intended to insure against just such economic or strategic contingencies. Second, the existence of an extensive system of state support, even in the form the Conservatives have given it, tends to some extent to shield the inefficient farmer against economic forces. Where the play of the market in inducing turnover is thus limited, insistence on minimum technical standards would be a way of reducing misuse or wastage of agricultural land. It can reasonably be argued that state subsidies ought not to be paid to definitely incompetent farmers when much better qualified men cannot secure a suitable farm.

A programme aimed at these relatively limited ends would have had to rest on minimum standards of husbandry and management suitable for normal peacetime use. These would have aimed (a) at keeping farm fixtures and equipment in a reasonable state of repair and the land itself in 'good heart' by keeping drains clear, weeds under control, etc.; and (b) at requiring some minimum standard of technical efficiency in such matters as stock management and breeding and in the use of crop strains. These standards would have been concerned with technical rather than economic proficiency, and they would have been fixed at a modest level and administered carefully and sympathetically. Their administration would have required a more systematic, though probably slower, use of the farm survey and a close coordination of the survey with advice and supervision. Dispossessions would have been necessary, but they need not have been numerous, so long as it was reasonably clear what the minimum standards were and that they would in fact be enforced. While other methods might accomplish the same objectives, such an advice-discipline programme as this would have represented a reasonable application of the principles of the Agriculture Act under peacetime conditions. But by the time efforts—rather half-hearted efforts, it is true—were made to move in something like this direction, the whole programme was almost dead, and the committees seemed too old to learn the necessary new tricks. This leads to the third and last question about the administration of sanctions.

(c) Why did the sanctions experiment fail, and was this failure inevitable? We have suggested that the principle itself was by no means indefensible and that the methods of application were on the whole equitable. Nevertheless, such unusual coercive powers were bound to become increasingly difficult to apply as 'normality' returned, and they called for skilled and delicate administration. During the war the justification for sanctions was obvious, and administration was thereby simplified. The standard to be applied was clear—maximum production with little regard to cost—and in those days of rudimentary procedural requirements, the means were ample. The Agriculture Act attempted a transition. Sanctions were an expression of the view that farmers were to be regarded as holding the land in trust for the nation, as the price review was an expression of the view that the public interest required agricultural stability. The standard was to be efficient production rather than maximum production, and the committee's wartime powers were limited. This transition would have been diffiicult in any event, but because of post-war conditions it was not made in 1948 when the committees were reconstituted on a statutory basis. The committees were immediately caught up in a series of post-war production drives and continued to wear their war hats—and the attitudes under them. This unquestionably made them more resistant to change than they otherwise might have been.

The importance of the committees' 'attitude' and 'morale' suggests the vulnerable character of committee administration. The basic assumption of the system was that such drastic powers could carry the support of affected groups only if they were entrusted to lay representative bodies. No doubt this was true, but it has to be balanced against the tendency of such bodies to be easily discouraged, quick to take offence, and sometimes unduly sensitive to outside opinion. The great emphasis laid in most discussions of sanctions on individual rights tends to obscure the fact that certain duties were laid upon farmers and landowners and that the committees were responsible for seeing that these duties were performed. The exercise of this responsibility confronted enormous hazards. At each administrative level disciplinary action was decided upon only reluctantly, and each of the lower bodies resented the frequent delays and lack of support of those higher up. The district committees—whose recommendations had to pass through the cautious hands of sub-committee, committee, and the Ministry—were the first to become discouraged; and as a consequence they (and the farm survey) had begun to deteriorate even when the committees were at the peak of their activity.

As time went on, reversals by the agricultural land tribunals began to mount, because of procedural defects, or different conclusions on the merits, or last-minute improvements on the farmer's part. Almost every committee had stories to tell of farmers, immune for years to committee advice and threats, who made gigantic improvements between the time of the final committee decision and the tribunal hearing. Buildings repaired, weeds cut, land ploughed, crops sown—and allowed to lapse into their former neglected state once a favourable tribunal decision was secured. Doubtless the committees exaggerated, but they were naturally dubious of quick improvements when their own lengthy efforts had been so fruitless. When the tribunal was deceived and the improvements were not lasting, the committee faced the dismal prospect of beginning again the whole process of inspection, advice, supervision, representation, and threats.

It was the fate of this part of the Agriculture Act to run foul of the courts' jealous distaste of certain features of delegated legislation and administrative justice and of a more general revulsion against state planning. The well-founded parts of judicial criticism related to general issues which were not confined to agricultural legislation and which need not have undermined the basic principle of agricultural self-discipline.[1] In so far as the courts and the Franks Committee went further and condemned by implication this principle itself, they revealed considerable ignorance of the real problem, as well as of parliamentary intention and rural opinion. Still less well grounded was the clamour from the urban press which chose to view the generally cautious and humane administration of a widely endorsed Act of Parliament by representative committees as if it were oppressive tyranny by Ministry officials. Distorted newspaper reports and recollections of stories of wartime injustice, strengthened by judicial *obiter dicta* and the often ill-informed criticism of the Franks Committee, managed to foster, in the towns, an impression of jack boots in the countryside which would have been comical in its ignorance and exaggeration had it not been so influential.

The result of all these forces was that all but a few of the committees had succumbed to a kind of psychological exhaustion long before sanctions were formally withdrawn. Yet the failure of this experiment cannot be attributed finally to the committees. They would have continued to toil at the task if they had had sufficient encouragement and guidance from the central Government. The qualification is crucial, for such representative bodies could not be expected to take full responsibility for disciplinary measures; nor did they have the capacity or the knowledge to direct the programme unaided. Unfortunately for that programme, the guidance which they received was fitful and ambiguous. The hostility of the committees to proposals to deprive them of ordinary administrative functions, discussed in the next chapter, did indeed complicate the task of giving the committees a lead in the area of sanctions. But the Ministry brought much of this on itself by its failure to prepare the ground carefully enough and by its unwillingness, once the committees had expressed their opposition, either to abandon the reform or openly to press it forward. The committees' sullen distrust of the Ministry engendered by this dispute was strengthened by the flabby and inconsistent advice they were given about the farm survey and

---

[1] Particularly objectionable (but nothing to do with the principle of sanctions) was the immunity given to the Minister of Agriculture in respect of his procedural errors.

sanctions—by their experience, for example, of being urged to renewed efforts in 1952 by the same Government which lost interest
in the programme in little more than a year. Perhaps the programme
was not worthwhile under peacetime conditions—that question the
reader may decide for himself—but it was not repealed out of any
deliberate conviction to that effect. It was repealed because those in
authority allowed events to decide for them.

CHAPTER VI

PARTNERSHIP IN THE FIELD

1

'FARMING from Whitehall' is the favourite accusation of those who dislike anything the Ministry of Agriculture is doing. Aware of the strong tradition of localism in agricultural affairs and of the large measure of voluntary co-operation necessary to the success of many agricultural programmes, national policy makers have been extremely sensitive to this charge. The county agricultural executive committees were Whitehall's reply. Through the committees the agricultural industry not only accepted extensive programmes of regulation and subsidy but shared in their administration. As we have seen, agricultural self-discipline through statutory sanctions has now been abandoned. The second aspect of this experiment, the committees as participants in local administration, still hangs in the balance.

Even when sanctions were at their peak, the farmer was likely to pay more attention to other aspects of the committee's work. For him 'the committee' was the place to apply for subsidies and grants and the telephone number to call when he wanted advice. Someone from the committee office inspected his methods of milk production, counted his subsidized hill sheep, punched the ears of his subsidized calves, and checked his subsidized corn acreage. He was aware that there actually were committees hovering somewhere in the background, and he probably knew some of the members, but he thought of the county committee, or the 'war ag' as he still called it, chiefly as a building full of civil servants.

Prior to the war, most advisory and regulatory programmes were administered by the county councils, while the Universities, aided by government grants, maintained provincial centres for research and specialized advisory services. The Ministry of Agriculture was responsible for some national programmes of assistance and regulation, but it had almost no field organization except for a small corps of land commissioners. Those officers, together with advisory and administrative personnel from the county councils, formed the nuclei of the staffs of the war agricultural executive committees formed in 1939. These committees administered subsidies, gave farmers technical advice, issued cultivation directions, and took possession of land where there was a failure to observe directions. They farmed some land themselves; operated labour and machinery pools; performed services on contract; and were responsible for the allocation of fertilizers, feeding stuffs, machinery, and other scarce agricultural requisites.

When peace returned, the committees' tasks changed only slightly at first. The new statutory sanctions seemed to require only minor alterations of procedure and scarcely any change in basic approach. The function of giving agricultural advice was neither handed back to the county councils, as some of them had hoped, nor given to a new independent agency, as the Luxmoore Committee on Post-War Agricultural Education had recommended.[1] Instead, a National Agricultural Advisory Service was established within the Ministry of Agriculture, and the local advisory officers continued to work under the committees' auspices. Similarly most of the post-war administrative and regulatory programmes were only slightly modified versions of their predecessors. A few of the wartime functions gradually disappeared, but many new ones were added; and a typical county committee was likely to have a dozen or more sub-committees dealing with such subjects as husbandry, estate management, labour, machinery, drainage, pests, milk regulations, technical development, hill farming, horticulture, and poultry.

A major organizational change did occur with the absorption of the local officers into the national civil service, but even here the committees felt little immediate effect. Their chief officer was still a person trained in giving technical advice, and he now became the county head of the new advisory service as well. Of his three assistants, one (also a member of the advisory service) was immediately responsible for the county's advisory programme; another (a member of the agricultural land service) was responsible for the administration of some improvement grants and for the application of sanctions;[2] while a third had charge of housekeeping services, the administration of most grants and regulations, and other miscellaneous matters.

The greatest change was the reconstitution of the committees themselves. The members of the 'war ags' were intended to be broadly representative of local agricultural interests, but in order to emphasize their responsibility to the Minister they were appointed without consultation with either agricultural organizations or county

[1] Minister of Agriculture and Fisheries, *Report of the Committee on Post-War Agricultural Education in England and Wales*, Cmd. 6433, 1943, Section III.

[2] The agricultural land service consisted of professionally qualified land agents and supporting personnel who were also immediately responsible for the management of publicly owned agricultural land and for the provision of advice on estate management. Because of the existence of a well established group of private land agents, the advisory functions of the Service were controversial and ill defined, and they never constituted an important part of its work.

councils.[1] After the war, however, when it was decided to establish the committees as part of a permanent system of peacetime regulation, it became important to ensure their representative character in some more formal manner, while retaining their status as agents of the Minister. Therefore the Agriculture Act of 1947 provided that the Minister must select three of the twelve members on each committee from nominees put forward by farmers' representatives, and two each from names suggested by representatives of landowners and workers. Although the Act did not say so, it was understood from the beginning that the National Farmers' Union, the Country Landowners' Association, and the two agricultural workers' unions would be the bodies asked for nominations.

Farmers' and landowners' nominees are selected by the county branches of their oganizations. The procedure is normally quite informal, with county branches sending names to their headquarters for transmittal to the Ministry. The usual practice is to submit at least twice as many names as there are positions to be filled, and only rarely do the organizations even indicate their preferences. The case of workers' nominees is different in two respects. They are, in the first place, selected by union headquarters on the advice of the district organizers (who are paid employees of the unions), and local branches and committees are seldom even consulted. In the second place, owing to a scarcity of suitable candidates, the workers' unions are seldom able to present more than one serious nominee for each vacancy. Thus in practice their preferences are known and accepted, although the Minister retains a rarely exercized right to ask for further names.[2]

The Minister appoints five members directly, one of whom must be a member of the county council. This appointment provides a link with the remaining agricultural activities of the counties, particularly the provision of agricultural education and smallholdings. There are no qualifications regarding the other direct appointments. The responsibilities of the nominated members and the directly appointed members are identical. The latter do not, for example, have a special obligation to represent the taxpayer or the public interest. The direct appointments are supposed to enable the Minister to select persons with special experience and to ensure that each

---

[1] Representatives of the workers' unions and the Women's Land Army on the wartime committees were selected, as a matter of convenience, by the organizations concerned.

[2] About two-thirds of the workers' nominees are from the National Union of Agricultural Workers and one-third from the Transport and General Workers' Union; about half of the total number are union officials. In a few counties the Minister chose a workers' union man as one of his direct appointees in order to ease union rivalry.

committee is fully representative of the county's agriculture.[1]

In order to secure a fuller picture of the composition of these bodies, a careful analysis was made of the membership of nine sample committees in 1955.[2] One fact which clearly emerged is that farmers made up a substantially larger portion of the membership than the statutory three-two-two ratio of nominated members might suggest. At the time of the study there was a vacancy on two of the committees, and their total membership was thus 106. This group included sixty-seven farmers, sixteen landowners, fourteen workers' union officials, eight land agents, and one agricultural worker. Moreover, all but two of the landowners were also farmers, and many considered themselves primarily farmers, thus raising the number of farming members to eighty-one, or about 75 per cent. Owner-occupiers outnumbered tenants by more than two to one, thus almost reversing the proportions in the country at large. Committee members were almost all large farmers (in British terms) and many of them very large ones. Among the seventy-six farmers for whom we have records, there were twelve with more than 1,000 acres and twenty-five with more than 500 acres, whereas there were only fourteen with less than 200 acres and only seven with less than 100 acres. Thus the 70 per cent of farmers who occupy less than 100 acres each were scarcely represented. Accompanying this disproportion in size was a tendency for most of the members' farms to be in the better farming areas of each county.

Most of the members were well into middle age. The average age of the farming members was fifty-six. Only four listed themselves as retired, but almost half were either in partnership, usually with a son, or were members of a private farming company; and a considerable proportion might fairly be classified as semi-retired. Of the total 106 members there were thirty-three of less than fifty years of age. The district committees, which were appointed by the county committees, consisted almost entirely of farmers; and if meetings attended in several parts of the country may be taken as typical, the average age of their active members was higher than on the parent bodies.

Typically a committee member is heavily engaged in other agricultural and public activities. The eighty-one members of our sample

---

[1] The Minister is advised on his appointments by a panel in each region consisting of the chief regional officers of the Ministry, the Minister's liaison officer, and the chairman of the committee concerned. Although practice has varied, it is not unusual for the Minister to take a personal interest in the composition of the committees.

[2] Because it was necessary to use various sources, there are some minor inconsistencies and omissions. While the figures are not to be taken as precisely accurate in every detail, they present a fair picture of the committees' composition throughout the post-war period.

committees for whom we have some information of this kind included twenty-seven members or ex-members of county councils,[1] twelve individuals co-opted to various county council committees, forty-six members or ex-members of other local authority councils, and twenty-eight justices of the peace. Most of the members were also active in one or more agricultural organizations, particularly the farmers, a majority of whom held positions of responsibility in the National Farmers' Union.

According to the National Farmers' Union, these representative bodies put agriculture 'in the proud position of being the only great industry that is self-governing through its three partners who are all represented on the County Committee'.[2] The committees are a form of 'self-government' only in a very qualified sense. In 1948 the Permanent Secretary of the Ministry explained to a Select Committee on Estimates that the members of county committees

are not delegates from, we will say, the National Farmers' Union or the Workers' Union. They are appointed by the Minister as his agents, and they are responsible only to him for carrying out the work that he delegates to them. They are his agents, and not in any sense representatives of bodies which had nominated them originally.[3]

Certainly the committees are not delegates, subject to instruction and recall, but the subtlety of committee administration lies precisely in their dual role as Minister's agents and sectional representatives.

The most notable instance of a purely sectional viewpoint occurred in connection with 'cottage certificates'. Under post-war procedure landlords could generally dispossess their cottage tenants only if they could demonstrate to a panel of the county committee that such action was agriculturally necessary. Although the Workers' Union was in principle entirely opposed to the 'tied cottage' system, these panels worked with very little friction between farmer and worker members—so little that in many counties the making of the decisions

[1] In 1947 there was an average of 2·7 county councillors on the English county committees and an average of over 3 on the Welsh committees. Political and Economic Planning, 'Agricultural Executives,' *Planning*, January 31, 1949, p. 226.
[2] *NFU Record*, March, 1948.
[3] House of Commons, *Eleventh Report from the Select Committee on Estimates, Together with the Minutes of Evidence*, 'Agricultural Services' (1948/49) (HMSO, 1949), p. 8. See also pp. xi–xii. While the committees were patterned in some respects on the county agricultural executive committees established during the First World War, the earlier bodies had been formed from the county council agricultural committees and had, according to Murray, owed their allegiance primarily to the county councils rather than to the Board of Agriculture. Murray, *Agriculture*, p. 8.

was delegated to a workers' union official or to the different members of the panel in turn.[1] However, after several years the National Union of Agricultural Workers decided that it could no longer be 'directly associated' with this work. 'Union representatives serving on these cottage panels have therefore been advised to resign from the panels forthwith.'[2] Most workers' nominees complied, regardless of their private opinions on the merits of the case and their duties as public servants. Being as a rule paid officials, they were in no position to disregard the 'advice' of their employer.

Comparable examples among the farmers' and landowners' nominees are extremely rare. They have seldom been used by their organizations as channels of pressure or even sources of information. The Committee on Intermediaries said that when a farmer thinks that he has been unfairly treated by the committee and appeals to the Union for help, 'the Union's first step will be to ask its nominees what reason the County Committee has for giving an unfavourable decision'.[3] But this was almost never the first step, and Union branches in fact relied more on formal channels than on personal links to pursue such inquiries. In 1949 the National Farmers' Union did report that, having failed to dissuade the Ministry from eliminating the committee-operated labour pools, it had advised county branches 'to do what they could through their representatives on County Agricultural Executive Committees to persuade the Ministry to take less drastic action'.[4] Taken as it stands, this statement suggests a misuse of the committee system. Members nominated by county branches are not supposed to be agents through which pressure can be brought on decisions of national policy. In fairness, it must be said that this was a rare exception to the Union's usual attitude. Sporadically, one of its branches has made a similar attempt. In 1951, for example, the Flintshire branch urged all Union representatives on the county committee to resign as a protest against the policy of the Ministry of Fuel and Power with regard to opencast coal mining.[5]

The Ministry did not expect committee members to cease to take an active part in the affairs of their organizations, and it saw no incongruity in a member holding the public balance in the morning and wielding the private sword in the afternoon. It suggested that if a member found himself in fundamental disagreement with a com-

---

[1] Slightly less than half of the applications for 'cottage certificates' were turned down by the committee panels. H. of C. O. R., 1953/54, Vol. 525, col. 2154.

[2] *The Land Worker*, May, 1951, p. 8. On the tied cottage see below, pp. 173–4.

[3] Office of the Prime Minister, *Report of the Committee on Intermediaries*, Cmd. 7404, 1950, p. 47.

[4] National Farmers' Union, *Year Book*, 1950, p. 86.

[5] *The British Farmer*, September 30, 1951.

mittee policy he should resign,[1] but few such resignations took place. In some counties committee members declined to stand for office in their organizations, but it was more usual for positions of authority to overlap. Sometimes the county National Farmers' Union automatically added all farmer members of the committee to its own executive body. Committee chairmen were often selected from the nominees of the National Farmers' Union or the Country Landowners' Association,[2] even when they were active local leaders of these organizations.

Overlapping membership of this kind had unfortunate results in some counties. That did not necessarily mean that the Union (or Association) had the committee in its pocket. In one county, for example, a strong committee chairman used his influential position in the Union to forestall criticism of his energetic sanctions policy. The opposite and admittedly more usual situation is typified by a committee which was dominated by a strong Union secretary, supported by the Union nominees, until his hold was broken by a new county agricultural officer. This committee had served farmers so well that it had accumulated one of the highest deficits in the country in its machinery and labour services. In the western counties especially some committees tended to think of themselves as a kind of special sub-committee of the county branch of the National Farmers' Union. Such unhealthy relationships were not usual in the country as a whole. If anything, they have been less common than might have been expected, considering the example set by the Ministry in its own dealings with Union headquarters.

2

At its peak the work of the committees fell into three main divisions: sanctions, general administration, and technical advice. It was the more or less routine administration of subsidies, grants and regulations that gave committee members the most satisfaction. Any number of them, when asked at the time of the Arton Wilson Committee investigations, whether they thought that the committees had a place in the future, replied, 'Of course they have, there is all this administrative work to do.' The proportion of the Ministry's staff serving in the field increased from less than 40 per cent in 1939 to 80 per cent

[1] Ministry of Agriculture and Fisheries, *Position and Responsibilities of County Agricultural Executive Committees* (February, 1949), p. 2. (Mimeo.) It is now the rule that members should not publicly criticize the Minister.

[2] In March, 1961, twelve chairmen were nominees of the National Farmers' Union and eight were nominees of the Country Landowners' Association. Many of the chairmen who are Minister's nominees originally came to their committees as nominees of one of the organizations and were later transferred to a Minister's seat.

in 1950. The total staff grew during the same period from 2,654 to 15,567.[1] As we have seen, many of the administrative duties were passed on from the 'war ags', with others added from time to time simply because the committees were a convenient hook on which to hang the Ministry's local activities. The organization was complicated, however, by a number of field services which continued to be separate from the committees, such as the veterinary services, the national milk testing service, and the agricultural wages inspectorate.

Immediately after the war the committees were responsible for a large number of trading services, including labour and machinery pools and the performance of certain operations on contract. These services were intended to help farmers (especially small ones) who were expanding output under difficult conditions. It was also hoped by some that they might lead the way to a more co-operative system of farming which would help to overcome the drawbacks of small farm units.[2] The committees' local knowledge helped them to suggest where needs for such services existed, but their local attachments often inclined them to go on providing them indefinitely and at unduly cheap rates.

The committees also administered many special subsidies, such as those for hill cattle and sheep, the ploughing of grassland, drainage improvements, marginal production, and hill farming. Many of these required merely routine investigation or the exercise of straightforward technical judgments; but others were aimed at farmers who had special problems or who could use assistance to especially good effect, and it was in these cases that the scope for local knowledge and experience was greatest. Nice decisions had to be made about the conditions and potentialities of particular farms and (equally necessary but much more delicate) about the capacities of their farmers. It had to be decided, for example, whether a hill farming scheme amounted to a 'comprehensive rehabilitation' of the unit and whether a farm could become enough of an 'economic unit' to justify an improvement grant.

A third group of administrative activities had to do with agricultural regulations about pests, injurious weeds, plant and crop diseases, and standards of milk production. Although most of this work was of a routine and technical nature and was left by the committees to their officers, a few regulations contained a strong discretionary element. This was especially true of the Milk and Dairies Regulations where the problem was gradually to enforce national standards of cleanliness in milk production without doing serious

[1] *Ryan Committee Report*, 1951, pp. 3–4.
[2] See R. S. G. Rutherford and F. W. Bateson, 'Co-operation in Agriculture' in F. W. Bateson (ed.), *Towards a Socialist Agriculture* (Victor Gollancz, 1946), p. 124.

hardship to individual farmers. Since the removal of a farmer from the list of registered milk producers might be tantamount to throwing him out of business, it was appropriate that the decision should be made by a representative body rather than by civil servants.[1]

In their administration of grants and regulations the committees could mediate between the Ministry's demand for national uniformity and strict compliance with regulations and farmers' preference for individual exceptions and lax administration. In the case of the milk regulations, the committees were usually able to maintain a steady pressure on sub-standard producers, while at the same time restraining their often impatient technical officers; but more often they tended, as might be expected, to be too soft-hearted. It was extremely difficult, for example, to persuade them that *any* farm was not an economic unit, and they were reluctant to discriminate between the needs of different farmers. An example is the marginal production scheme, which was introduced in wartime to help farmers who had poor land or other production difficulties and which was continued until 1959. Some county committees found it easier to use up most of the money in grants for various specified operations carried on by any farmer (which the scheme permitted) rather than to investigate the awkward question of which farms most warranted this assistance.

Contrary to the general impression, the committees were more open to criticism in their ordinary administration than in their imposition of sanctions. They inevitably collected a great deal of information about other farmers' affairs, and they were largely ignorant of the unwritten rules telling the professional civil servant when to talk and when to be silent. They talked; indeed they tended to become a kind of switchboard for the gossip of the farming community. Nor was favouritism entirely absent. Where only small questions of justice were at issue, committees sometimes allowed themselves to forget the demands of impartiality in order to reward friends and annoy enemies.[2]

The extent of the committees' authority over their officers was not clearly defined, though their broad wartime powers of appointment

---

[1] There was provision for appeal from the committees' decisions to *ad hoc* appeals tribunals composed of an independent chairman, a representative of consumers, and a representative of producers: but these tribunals were not widely used.

[2] A Gloucester agricultural contractor told a Select Committee on Estimates in 1948: 'As you know this machinery is allocated by the committees and the committees are controlled by farmers; of course they allocate them to themselves and to their friends. That is not only happening in my county but I would say in every county in the country.' *Eleventh Report from the Select Committee on Estimates*, 1949, p. 183. Allegations of such glaring misbehaviour were more frequent during and immediately after the war than in later years.

were eventually reduced to a merely advisory role as a result of strong pressure from the staff side of the Ministry's Whitley Council. Although from one point of view agents of the Minister, from another the committees were an asymmetrical addition of a group of laymen to the lower level of the administrative hierarchy. Thus the local civil servant had somehow to serve his committee, the Ministry divisions concerned with local administration, and (if he was an advisory officer or land agent) his professional service as well. These circumstances forced him to take on many of the attributes of a petty politician, and his own inclinations sometimes led him in the same direction. The problem was most acute, and the opportunities greatest, for the county agricultural officer. He was rarely awed by his committee, but neither was he attached by habit or background to the Ministry. By playing the one against the other he could usually control the committee, while at the same time forestalling or modifying decisions of higher authorities to an extent impossible for ordinary civil servants of comparable rank.

A frequently critical view of the committees' administrative capacities did not prevent local officials from opposing any attempt to reduce the committees' powers. The Ministry of Agriculture's field services were mainly composed of technical officers whose importance grew considerably during the war and who fought hard to retain their key position in local administration. They shared with the committees a tendency to see the public interest from a rather narrow agricultural point of view, a tendency less justifiable on their part than on the committees'. Some believed that the Ministry's programme was essentially technical, and they feared that if the technicians lost control in the field (as, they ruefully reflected, they had lost control at headquarters) advisory and technical work would be subordinated to 'administrative' considerations. They sought therefore to maintain the committees' place in local administration as the best means of retaining their own influence.

The committees themselves were extremely sensitive about their administrative prerogatives. Some members resigned because of 'interference' by the Ministry,[1] and the possibility that others might do the same put the committees in a strong position. Of course the intention that these unpaid bodies would act as some kind of a check on the Ministry was implicit in their establishment. What was not sufficiently guarded against was their tendency to use their influence

[1] Captain George Walmsley, for example, resigned as chairman of the West Suffolk County Committee on grounds of 'rank interference' by senior civil servants. 'No self respecting person,' he said, 'working in a voluntary capacity would tolerate the situation. The present system of centralization to the last comma from Whitehall militates against committees doing any useful work in the counties on their own initiative.' The Farmers' Weekly, December 9, 1949.

in all kinds of trivial cases. Ordinary administration was frequently obstructed by committee inaction or 'misinterpretation' of instructions, by protests to the Minister on minor questions, by subterranean conflicts and intrigue. Much time and energy had to be spent pacifying the committees, irritated by some new rule or decision from Whitehall. Matters which in other Departments would cause scarcely a flurry were accompanied by intricate calculations of 'how the committees will take it' and 'how it can be put over'. Whitehall's response was an increasing and sometimes exasperating secrecy about its intentions.

As long as it was necessary to expand food production rapidly, to administer a politically delicate sanctions policy, and to develop new and complex schemes of direct grants, the committees' value outweighed their administrative drawbacks. Once these needs became less important the balance of advantage shifted. In 1949 a Select Committee on Estimates drew attention to the heavy losses incurred by the committees in their trading services.[1] Disquiet about the Ministry's rapid and confused growth, the high administrative cost of certain agricultural grants, and the inefficiency of committee administration led to the appointment of two independent investigating committees within five years.

The first of these, the Ryan Committee, proposed that the committees should shed the responsibility for both the advisory programme and ordinary administration, concentrating on the exercise of sanctions and a vaguely defined 'leadership in the industry in the counties'.[2] It proposed that separate county offices should be established as the Ministry's local administrative units. The committees would aid by ' "selling" the scheme to farmers generally and . . . advising or arbitrating on particular cases where there may be doubt or dispute'.[3] The Ryan Committee blandly hoped that the committees would 'recognize the advantage to be gained by being freed, so far as possible, from pedestrian tasks', but the committees' attachment to their pedestrian tasks was common knowledge.

The Ryan recommendations were acceptable to Ministry headquarters, except for the heads of the advisory service, and preliminary steps were taken to implement them. However, little effort had been made to persuade the committees or even to assess the strength of the committee-advisory service opposition. At the next annual meeting of committee chairmen the Minister was bluntly informed of the

---

[1] *Eleventh Report from the Select Committee on Estimates*, 1949.
[2] *Ryan Committee Report*, 1951, p. 26.
[3] *Ibid.*, p. 12. The Ryan Committee thought, however, that the committees should remain responsible for considering each case arising under the Milk Regulations.

committees' hot opposition. Retreating to his rooms, the Minister doubtless contemplated the picture of his whole local organization up in arms against him, and he determined to move very cautiously. County offices were not established, but the committees' authority was gradually shaved away by increasing the number of detailed instructions from Whitehall and broadening the power of local officers to make final decisions in certain cases.[1] Committees were allowed to continue their trading services only if they could operate them without loss, a condition which necessitated drastic curtailment.

The sharp acrimony characterizing this dispute arose less from the contents of the Ryan Report than from beliefs about its motivation. It was widely believed among the committees and many of their local officers that the Ryan investigation was a scheme of the Ministry's Establishments Division to get rid of the committees altogether and to force the Ministry's local organization into a more orthodox pattern, thus strengthening the authority of Establishments. However overplayed, this supicion had its particle of truth. The report did not adequately lay to rest the suspicion that as mere advisers and critics the committees might be ignored, while as administrators their views had at least to be considered.

The second committee of inquiry, like the first, owed its existence to some critical comments by a Select Committee on Estimates.[2] The Ministry was stimulated to appoint the Arton Wilson Committee to investigate its field organization in the hope of forestalling the fuller Parliamentary investigation which the Select Committee threatened. Reporting in 1956, the Arton Wilson Committee strongly recommended that the committees should cease to be responsible for the routine administration of grants, subsidies, and trading services 'or in any way to supervise the civil servants engaged on this work'. The committees would instead act as courts of appeal 'to which an aggrieved farmer could state his case against the official's decision' and as bodies to assist in dealing with particular local problems such as the development of rabbit clearance schemes. These 'appellate' and consultative functions, together with the administration of sanctions and other statutory regulations were to be performed by a small 'executive panel', while the main committee concentrated on

---

[1] The executive assistants to the county agricultural officers (who would have headed the county offices had they been established) were made directly responsible for some matters to the appropriate headquarters division rather than to the county agricultural officer or the committee. Needless to say, this further complicated the administrative situation and would have been intolerable on any long-term basis.

[2] House of Commons, *Sixth Report from the Select Committee on Estimates, Together with the Minutes of Evidence*, 'Regional Organizations of Government Departments' (1953/54) (HMSO, 1954).

technical development and advising the Minister on broad agricultural policy.[1]

This time the Ministry moved with more prudence but also more vigour in acting on the report. The committees were seen individually before any general body of opinion had crystallized. There were naturally some protests, but the committees were well aware that their importance had declined drastically during the five years since the Ryan report. In the event the routine administrative work was surrendered with scarcely a struggle.

Following the Arton Wilson recommendations the Ministry's organization has been considerably streamlined. The administration of most grants and regulations is now concentrated in thirty-two divisional offices, most of which cover more than one county. Seven regional controllers with the rank of assistant secretary have been appointed to control local administration and co-ordinate the work of the Ministry generally in their regions.[2] Technical staff retain direct access to their superiors on purely service and technical matters. These arrangements overcame the administrative drawbacks resulting from the varying size of the counties and they also, of course, remove administration one stage further from the influence of the committees, which retain administrative responsibility only for milk, pests, and various minor statutory functions. The committees also give advice on technical development and the advisory programme, on the local implications of policy, and on borderline grant and subsidy cases. In addition they hear complaints from farmers about administrative decisions.

3

The third part of committee work was responsibility for the provision of technical advice. The close institutional connection between the committees and the advisory service has been noticed. The district committee acted as sponsor of the young advisory officer, introducing him to farmers, publicizing his meetings, and finding farms for demonstrations. Its members instructed him in local agricultural conditions and warned him of his farmers' idiosyncrasies and prejudices. He could expect a few members at least to be enthusiastic about seeking out and acting upon his advice, and their farms might become public demonstrations of his competence. The need for this kind of assistance declined somewhat as the advisory service gained

[1] *Arton Wilson Report*, 1956, pp. 8–9.
[2] The Welsh Secretary performs the same function in Wales. The extent of regional co-ordination is still rather uncertain. The Fisheries Department, for example, remains substantially independent, and the veterinary services, traditionally hostile to any 'outside' supervision, have resisted regional control.

stature, but the promotion of many of the best field officers to positions in the service's inflated provincial hierarchy tended to draw
experience and maturity out of the field, thus maintaining the need
for the committees' help.

On the other hand, district advisory officers performed much work
that was not strictly advisory, such as processing applications for
grants and inspecting the acreage of crops on which subsidy was
claimed. They frequently assisted their district committees with the
farm survey, and sometimes made recommendations regarding the
imposition of sanctions. Although some advisory officers thought
that their administrative chores gave them valuable contacts, most
complained that they only stole time from their real work and complicated their relations with farmers. It was this overlapping of functions which alarmed the Ryan Committee and led it to recommend
that the advisory service should have a separate county organization.
While the committees were to continue 'to popularize its work with
farmers, to help the Service to appreciate the sort of advice that is
wanted and to co-operate in its activities in the county', advisory
officers were no longer to compromise their reputation for impartiality by serving as officers of the committees.[1] The extent to which
advisory work was really hampered because of this connection is
difficult to judge. No doubt some farmers did avoid advisory officers
on the principle that it was prudent to stay clear of the whole lot from
the 'war ag'. On the other hand, they were generally the ones least
likely to ask for advice in any case.

This recommendation of the Ryan Committee was not formally
implemented, but from 1951 onwards there was a steady process of
internal separation. This internal separation, together with the decreasing importance of production targets, helped the advisory service to escape from its close identification with the promotion of
Government policy. More attention was paid to the farmers' individual interests and also to the economics of the whole farm as a
necessary framework for technical advice, although many advisory
officers, like many committees, were slow to see that their task was a
more complicated one than showing farmers how to raise more corn
and better grass.[2]

The Ryan Committee hoped to accomplish objectives which were
probably incompatible: the continuation of an energetic advice-

---

[1] *Ryan Committee Report*, 1951, p. 28; see also pp. 13–22.

[2] In 1954 the Ministry of Agriculture issued a handbook on farm management,
The Farm as a Business, which marked the transition from a 'production' to an
'economic' approach in the giving of technical advice. The provincial economists
attached to the Universities also offer economic advice to individual farmers, but
this is done on a very small scale; they have concentrated mainly on providing
basic economic and financial data and on helping to repair gaps in the technical
advisory officers' knowledge of economics.

sanctions programme and the establishment of an independent advisory service. Five years later the problem presented itself to the Arton Wilson Committee in quite a different form. As a corollary of the reduced significance (and subsequent abolition) of sanctions, the committees were left with technical advice as their one remaining function of importance. 'If . . . the partnership between State and industry is to survive, both will have to concentrate on technical development; and the CAEC or some equivalent body, can admirably be harnessed for the purposes.' The committee member should be 'younger than in the past, with a mind especially alive to technical and scientific development'. While the Arton Wilson Committee recommended larger units of local administration, it thought that the committees and the advisory service should continue to be based on the counties, 'because in our view the nature of their work is unique and can only be carried out effectively within units shaped to suit the tradition and practice of agriculture'.[1] However, it was now the committees that were to be 'harnessed' to the advisory service rather than the other way around.

These recommendations were well suited to the Conservative Government's emphasis upon economic efficiency as the prime goal for British agriculture. Both the committees and the advisory service have been relieved of administrative responsibility.[2] This has left the county agricultural officer, for fifteen years the key figure in local agricultural administration, in charge only of his county unit of the advisory service. At first the committees, and some of the advisory officers too, resented this curtailment of their responsibilities. However, Government efforts to introduce younger and more technically progressive farmers gradually changed the committees' attitudes, while at the same time improving their value to advisory officers.[3]

4

As in the case of sanctions, so in local administration and technical advice, the transition from a wartime expedient to a tenable long

[1] *Arton Wilson Committee Report*, 1956, pp. 7, 10–11, 13.

[2] The Arton Wilson Committee also recommended that the agricultural land service be relieved of its administrative and advisory duties and turned into a compact body of professional land agents for the government. The land service beat off this threat and continues as a quasi-professional service with mainly administrative duties and some vaguely defined responsibility for advice on estate management.

[3] For the first time, long-standing age limits (60 for new appointments and 67 for reappointments) were enforced, and the average age of committee members declined, standing in 1960 at 53. Information from Ministry of Agriculture, Fisheries and Food.

term basis was not made in 1947. It had been expected, perhaps short-sightedly, that the committees' routine administrative work and the trading services would rather quickly disappear and that there was, therefore, no necessity of setting up a local organization to preside over their demise. These functions did not disappear, and the com-mittees found themselves performing a wide variety of tasks which had been hastily improvised to meet wartime emergencies. They vigorously opposed each reduction in their duties and every new central control. With the Arton Wilson reorganization and the abandonment of sanctions, the question became whether the committees were to enter a new stage, serving a subordinate but still significant function in agricultural administration, or whether they had been right in thinking that they were to be sapped of any real importance.

During the years of their greatest activity the committees were an effective force in aiding, advising, and checking the bureaucracy. The difficulty was, as we have seen, that they also got in the way of good administration. Is there some function for them now lying between a badly performed executive responsibility on the one hand and an insignificant, purely formal advisory responsibility on the other? The dismal history of other bodies advising on local adminis-tration warns against any high expectations,[1] and it would be wrong to give the impression that the greatest issues are at stake. Agricul-tural administration will not fall to the ground if the committees disappear altogether, and its problems will not be solved even if they are used well. Moreover it is well to be sceptical of every advisory body. Public administration today needs fewer of these, not more. It is all too easy for a democracy to spawn useless devices for consulta-tion based on vague notions of 'democratic administration'. Without any doubt lay participation in public administration can promote a broader appreciation of public needs and a deeper understanding of the responsibilities of citizenship in a democracy, but this cannot be shammed. There has first to be something for the laymen to do.

According to the Arton Wilson Committee, one of the main jobs of the reformed committees would be to serve the Minister as 'prac-tical advisers'. 'We consider that the Minister's responsibilities to-wards agriculture call for a body of local advisers, having their roots in farming, to help in the shaping of agricultural policy.'[2] This con-ception of the committees did have a certain reality in wartime. As his direct agents, the 'war ags' had access to the Minister, and a dis-tinguished group of liaison officers served as links between the lay-

---

[1] See Enid M. Harrison, 'Local Advisory Committees,' *Public Administration*, Spring, 1953, p. 65.
[2] *Arton Wilson Committee Report*, 1956, pp. 8, 11–12.

man at the top of the organization and those at its base.[1] After the war periodic conferences between committee chairmen and the Minister were instituted in an effort to maintain close contacts, and Sir Thomas Dugdale reintroduced the liaison officer system, but the new officers did little. Under peacetime conditions the 'direct agent' theory became increasingly fictional, and the channels of communication between committees and Minister tended to become choked with administrative trivia.

Ministers of Agriculture might indeed have found advantages in developing the influence of the committees as a counterweight to their powerful friends in the National Farmers' Union. But the Union would certainly have strongly opposed such a development—the history of the interwar Parliament of Agriculture is in point here[2]—and nothing like it ever occurred. Such influence as the committees had was confined to the services for which they had direct responsibility. They were never seriously regarded as a significant source of advice on general policy, nor is there any likelihood that they will become such a source in the future.

With respect to more specific, practical, and local questions, however, there is still a place for lay participation at the local level, although it is now a distinctly subordinate place. Moreover, there is evidence that the Ministry is making genuine efforts to utilize the committees. A small standing committee has been established under the chairmanship of a Parliamentary Secretary to provide a focus for questions about the committees' work, and headquarters actively encourages local officers to foster the committees, keep them informed, and make use of them. The committees have been encouraged to take an interest in such matters as the use of poisonous sprays, rural transport and housing, and the work of the Ministry's experimental farms. They have been especially helpful in programmes which require a large measure of voluntary support. Many committees have taken the lead in forming rabbit clearance societies, and some have participated closely with National Farmers' Union branches in campaigns against foot and mouth disease and in forming machinery syndicates. With the gradual elimination of the 'old guard', the committees have become increasingly competent to take

---

[1] Sir Anthony Hurd, who was one of the wartime liaison officers, has described the system in some detail in his *A Farmer in Whitehall* (Country Life, 1951), ch. 4. 'Every month the Minister held his liaison officers' conference. At these he took us into his confidence regarding the national situation, and what we learnt from him at these meetings was invaluable in getting policy across to the county and district committees, and seeing as far as we could that all kept in step. He then demanded reports from all of us of progress in our counties, of difficulties, and every possible suggestion for improvement was thrashed out.' p. 33. Some of the wartime liaison officers worked almost full time at this job.

[2] See above, p. 39.

part in the advisory programme. Finally, although the committees do not (and constitutionally cannot) function as independent courts of appeal, they have had some effect upon administrative decisions. In the two years 1959–60 they heard some 800 representations from farmers and secured reversal or modification of the official decision in 150 of these cases.

The committees have survived the shock of a drastic transformation; they have been revived and put to their new work. Two characteristics of the Ministry's present organization give some ground for thinking that these bodies will be used well, perhaps even imaginatively. On the administrative side, the regional controllers confront a task of extraordinary difficulty and complexity in co-ordinating the numerous field services, some of which are traditionally almost autonomous. The county committees, wisely used, serve as the regional controller's natural ally, providing him with an independent source of information and support. On the advisory side, it is clear that the small cadre of 1,350 advisory officers still needs some system of regular association with influential and progressive farmers who can support and amplify their work, experiment with new ideas, and contribute their local experience and practical outlook.

In spite of the county committees' extremely difficult tasks of balancing general and particular interests, and in the face of some just criticism of their administration, they established for themselves a respected place in the agricultural community. They accumulated valuable experience with local administration and advisory work, as well as some ability to see the different parts of agricultural administration in the county as one connected whole. This kind of standing and experience is difficult to achieve in local representative bodies, and easy to lose. Partnership in the field must now be differently conceived and more narrowly interpreted, but the committees can still contribute worthwhile local participation to a sensitive field of public administration.

CHAPTER VII

THE WORKERS' PLACE IN THE SUN

1

DESPITE their numerical preponderance, farm workers are a much weaker force than farmers.[1] The farm worker has little history beyond poverty and remorseless labour. The Enclosure Movement and the Industrial Revolution between them wrought the destruction of the independent yeomanry and peasantry of England and substituted a landless wage-earning class. The extent of the farm workers' social and economic dependency right down to the second world war is easily forgotten by those whose view of labour history is derived from the different circumstances of the industrial worker. Exiles to remote villages in the Second World War were startled by the extent to which squires and their ladies still presided over the lives and morals of their villagers.

In this century the condition of the farm worker gradually improved. He was helped by the sudden importance of agricultural production in the First World War, by the swelling tide of welfare legislation, by refraction from the gains of industrial workers, and by his own efforts at unionization. Yet his pay, his amenities, and his social status remain relatively poor, and his unions are divided and irresolute. He has yet to find his place in the sun.

In some ways it was easier in the bad old days. The desperate circumstances of agricultural workers in the past are an oft-recounted part of their unions' lore. The intellectual frustrations of today can be forgotten in a return to the certainty of yesterday when, harsh as the issues were, right and wrong were clearly defined. The six agricultural workers of Tolpuddle who were transported in 1834 for taking an illegal oath in the formation of 'The Friendly Society of Agricultural Workers' could make a defence that, in dignity and right, is difficult to rival today.

My Lord, if we have violated any law, it was not done intentionally; we have injured no man's reputation, character, person or property; we were uniting together to preserve ourselves, our wives and children from utter degradation and starvation. We challenge any man, or any number of men, to prove that we have acted or

[1] The number of whole time, regular agricultural workers recorded for the UK in 1958 was 538,000. (*Agricultural Statistics*, 1958–9, HMSO, p. 22). This compares with the estimate of 300,000 full-time farmers given in Chapter I.

intended to act, different from the above statement.[1]

Agricultural workers contributed these 'Tolpuddle martyrs' to trade union history, but they were slow to profit from the sacrifice themselves. Efforts during the nineteenth century to organize agricultural workers, notably by Joseph Arch's National Agricultural Labourers' Union in the 1870's, enjoyed some temporary success, but not until 1906, with the initiation in Norfolk of the Eastern Counties Agricultural Labourers' and Small Holders' Union, was a lasting union formed. Four years later, having established branches in other parts of the country, the union was reconstituted on a national basis, and adopted its present name, the National Union of Agricultural Workers, in 1920.

Two strikes and two wars provided the main events of the Union's history before 1945. In 1910 agricultural workers in Norfolk struck in an effort to enforce their claim for a raise of one shilling a week and a Saturday half holiday. (The average weekly wage was then 14 shillings.) They held out for six months, but the strike ended with conditions unimproved and the Union seriously weakened. War accomplished what a strike had not. Thanks to a shortage of labour during the First World War and to the introduction of the Central Wages Board by the 1917 Corn Production Act, average weekly wages in the eastern and north-eastern counties increased from 15s. 3d. in 1914 to 37s. 3d. in 1919. Union membership also increased, more rapidly than ever before or since, rising (according to the official figures) from 4,141 in 1910 to 126,911 in 1919.[2]

The gains proved to be short-lived. The repeal of the Corn Production Act in 1921, including the provisions for the Wages Board, and the post-war agricultural depression resulted in a decline in both farm wages and Union membership. In 1923 the Union again went on strike in Norfolk and certain other parts of the country. A settlement was negotiated by the leader of the Labour Party, Ramsay MacDonald, but it did not effectively prevent victimization of strike leaders, and the Union was again weakened. Moreover this strike, like most disputes between agricultural workers and farmers, had an air of unreality. The Union lacked the strength to secure or to police a satisfactory settlement by direct pressure on the farmers. The strike was a tactical move, but the issue was decided elsewhere—at the level of state agricultural policy. In 1924 the minority Labour Govern-

[1] Reg. Groves, *Sharpen the Sickle: The History of the Farm Workers' Union* (London: The Porcupine Press, 1949), p. 20.

[2] *Ibid.*, pp. 245, 252. These membership figures are estimates compiled by an officer of the Union. Groves points out that the early figures are unreliable, since the small office staff 'could only add on new members to previous figures without being able to record losses.' Nevertheless there can be no doubt that the gain in membership was immense.

ment re-established statutory machinery for fixing minimum wages, this time on a county basis, and wage rates were stabilized. 'The strike,' one Union leader said, 'won us the Wages Boards back.'[1]

The low point of Union strength between the wars was in 1924 when membership dropped to 29,000, remaining at little more than this figure until 1936 when it began slowly to climb. During the second world war the machinery for fixing minimum wages was again centralized, and although agricultural workers suffered the restriction of being compelled to remain on the land, they were compensated with a sharp rise in the minimum wage. Workers were confident that this time their improved position would be maintained, with a Labour Government in office and agricultural prosperity guaranteed by statute. While workers received only a brief mention in the basic Agriculture Act of 1947, the Agricultural Wages Act of the same year continued the central wage fixing machinery. The Union was stronger than ever before, and its historian wrote in 1948 that

by the end of 1947 the membership figure had reached 162,533 and was fast moving towards the 200,000. That this growing membership has been held, unlike the thousands who joined at the end of the First World War, shows that the Union organization has been built on a sound foundation.[2]

In fact, these optimistic expectations proved mistaken. The Union did not suffer anything like the drastic decline after the First World War, and in the light of the changed position of agriculture such a development was and is extremely unlikely. However, membership did fall, and in its evidence to the Royal Commission on Common Land (1957) the Union claimed about 150,000 members. Asked what proportion that was of the total number of agricultural workers, the Union's spokesman estimated that 'somewhere between 30 and 50 per cent of the actual employed workers are members'.[3] This estimate is certainly exaggerated. On the basis of 1959 subscription income it would appear that the Union's maximum possible membership did not exceed 30 per cent of the agricultural labour force,[4]

---

[1] *Ibid.*, p. 205.

[2] *Ibid.*, p. 229.

[3] Royal Commission on Common Land, *Minutes of Evidence* (HMSO, 1957), November 28, 1956, pp. 636–7. In 1959 the Union declared a membership of 147,938 to the Registrar of Friendly Societies.

[4] If all Union members had been regular adult male workers paying full subscription rates, their numbers would have been about 112,000 or just under 30 per cent of the adult male labour force at that time. Some members, of course, were actually women or juveniles who paid lower subscriptions, but while this fact points to a somewhat higher membership, it can hardly have increased the proportion of all workers who belonged to the Union.

while in fact a considerable number of its members are not agricultural workers at all. The proportion of farm workers who are unionized still seems to be under a third, even allowing for the fact that some belong to a different union. This makes a striking difference not only from industrial workers but also from the highly unionized farmers. The National Union of Agricultural Workers itself has still to establish the solid organization, the consistent objectives, and the sound strategy which are necessary for effective political action.

The difficulties of organizing agricultural workers are considerable. The worker's education and upbringing have generally taught him to be satisfied with a humble station—and to the consternation of his Union, he may *be* satisfied and therefore slow to see the advantages of trade union organization. The fact that many intelligent and ambitious workers leave agriculture, or buy a precarious independence by accepting the drudgery of a small-holding, deprives the Union of potential local leaders. Even the physical problems of organization are formidable. Thinly broadcast over the countryside and working long and often irregular hours, farm workers find it difficult to attend meetings and perform Union work. The organization is often hard pressed even to keep in touch with its members. Conditions have not altogether changed since George Edwards, the Union's first general secretary, reported cycling over a thousand miles during the year on Union business.

The villages are so scattered, and the labourers live in such isolated districts, with no opportunity to make themselves acquainted with the great social questions of the day. The distances to be travelled to get to the villages will always make it more costly to organize the Agricultural Labourers than it does the mechanics and workers in the towns.[1]

The proportion of the Union's energy that has to be spent in organizing workers helps to explain its weakness. The Union has no less than 3,700 branches, each of which sends a delegate to a district committee, although in practice the branch secretary often delegates himself. The district committee in its turn elects one or two representatives to a county committee. One of the main tasks of these small branches is to collect subscriptions, which is a difficult task in itself.[2] Branch chairmen are paid a small stipend and branch secre-

[1] Eastern Counties Agricultural Labourers and Small Holders' Union, *Report and Balance Sheet for Year Ending December 31, 1906*, p. 4.

[2] In 1960 the leadership persuaded the biennial conference to agree that the monthly contribution should henceforth be the same as the minimum hourly rate of pay. *The Land Worker*, April, 1960, pp. 4–5; July, 1960, p. 2. The first automatic increase (to 3s. 8d.) followed the wage award in 1961.

taries earn 10 per cent of all collections made plus certain bonuses. These payments amounted in 1959 to over £30,000, or about 14 per cent of the Union's total income from contributions.

Union leaders have begun to question whether this dispersed system is still the most effective way of maintaining membership and income. The commissions paid to branch secretaries have less value than when times were hard. Many of the older members who collected subscriptions and kept their branches together, sometimes for three or four decades, have died or retired.[1] Television and other competitors for the workers' leisure time have seriously reduced attendance at branch meetings, thus increasing the difficulty of making collections. Under these circumstances the Union has experimented with alternative methods of collection. In some places 'mobile collectors' equipped with motor-bicycles have been appointed, and in other areas there are full-time collectors.[2] These experiments have been introduced cautiously out of fear that they might further debilitate the local branches

In fact, however, the level of local participation has always been low, especially in the more recently organized areas. Many branches never meet, their business being conducted entirely by the branch secretary, if there is even a secretary.[3] There is seldom any competition for the local elected positions. The organizers find lay leaders, especially among the younger workers, only with the greatest difficulty. In the past, the Union relied heavily on financial inducements and on the loyalty of founder-members for such local lay leadership as it was able to muster, and it has found as yet no satisfactory substitute.

With a few exceptions the real local leaders are the forty full-time, paid organizers. The Union has never made a clear distinction between paid officials and elected representatives. Unlike the National Farmers' Union, there is no occupational requirement for membership, and the organizers and headquarters staff are members as well as employees of the organization.

Although assigned and paid by headquarters, the organizer *is* the National Union of Agricultural Workers on the local scene, and is

---

[1] Examples can be found in almost any recent issue of *The Land Worker*. See for example the report in January, 1957 (p. 12), of the retirement of a branch secretary in Lincolnshire who had attempted to refuse the position when the branch was formed in 1918: ' "You can forget about me, I cannot do it" . . . But eventually he agreed to do the job—and has been doing it ever since.'

[2] See *Ibid.*, September, 1959, p. 8; July, 1960, p. 12; September, 1960, pp. 10–11.

[3] An examination of voting at Union elections suggests that the astonishing proportion of about four-fifths of the members vote, but this is explained by the fact that those who do attend the relevant branch meeting cast the votes of the entire branch membership. Thus the true inference is that one-fifth of the branches are too inactive to participate in elections at all.

so regarded by himself and by others. Inevitably this situation gives rise to the charge that the Union represents the views of a small group of paid 'agitators' rather than those of agricultural workers, although the Union has pointed out that all of its organizers have been drawn from the workers' ranks.

At the national level many of the workers' leaders have had a more tenuous connection with the land. Only one of the Union's four Presidents was an agricultural worker, although another worked on the land as a child. The first was a Liberal Member of Parliament, the second a leader of the Boot and Shoe Operatives' Union and later a Labour Member of Parliament for an urban constituency, the third a Labour Party organizer who resigned from the Presidency to become the Union's general secretary. Since 1929 the President has been Mr E. G. Gooch, who was treasurer for the Union during the 1923 strike. He was variously a blacksmith, printer and journalist before becoming a Labour Member of Parliament. He receives an annual 'honorarium' of an undisclosed amount.

The general secretary is a full-time, paid official, but he is elected by the branches and serves 'during the will and pleasure of the members,'[1] although the post is regarded in practice as a permanent one. He is by far the most influential person in the Union, controlling the organization, guiding its deliberations, and articulating its politics. The early occupants of this post had agricultural backgrounds, although they came to the Union by way of political or trade union work. Mr Harold Collison, the present general secretary, was an agricultural worker and lay leader of the Union before becoming a Union official.[2]

The Union's Executive Committee consists of twelve members who are elected biennially by the local branches, grouped for this purpose into twelve regions. The long tenure of many members of the Executive has been the object of much criticism, but suggestions for limiting the right of re-election or imposing a retirement age have always been rejected.[3] In 1956 and 1958 two of the oldest members retired, but there remained three more who had served at least twenty years. In 1952 the Gloucestershire county committee submitted a resolution to the biennial conference criticizing 'the virtual impossibility of the ordinary farm working members attaining the office of Executive Committee member. . .'. This was rejected on the advice of the platform, whose spokesman argued that 'some members

[1] National Union of Agricultural Workers, *Rules* (1953), No. 30.
[2] Collison's predecessor, however, was a Londoner who became concerned with the plight of agricultural workers while doing military service in East Anglia during the First World War. A number of the Union's organizers and officials first came into contact with the land as conscientious objectors during the two world wars.
[3] *The Land Worker*, August, 1952, p. 14

of the Executive Committee were not farm workers now but had
been farm workers, and knew as much about farm work as most
delegates'.[1] In 1954, a different type of resolution suggested that 'a
possible solution to this regrettable situation is a full-time, paid
Executive Committee and Presidency',[2] but the Executive took the
reasonable view that this expedient would hardly reconcile farm
work with Union leadership.

The Union's principal internal problem has been the conflict between local organizers and the national leadership. This competition
springs partly from different political attitudes—the organizers tend
to be more militantly left-wing than headquarters—and partly from
the power vacuum which results from the passivity of the rank and
file. In the Union's early days organizers sat on the Executive Committee, but paid officials are now debarred from elective office.[3] The
leaders control national policy and finance and enjoy the advantages
of wide publicity;[4] but the organizers are in immediate and constant
contact with members, upon whose opinions they have considerable
influence.

The leaders have done what they can to discourage consolidated
action by local organizers, and to lessen the organizers' influence
upon the rank and file. They discouraged co-operative action by
adjacent counties because this would have widened organizers' contacts.[5] Instead, they have stressed an extra-constitutional device,
the county conference. This is an annual meeting of branch officers
which is normally attended by an Executive Committee member and
the general secretary or president. The organizer is also present and
reports on his activities, but at this meeting he stands in the shadow
of the national figures. The main reason for this addition to an already complex hierarchy is that it provides a way for the national
leaders to establish direct contact with a core of members in each
county. The leadership has also been protected by a rule prohibiting
the issue of circulars save by written permission of the general secre-

[1] *The Land Worker*, August, 1952, p. 14. In the same year a Yorkshire branch
submitted (but did not move) a resolution that any member standing for election
to the Executive must be an agricultural worker 'or in a subsidiary occupation of
it, and must state his exact occupation on the ballot form'.
[2] National Union of Agricultural Workers, Biennial Conference 1954, Com-
posite Resolution No. 15.
[3] There is still some going back and forth, however. In one case a member of the
Executive resigned to take employment as an organizer for the Union; and the
Union's vice-president, a newly created post, was an organizer before his election
to the House of Commons in 1959. *The Land Worker*, June, 1956, p. 4; June,
1960, p. 11.
[4] Readers of *The Land Worker* in 1957, for example, were favoured with an
average of almost two photographs per issue of the general secretary and a
slightly smaller number of the President.
[5] This was proposed by the 1952 Biennial Conference, but not acted on.

tary or Executive Committee, which has been interpreted in a way that gives an enormous advantage to sitting members of the Executive Committee seeking re-election.

Part of the reason for these defensive postures by the Union's leadership is to be found in the activities of a group of petty Marxist politicians who have infiltrated the Union through their willingness to perform routine chores. Most of the organizers are not Marxists, although in a few counties—notably Dorset[1]—the local organization has a Marxist flavour. However, organizers share with this small Marxist group an impatience with the conservatism and entrenched position of the leadership. The Union's biennial conferences often produce vigorous attacks on the leadership, which are helped by the pliability of a majority of the delegates. Very often, as with the Farmers' Union, unpalatable resolutions passed by the conference can be shelved or even ignored.[2] This situation, however, undermines the claim of the Workers' Union—a claim which the farmers' organization never makes in the same way—that their conferences are the real instruments for democratic policy-making.

The ease with which a conference can be goaded into attempted rebellion, despite the institutional defences which the leadership has erected, indicates the Union's basic weakness. The structural rigidity at the top is an attempt to compensate for the lack of solid foundations, and it is this lack, not the 'communist threat' or 'the undue influence of organizers', that is the Union's real organizational problem. If the leaders gave up the rather undemocratic means by which they stay in office they might be replaced by a group less genuinely interested in the welfare of agricultural workers. On the other hand, these devices of entrenchment reduce the possibility of intelligent and responsible criticism and keep the Union politically immature.

The organizational weakness of agricultural workers is aggravated by union competition. The vast Transport and General Workers' Union contains pockets of agricultural members, particularly in the north and west. Separate membership figures are not published for its agricultural group, but reliable estimates suggest that it is not larger than 20,000. An accommodation between the two unions might be reached if the Transport and General ceased to organize agricultural workers in return for a similar withdrawal by the National Union of Agricultural Workers in relation to other rural workers.

[1] See *The Land Worker*, October 1955 and the motions put forward by Dorset branches at the 1952 biennial conference.

[2] For example in 1956 conference passed a resolution that Wales should have separate representation on the Executive Committee. The President indicated that the decision might not be implemented, and it was not. *The Land Worker*, July 1956, p. 10.

The Agricultural Workers' Union professes not to know how many non-agricultural workers it contains, but its opposition to a 'sharing' agreement and its statistical reticence strongly suggest that the numbers are quite considerable. At any rate, it relies heavily on non-agricultural members to man its local organization in certain areas.

2

The basic aims of the National Union of Agricultural Workers are, in the words of its general secretary:

to put the farm worker on a level at least with the town worker, to free him from the master-and-servant relationship which is implied by the tied-cottage system, to give him the same independence and the full social services enjoyed by others, and the same opportunities of playing a full part in the duties of citizenship.[1]

Practically these aims amount to a claim for parity with the industrial worker in wages, living conditions, and social status. The most obvious demands relate to wages, but in other fields too there is a desire to escape from a dependent, underprivileged status. Thus the abolition of the tied cottage is demanded as part of 'the struggle for the full rights of free men and citizens. . . '.[2] The unsuccessful campaign for equal representation with farmers on the County Agricultural Executive Committees was a claim for 'a fair share in the control of our industry',[3] more as a matter of principle than because the Union had any particular objectives to implement. Time and again the Union has demanded, and usually received, representation on committees and bodies whose work only remotely impinges on the interests of farm workers. It is, as a matter of fact, hard pressed to provide suitable representatives, and in the counties the district organizers have so much work of this kind that their other duties are adversely affected; but the desire to gain prestige, to acquire 'status', is paramount. 'We want parity for our people', said one rural delegate to a Labour Party Conference, 'in every aspect of country life from the village dog show to the county hall. . . '.[4]

The same sentiment manifests itself in what might seem to the outsider trivial ways. Let some journal refer to the agricultural

---

[1] Harold Collison, 'Towards Our Goal,' *Ibid.*, September, 1953, p. 7. For the Union's programme see, *Health and Wealth Under Our Feet*, The Agricultural Programme of the National Union of Agricultural Workers (Revised, March, 1956).

[2] *The Land Worker*, September, 1951, p. 5.

[3] *Ibid.*, May, 1947, p. 5.

[4] *Report of the Fifty-Second Annual Conference of the Labour Party* (Transport House: London, 1953), p. 137.

'labourer', for example, and the Union instantly arises to denounce what it believes to be the connotations attached to that word—an unskilled, unlearned, insensitive drudge, roughly equivalent to a dray horse. Fair treatment in every respect, large and small, is the Union's great objective. 'Our members really do serve the country with a conscientiousness and integrity which entitles them to fair treatment. For too long agricultural workers have been the forgotten men and the poor relation in the industrial world.'[1]

The concrete application of these general aspirations is anything but easy. The first, simplest, and safest policy is to press for higher wages, though even that is not free of complications. The weakness of their organization and the dispersed structure of farming long ago forced the workers to turn to Government for assistance, but it was not until the Agricultural Wages (Regulation) Act of 1947 that they gained their first objective of a national board with unfettered discretion to fix minimum wages.

The Agricultural Wages Board consists of eight representatives each of employers and workers, and five independent members appointed by the Minister of Agriculture. It has power to fix minimum rates of wages, overtime rates, and holidays for agricultural workers.[2] The employers' representatives are named by the National Farmers' Union. Five of the workers' representatives are selected by the National Union of Agricultural Workers and three by the Transport and General Workers' Union.[3] Both the farmers' and workers' organizations give instructions to their representatives, and each group votes as a bloc. For most practical purposes the decisions of the Board are made by the independent members who are in effect arbiters. They too act as a bloc, holding private discussions with each side before announcing the terms they are prepared to support.

The Union's preference for national wage-fixing arises mainly from organizational considerations. There is a closer matching of strength and capacity between the headquarters of the workers' unions and the Farmers' Union than there is between the respective local branches, where slender finances, weak local leadership, and rural traditions of deference inhibit the workers in prosecuting their

[1] Harold Collison in *The Land Worker*, May, 1958, p. 9.

[2] There is nothing to prevent the Board from fixing different rates for different areas, but it has not generally done so. Successive transfers of authority to the Board have left the county agricultural wages committees, which formerly exercised the wage-fixing powers, with little to do but execute and allow minor exceptions to the Board's orders.

[3] The division of seats between the two workers' unions was determined in 1924 on the basis of a recommendation of the Trades Union Congress. Although the five-three ratio does not now accurately represent the proportion of agricultural workers in the two unions, the National Union of Agricultural Workers has not attempted to increase its representation, preferring to fry its jurisdictional fish elsewhere.

case. Centralization has been necessary to the workers' first goal: 'machinery which enables us to meet the farmers in wage negotiations on something like equal terms'.[1]

The inter-war county wages committees were required to fix wages sufficient 'to promote efficiency and to enable a man in an ordinary case to maintain himself and his family in accordance with such standard of comfort as may be reasonable in relation to the nature of his occupation'.[2] This language put the emphasis on the needs of the individual worker, where the Union thinks it ought to be, but it also seemed to assign him a permanently low station. The present legislation provides no limitation or guidance of any kind. The Board is free, as the Labour Minister who sponsored the 1947 Wages Act explained, 'to take into consideration any single factor or any combination of factors. . . '.[3] While the Workers' Union favoured this policy, it has not always liked the results. In 1954 the general secretary went so far as to claim that the independent members had failed to consider the workers' case 'on its merits' and 'must have allowed considerations outside those which it is their duty to consider to influence their decision',[4] although there seemed no basis for the allegation beyond the Union's disappointment.

During the past half century the earnings of agricultural workers has shown a steady, although somewhat irregular, improvement; but the major gains were made during and immediately after the second world war. Farm wages in 1950 were almost three times the 1938 level, whereas wages generally were not quite twice as high.[5] This was a considerable advance, but since about 1948 the farm workers have been mainly engaged in holding their new position. The difference between average weekly earnings in agriculture and in manufacturing industry was much the same in 1959 as it had been ten years earlier. As reported by the *Ministry of Labour Gazette*, earnings in manufacturing industry were on both occasions about 38 per cent higher, although it is generally agreed that the farm worker has some compensatory advantages in lower housing and transport costs. Improved as his position is, he is still a considerable distance from his goal of 'parity'.

When dissatisfied with the results of the statutory machinery, the workers' representatives toy with the idea of abandoning it. However the Agricultural Wages Board has not prepared the way for voluntary

[1] *Ibid.*, April, 1950, p. 5.
[2] Agricultural Wages (Regulation) Act, 1924, sec. 2(4).
[3] H. of C. O. R., Standing Committees, 1946/47, Vol. I, col. 16.
[4] *Manchester Guardian*, June 21, 1954; *The Land Worker*, July, 1954, pp. 3–4.
[5] See E. Mejer, *Agricultural Labour in England and Wales* (University of Nottingham, Department of Agricultural Economics: 1939, 1951). Part II of this study contains a detailed analysis of farm workers' earnings during the period 1917–51.

negotiation, although that was the original intention, and the workers' experience with this method after the First World War left them fearful of repeating the experiment.[1] Union leaders usually explain that their chief concern is the enormous problem of enforcing voluntarily agreed wages, but they are also uncertain about the real strength of their Union. They are fond of pointing to the 'restraint' shown by agricultural workers compared with frequently striking workers elsewhere and of hinting that this gigantic force might some day have to be unleashed; but while the Union is certainly much stronger now than ever before, it is doubtful whether it has either the membership or the militancy necessary for a successful strike.

Another route towards the goal of parity with industry would be a statutory wages structure with special rates for extra skill, responsibility, and unpleasantness. The Board has the authority to introduce such a system, and as long ago as 1946 the independent members suggested it to the farmers' and workers' representatives. The farmers were dubious, and the workers' representatives were divided. The Transport and General Workers' Union favoured the idea, but the National Union of Agricultural Workers was long unwilling even to discuss it, and claimed that its rival's position only showed that 'the discussion of agricultural questions should be left to people who have some understanding of the industry', since 'all sensible farmers and farm workers know that the grading of jobs in agriculture is impracticable.'[2] In reality Union leaders were most concerned not with these practical problems, but with the dangers that the objective of a satisfactory minimum wage (on which the Union's egalitarian traditions laid all the emphasis) might be side-tracked and that a wages structure might cause serious internal differences. Gradually, however, they saw that concentrating on a minimum rate was an unrewarding policy, and in the spring of 1956 the Executive Committee recommended that a wages structure was both practicable and desirable.[3]

The Executive's report was sent to the counties and branches for discussion, and many district organizers conducted intensive campaigns in favour of a wages structure, while a few quietly discouraged the idea. The debate on this question was the focal point of the 1956 biennial conference. The hard core of the opposition to the executive centred around two groups. The first was composed of delegates from East Anglia whose conservative bias against innovation was strengthened by the fact that many workers in this part of the country al-

---

[1] When the Corn Production Act was repealed in 1921, provision was made for local voluntary conciliation committees, but the experiment was unsuccessful and wage-fixing reverted for a time to the hands of employers.

[2] *The Land Worker*, September, 1949, p. 6.

[3] *Ibid.*, March–April, 1956, pp. 10–11.

ready enjoy rates above the minimum. Joining them in a strange alliance was the small Marxist group, fearful that a wages structure would weaken the class consciousness of agricultural workers and thus increase the already considerable difficulties of fostering the doctrine of class conflict. In spite of the general secretary's well reasoned summary and strong appeal for a vote of confidence, the platform was defeated.

Between 1956 and 1958 the Union carried on a campaign to convince the waverers and the East Anglians of the justice of the wages structure proposal. The most articulate section of the membership of course remained opposed, and they filled the correspondence column of *The Land Worker*. '. . . to adopt such a principle makes Socialism impossible. Let us be clear in our minds and repeat that a wages structure means reward for ability. It is the foundation of, and results in, the "haves" and the "have nots".'[1] Few agricultural workers are really opposed to reward for ability, and two more years of steady Union propaganda were enough to persuade the 1958 conference to support, by a small majority, the principle of a wages structure.[2] A committee was appointed to frame proposals, which the Union finally put to the Board in 1961.[3] By this time Union leaders were thoroughly convinced of the desirability of some kind of wages structure, but they were moving very cautiously into what was likely to be one of the most critical periods in the Union's history.

3

Behind the wages issue lies a more fundamental question about the farm worker's future. Towards what sort of 'promotion ladder' should he strive ? Should he aim to become a farmer, with his Union seeking to maintain a large number of smallholdings and small farms as the steps between worker and farmer ? Or should he seek his advancement as a worker, with his Union favouring more large farms and thus more specialized and responsible positions for the capable and ambitious workers ?

Traditionally agricultural workers have had much sympathy with the smallholdings policy. The ambitious farm worker wanted to farm, and the smallholding was his opportunity to do so, even though it offered him a barely sufficient livelihood and only a remote prospect of some day moving on to a better farm. Among the relatively few achievements of Joseph Arch's National Agricultural

[1] May, 1958, p. 15. For another example see September, 1957, p. 15.
[2] *Ibid.*, June, 1958, p. 9. In 1960 the Union's commitment to a wages structure was confirmed, though the opposition was still able to attract one-third of the delegates. *Ibid.*, June, 1960, p. 9.
[3] *Ibid.*, February, 1961, p. 4.

Labourers' Union was the smallholding legislation of the late nineteenth century.[1] Smallholdings sentiment was still considerable after the second world war, and the Workers' Union gave its support to Part IV of the 1947 Agriculture Act which provided national assistance for the county councils' smallholdings programme. Even though little use has been made of this legislation, it has become somewhat embarrassing to Union leaders. To the extent that they take their socialism seriously, they are reluctant to encourage turning workers into petty capitalists. More important perhaps, they have no great enthusiasm for a movement which seems less likely to provide the first rung of a 'ladder of promotion' than to establish a permanent class of subsistence-level farmers. Apart from everything else, such a class would provide poor materials for unionization.

Testifying before the Royal Commission on Common Land, Mr Dennis Hodsdon, the editor of *The Land Worker*, explained that, while more agricultural workers are 'coming to regard their livelihood in the way an industrial worker does', it would not be right to assume that there is now no land hunger among agricultural workers. 'There is a difference of approach within the Union on this.'[2] The difference is well illustrated by the following letters written to *The Land Worker*.[3] The first is from a smallholder.

Membership of our Union is open to smallholders. The only hope farm workers ever have of becoming farmers is by taking the risk of starting on a small farm. Obviously for the first few years the income is likely to be less even than the minimum wage, but despite the difficulties, many in fact eventually succeed in making a fair living, by courage, hard work, and efficiency.

. . . .

I believe that the NUAW could do a great job by really taking up the problems of the family farmer and smallholder, and could help to win these hardworking people as our allies in the struggle for Socialism and progressive farming.

Another correspondent asks in reply:

But wherein lies the best interest of the farm worker of tomorrow? The maximum government help for the small man or the gradual amalgamation into larger holdings, backed with plenty of capital

[1] Small Holdings Act, 1892. This merely permissive legislation was followed by the Small Holdings and Allotments Act, 1908, which required county councils to establish smallholdings programmes.

[2] Royal Commission on Common Land, *Minutes of Evidence* (1957), pp. 630, 632–3. See also Mejer, *Agricultural Labour in England and Wales*, Part I, pp. 64–67.

[3] February, 1957, p. 14; March, 1957, p. 15.

which requires large numbers of foremen and managers? Are we heading for a peasant agriculture, or do we, as workers, stand to get a better standard of living for our families with larger farms . . . ?

I think the small farm is finished as a method of advancement for farm workers. . . . As far as I can see, it is the big farms that provide the good jobs, adequate machinery and well kept cottages.

The desires of those 'few individuals who are not happy to call any man master'[1] deserve consideration by the Union as well as the Government; but it is probable that the present number of agricultural holdings will fall, not increase, and it is certain that Governments will not willingly add to the number of subsistence farmers. In these circumstances, the interest of farm workers generally would seem to lie in an agriculture organized more nearly along industrial lines. This policy would require fewer and larger farms, a somewhat smaller but more concentrated labour force, and an effective promotion and wages ladder for the better workers. Such a system might reduce some of the intangible advantages of rural employment, which lie precisely in its dissimilarity from the industrial pattern; but these advantages are connected with just those traditions of agricultural employment which the Union would like to eliminate. What seems certain is that a more large-scale and rationalized system of agriculture would boost the average workers' earnings and facilitate unionization among those who remain on the land. It might even enable the farm workers to realize their cherished aim of parity with industrial workers in standards of living. The wages structure proposal and other evidence indicate that workers' leaders are beginning to think along these lines,[2] but there is still too much uncertainty and division of opinion for the Union to speak with conviction on the crucial question of how agriculture should be organized.

It is this uncertainty that accounts for the peculiar character of the Union's concern with the related issue of land nationalization. Hardly any workers' leader would express outright disagreement with the traditional and well-worn view that the Union's present policy is 'a halfway house, untenable in modern conditions' and that nationalization is necessary to remedy 'the fundamental unsoundness of present-day agriculture. . . '.[3] The accepted formula is that, while the principle of nationalization is right, the time is not. 'We do not ob-

[1] Royal Commission on Common Land, *Minutes of Evidence* (1957), p. 633.

[2] See the article by the editor of *The Land Worker* in the September, 1957 issue (pp. 10–11), 'Which Way?'; and compare the statements on smallholdings in the original (1953, p. 17) and the revised (1956, p 21) versions of *Health and Wealth Under our Feet.*

[3] Groves, *Sharpen the Sickle!* p. 235.

ject to land nationalization in principle but we very much doubt whether wholesale nationalization is practicable at present. . . .'[1] Nonetheless a resolution in favour of immediate and complete nationalization of land was defeated by only two at the 1950 conference. Four years later it was decided by a small majority that 'increasingly greater areas of land shall be taken under public ownership and control'. In 1956 the conference accepted a more specific resolution on nationalization, opposed by the platform, which called on the next Labour Government to make a start 'by nationalizing some selected large estates to be developed as models for the future of public ownership and by transferring farms at present under the control of the National Coal Board to an Agricultural Land Board'.[2] The difficulty is that nationalization has to be discussed in terms of some notion of what the government should do with the land when it gets it, and there has been little discussion of this point in the Union. The principle continues to be supported, with decreasing enthusiasm, by the leaders because it is part of Union lore and because its abstract quality masks, at least for the time being, harder questions.

4

Although the Workers' and Farmers' Unions are about the same age, they represent quite different levels of organizational maturity. For the workers these are still very much days of 'each against all'. Legal services and other benefits, which played such a large role in the early days of the National Farmers' Union, are still given great prominence by the Workers' Union. Each issue of its journal contains long lists of benefits and services received by individual members, together with two or three pictures of injured but smiling workers receiving from a Union official a cheque for damages obtained with Union assistance. Matters such as these are tangible, easy to understand, and uncontroversial.

Similarly in choosing the policies to be given greatest weight, the Union seeks out the narrower issues which do not expose cleavages of opinion but promote organizational strength and unity. One of its major propaganda themes during the post-war period has been the 'drift from the land'. In the seven years between 1951 and 1958, about 150,000 full-time workers quit the land, representing an average annual loss of 3 per cent.[3] In part the Union uses these figures to buttress wage claims: it argues that wages must be higher to hold the

[1] *The Farmers Weekly*, July 24, 1953, p. 30; See *The Land Worker*, September, 1953, p. 4.

[2] *The Land Worker*, July, 1950, pp. 6–7; July, 1954, p. 7; June, 1956, p. 9.

[3] *Agricultural Statistics*, 1958–9, HMSO, 122.

agricultural labour force.[1] This is also an easily dramatized issue. The picture drawn by the Union is one of an industry where workers' pay and conditions are so bad that they leave in busloads. The implied slur on those who remain will lead, it is hoped, to greater support for the organization that is trying to make agricultural employment worthy of self-respecting men.

On examination, however, this criticism of the rural exodus appears somewhat questionable. It is true that the decline of the rural population produces some real economic and social difficulties; it intensifies, for example, the problems of providing satisfactory public services. Moreover, in so far as the abler and more energetic workers quit the land, agriculture suffers—and the Union suffers even more. Initially, therefore, the exodus hurts more than helps the Union. However, as agricultural labour becomes scarcer its value increases, and in the long run a better-paid class of agricultural workers would benefit the Union as well as individual workers.

Another major object of Union rhetoric has been the 'tied cottage', which is reserved for workers employed by the farmer-landlord. The Union's journal is filled with reports of evictions from these cottages, complete with photographs of the worker, family, and aged relatives contemplating their ejected possessions by the roadside. The Union's unyielding hostility to this system has been expressed in hundreds of resolutions, and its temper is maintained by a barrage of indignant articles and speeches. Even here, not all members agree with the Union, because tied cottages are let at very low rents.[2]

Apart from the genuine hardships which the tied cottage system does sometimes produce, it is identified with the continuation of a dependent social status for the agricultural worker. By means of the tied cottage, in the Union's opinion, the farmer's influence extends beyond employment to the private and family life of his workers.[3] The tied cottage system both strengthens and symbolizes the unusually close relations between farm workers and their employers. Living on the farm, a worker tends to enjoy easy (which is not to say equal) social relations with the farmer. Whether or not this relationship is a good one, it is certainly not helpful to unionization. How-

[1] The Union recognizes of course that mechanization and the more efficient use of manpower partially offset the loss of labour, but it contends that the position is rapidly approaching 'where the men are just not there'. Harold Collison in *The Land Worker*, November, 1955, p. 4. More pointedly, the Union argues that a declining need for labour is an argument for a smaller number of farmers as well as workers, although in fact the number of farmers has remained fairly stable for decades. *Ibid.*, December, 1960, p. 3.

[2] See W. J. G. Cowie and A. K. Giles, *Accommodation of Rural Workers*, University of Bristol, 1960.

[3] The argument (to which certain defenders of the system are prone) that the Prime Minister and the Archbishop of Canterbury also live in 'tied cottages' has never seemed to the workers a proper analogy.

ever, as one delegate to the 1954 Labour Party Conference said, 'You cannot live for ever on the tradition of the Tolpuddle Martyrs. You have to have something more constructive in your policy than the tied cottage.'[1]

The National Union of Agricultural Workers has always been within the curtilage of party politics. It was founded largely by Liberal politicians, and 'at least some of those present', *The Land Worker* remarks, 'were as concerned about the political possibilities of such a Union as they were about the effect it could have on farm workers' conditions . . '.[2] The Liberals were soon replaced by Socialists, and the Union's growth was characterized by a dependence upon the Labour Movement. Most of its present leaders are active in the Labour Party. Its President was chairman of the Party in 1956 and is one of the two Union leaders who (in 1961) are also Labour Members of Parliament. Most of the organizers are active in local Labour Party groups, and *The Land Worker* vigorously urges its readers to vote Labour in national and local elections.

Developed and nurtured by Labour, the Union found that it carried disappointingly little weight when Labour came to power in 1945. It appealed in vain to earlier Labour principles for equal representation with farmers on the county committees.[3] More important, it failed to persuade the Minister of Agriculture to intervene in decisions of the Agricultural Wages Board: 'farm workers . . . expect Labour Ministers to be different in some ways from Tory Ministers, and . . . simply cannot believe that the Wages Board is beyond Government influence'.[4] It failed to get the tied cottage abolished. The last perhaps rankled more than anything else. The Union had expected that Labour would destroy this remaining manifestation of the master-servant relationship. Yet when the opportunity came, the shortage of housing and the farmers' opposition convinced the Labour Government that such action would be inexpedient.

The workers complained that Mr Tom Williams, Labour's Minister of Agriculture, clung too tightly to the skirts of the National Farmers' Union and consulted the Workers' Union too little about matters of agricultural policy.

The Minister of Agriculture has leaned too much on farmers. Let

[1] *Report of the Fifty-Second Annual Conference of the Labour Party*, 1953 p. 144.

[2] May, 1956, p. 14.

[3] The Minister of Agriculture read the Union's president a lecture in practical politics. 'Neither of us in 1926 ever dreamed, when recording our opinions then, that we should be in charge of a Bill of this magnitude and importance.' H. of C. Standing Committees, 1946–7, Vol. 2, Cols. 1088–9, 1094.

[4] *Ibid.*, March, 1946, p. 2.

him lean our way for a while and he will be surprised at the response he and the Labour Party will get. We want a much larger share in the running of the industry.[1]

In a similar vein, the Union's journal criticised the Labour publication, *Fact*, for accepting Farmers' Union figures on farm workers' earnings, instead of asking the Union for information.[2]

During the years of Conservative Government the differences between the Union and Labour naturally seemed less acute. The Union pressed its own candidates for Parliamentary contests upon the Party and participated more closely in the formulation of its agricultural statements. On the question of the tied cottage Mr Collison reported to the membership in 1958 that 'good progress has been made in consultation with our friends of the Labour Party, and we now have the assurance that when Labour is returned to power the problem will be dealt with at last—as part of the Party's housing policy'. Even in opposition, however, the Labour Party was unwilling to abolish the tied cottage system outright.[3]

As one reaction to Labour's indifference, the Union has taken to stressing its responsibility to promote its members' interests regardless of what Government is in power. Referring to the new minimum wage promulgated by the Agricultural Wages Board at the end of 1953, the general secretary said, 'Our gains would have been much less had we expected the employers or any of the political parties to do for us what we have done for ourselves.'[4] In 1957 for the first time Union representatives appeared before the Conservative Parliamentary agricultural committee to put the workers' case on the proposed safety regulations for agriculture. Complaining that the workers had not been consulted about the 1958 Agriculture Act, the Union's President suggested that 'it will even pay the Tory Party to talk sometimes to the representatives of the farm workers'.[5]

It is doubtful, however, whether the workers have open to them the possibility of 'going it alone'. Their intrinsic economic and organizational weakness requires them to seek allies. As long as they concern themselves primarily with employer-employee issues, such as wages

[1] E. G. Gooch, *Ibid.*, June, 1950, p. 3; see also September, 1949, p. 10. In retrospect, Mr Williams's methods of consultation seemed better. In 1958 Mr Gooch complained: 'It is now on record that the Minister proceeded with the new Agriculture bill without consulting the third partner in the industry—the farm worker. Under the Labour Government the NUAW were treated as equal partners in this respect and our opinions sought.' *Ibid.*, May, 1958, p. 8.

[2] *Ibid.*, May, 1949, p. 7.

[3] *Ibid.*, May, 1958, p. 4. Labour's intended solution is to prohibit owners from taking possession of tied cottages until the local authority can offer alternative accommodation. See *Prosper the Plough* (Labour Party, 1958), p. 36.

[4] *Ibid.*, September, 1953, p. 4.

[5] H. of C. O. R., 1957/58, Vol. 584, cols. 1141-42.

and the tied cottage, they can find the necessary allies only in the Labour Movement, however unsatisfactory the results. But they must also concern themselves with the prosperity of agriculture, and this need suggests that they might make common cause with the National Farmers' Union. Thus while Mr Gooch has argued that Labour 'is not just the industrial party' but the best friend of 'those who work and live in rural England', he has also emphasized the 'community of interest' between farm workers and farmers and the need for 'the greatest possible degree of unity' within agriculture.[1] The shadow of an immense urban majority falls across the interests of agricultural workers as well as those of farmers and landowners.

As an examination of their programmes will demonstrate, the farmers' and workers' unions agree on many basic questions of agricultural policy. The farmers accepted the wartime proposal for a national minimum wage in return for an assurance by the workers' representatives that they would support the farmers over agricultural prices.[2] The Workers' Union backed the farmers' demands for closer guarantees which culminated in the 1957 Agriculture Act. It has also opposed the rerating of agricultural land on the grounds that this would cause a rise in food prices and thus 'create a rift between town and country which would be extremely undesirable and not in the interests of farming'.[3]

Representatives of the two organizations have discussed the possibility of closer co-operation, but any coalition would require that the Workers' Union drastically loosen its bonds with Labour. Powerful traditions, sentimental attachments to socialist doctrines, and a real doubt of the wisdom of allying itself with the employers influence the Union against such a course. Moreover, while the Farmers' Union would doubtless be happy to see the workers cut their ties with Labour, it has not as yet greatly needed their support.

Thus the organized workers are still torn by doubts and differences. Ought the agricultural workers' place in the sun to be sought alongside his industrial comrades or through a closer relationship with his farmer-employers? Is his best political strategy to commit himself to one camp or the other, or to maintain the cautious policy of keeping one foot in each? The primary problem is that both of these allies are uncomfortably strong and therefore somewhat unreliable. More fundamentally, the Union's voice is weak because its leaders have been unable to decide where the interests of agricultural workers really lie.

[1] *The Land Worker*, July, 1955, p. 4; E. G. Gooch, 'Farm Labour Since 1894', *The Journal of the Ministry of Agriculture*, September, 1954, p. 275.
[2] Mejer, *op. cit.*, Part II, p. 74.
[3] *The Land Worker*, April, 1955, p. 11.

CHAPTER VIII

GENTLEMEN, LIMITED

1

THE third of the 'partners' recognized by the 1947 Agriculture Act is the agricultural landowner. To some it may seem surprising that landowners still aspire to a principal place in agricultural policy-making. Their importance in any economic or functional sense has fallen far behind that of the farmers, while they have little numerical weight when compared with either farmers or workers. Politically, landlordism in agriculture has been for many decades under a heavy cloud.

Such continuing importance as landowners possess derives from two sources. Despite a steady increase in owner-occupation, the landlord-tenant system still covers about 60 per cent of the total agricultural area. This system, which is largely peculiar to Britain, has often been admired because it brings in landlords' capital, in the form of fixed equipment, to help out the frequently slim financial resources of family farmers. It thus increases the supply of agricultural capital and benefits many farmers, particularly if they can rent their land and fixed equipment on favourable terms. Given the increasing capital requirements of agriculture, the theoretical advantages of this arrangement remain cogent,[1] but its actual utility depends upon the ability and willingness of landlords to play their part satisfactorily—a question about which there has for long been a considerable amount of doubt.

Secondly the larger private landowners continue to possess considerable influence and prestige. Their numbers are not large, since it is improbable that there are more than three or four thousand estates in England and Wales in excess even of 500 acres.[2] Some of them, however, still carry on actively the traditions of their ancestors, although in a much less autocratic spirit. Leading landowners retain a broad interest in agricultural welfare and progress, and on such difficult issues as European integration sometimes display a more statesmanlike attitude than farmers' leaders. They also possess an organization, which by studied moderation and careful attention to detail, has managed since 1945 to be surprisingly successful.

---

[1] A recent, well-argued but not uncritical defence of the system is to be found in Graham Hallett, *The Economics of Agricultural Land Tenure* (Land Books, 1960).
[2] Authors' own estimate based on unpublished data.

These continuing assets have to be viewed against a history of severe and prolonged decline. The British landowner toppled from a very high eminence. The Ricardian theory that a rising population would redound to the agricultural landlords' benefit through rising rents proved true for a large part of the nineteenth century. Agricultural landowners of this age were both prosperous and autocratic. They controlled the cropping and other operations of their tenants, whom they could evict at will. They employed large staffs of estate workers and domestics, and the activities of the village revolved completely around the manorial splendours of the 'big house'. This autocracy was tempered only by the personal interest of many landowners in agricultural techniques and development. Landowners were the scientific and economic leaders of agriculture, as well as its principal beneficiaries.

Their decline followed upon economic disaster and political change. The average agricultural rent in England and Wales rose from about 20s. per acre in 1840 to 34s. in 1870, before the influx of cheap food. By 1900 rents had fallen again to about 20s., and they never again reached the 1870 level until the early 1950s, by which time the real value of the same income had drastically declined.[1]

Simultaneously, a long series of Acts increased the rights of agricultural tenants. Measures passed in 1875 and 1883 assured them of compensation for improvements, a 1906 Act gave them freedom of cropping, and the 1920 Agriculture Act guaranteed them compensation for unreasonable disturbance and introduced machinery for rent arbitration.[2] These measures reflected the growing democratic and reformist temper of the age by protecting the interests of a highly dependent group. Their justification was further strengthened, however, by the passing of the landlords' technical leadership and by the need for tenants to have greater freedom of action if they were to survive economically. This was also a period when agricultural landowners incurred much political unpopularity. The Liberal Government of 1906–14 not only increased death duties considerably, but seriously considered nationalization of the land.

In 1907 a small group of Lincolnshire estate owners banded together as the Central Land Association in order to combat this Liberal threat. The Association displayed from its inception a somewhat high-minded, moderate, and politically aloof attitude. Some members broke away to found the Land Union, a body which allied itself with the Tories and vigorously fought the Liberal schemes of land taxation on behalf of both rural and urban landowners. The Association, however, would not be drawn closely into party politics

---

[1] Hallett, op. cit., p. 52–3.

[2] These measures were consolidated by the Agricultural Holdings Act of 1923, which governed landlord-tenant relations until 1947.

and refused to compromise its concern for agricultural welfare by an alliance with urban landed interests. The logical culmination of this approach came in 1949, when its title was changed to the Country Landowners' Association.

In its early years the Association was a small body of influential men, many of whom sat in Parliament.[1] One of its main concerns, which it has never abandoned, was to awake landowners to a recognition of both their rights and responsibilities. This was an essential first step at a time when many owners prized their land largely for sport and amenities, lived off capital or urban profits, and neglected their estates. The Association, however, was at first too small to have much effect, although its membership rose after the First World War to 8,000 in 1925.

The Association's main achievements in the inter-war period concerned taxation. In 1925 it was instrumental in securing the exclusion of agricultural property from the general increase in death duties which occurred at that time. This concession was partly based on technical arguments about valuation, but in the main it represented a recognition of the special value and vulnerability of the individually-owned agricultural estate. The Association also joined with the farmers' and workers' organizations to press successfully for the complete derating of agricultural land and buildings. This campaign was actually praised by the Minister of Health (Mr Neville Chamberlain) as a remarkable example of co-operation between three different classes.[2]

The Association could not, however, arrest the steady deterioration of landlordism. By 1939 the value of the institution was very much in question. The dilapidated condition of the land's fixed equipment, which was strikingly demonstrated by the findings of the wartime National Farm Survey, bore witness to the inability of many landlords to perform their economic function. The continuing decay of the larger estates reduced the opportunities for scientific management or rational reorganization of unsatisfactory holdings. It was technical considerations which now caused such agricultural experts as Sir Daniel Hall and Dr C. S. Orwin to conclude that the only effective remedy was land nationalization.[3]

The advent of a Labour Government after the war posed a new threat to landowners. While anxieties about land nationalization

[1] By 1910 the Association had 1,000 members, of whom over 100 were Members of Parliament. Twenty of the thirty members of the Executive had to be Members of Parliament, but so as to preserve political balance not more than twelve could belong to the same party. Recorded in a short history of the CLA issued at its golden jubilee (1957), p. 9.

[2] *Ibid.*, p. 23.

[3] Sir D. Hall, *Reconstruction and the Land* (Macmillan, 1941). C. S. Orwin, *Speed the Plough* (Harmondsworth, 1942).

proved groundless, the 1947 Agriculture Act provided for the supervision and dispossession of inefficient landlords, while further reducing their rights in relation to tenants. A landlord could only terminate a tenancy if he could make out a satisfactory case to a county agricultural committee or, on appeal, to an agricultural land tribunal. All disputes over rents were to be dealt with by arbitration, but landlords could be ordered to provide new fixed equipment which was necessary for efficient farming. In response to these circumstances, the Association, which had been a rather exclusive club, set about transforming itself into a modern fighting union. We will first examine the character of this organization and then consider its achievements in recent years.

2

The Country Landowners' Association is an organization of owners, not landlords. The distinction is central to the Association's strategy and achievements. Its leaders are agricultural landlords, but 75 per cent of its members are farmers who own their own farms.[1]

The Association has welcomed owner-occupiers into its ranks for two reasons. First, they furnish the numerical support and subscription income[2] without which it would be a very weak organization indeed. Secondly, they broaden the Association's political appeal. By stressing the virtues of land ownership as such, and by even favouring a broader diffusion of ownership through tenants' purchases of their holdings, the Association can rally a much stronger support against the threat of land nationalization. This danger played a most helpful part in its post-1945 recruitment campaign. Without the numerous owner-occupiers who anxiously joined it while Labour was in power, the Association would be a much weaker force today.

In theory it might be supposed that the steady extension of owner-occupation would trespass upon the landlord-tenant system, whose virtues are so dear to the landowning traditions of England. The Association's contention, however, is that there is plenty of room for both systems of land tenure to co-exist, and indeed that this arrangement adds 'strength and flexibility' to the pattern of rural life.[3] The Association, recognizing the declining position of the large landowner, takes comfort in the idea that 'it is for his former tenants who are now in increasing numbers buying and working their farms

[1] CLA, *Your Land, the Answer to Tomorrow's Problems*. (Leaflet, n.d.).
[2] Subscriptions are of course graded according to the area owned. The annual rate ranged in 1960 from £2·2 for a unit of below 50 acres to £75 for an estate of more than 15,000 acres.
[3] CLA, *Policy and Objectives* (1955), p. 20.

to carry on the old traditions of care of the land and service to the rural community'.[1]

These arguments are quite sincere. The estate owner shares with the owner-occupier a common interest in agricultural welfare and rural traditions. If he must sell land, he would genuinely prefer to sell to someone who joins in these concerns rather than to some smaller landlord whose links with agriculture itself may be minimal. These attitudes explain why an Association whose leaders are large landowners and whose members are mainly owner-occupiers can work harmoniously. They also explain the emphasis upon ownership rather than landlordism. Indeed, in an organization which still radiates an atmosphere of 'noblesse oblige', the odd man out is the petty landlord without agricultural roots.

Nonetheless, there can be no pretending that the interests of the estate owner and the owner-occupier are actually similar. Former tenants may indeed carry on some of the old rural traditions, but they will do so as farmers not landowners. Owner-occupiers look primarily to the National Farmers' Union to support their interests. Even those relatively few owner-occupiers who are active in CLA branches are frequently ex-local dignitaries of the Farmers' Union. It is not surprising that the suspicion should sometimes arise that the owner-occupiers are mainly of use in protecting the interests of the large estate owners.

The presence of the 'small fry' . . . in its ranks justifies the CLA in claiming that it represents all landowners, large and small. During the past six years, this has been decidedly useful. The 'small fry' are naturally gratified at being of assistance to their larger brethren, and they trust that they may continue to be so. If they ask in return 'What does the CLA do for them?' it is in no spirit of criticism. Not at all.

· · · · · · · · · · · · · , · · · · · · · · ·

What, then, can the CLA offer to small owners and owner-occupiers, if woodlands, estate management and surtax relief are out? There is no need for help on the farming side. . . .[2]

The Association's answer is to point to the numerous services which it offers in connection with problems of the ownership of agricultural land, whether on a large or small scale. These include guidance on legal matters, taxation, Government grants, and town and country planning controls, and specialized advice on these matters has certainly been more needed since 1945. In addition, the Association fights hard over those issues of public policy which con-

[1] 'A Great Tradition', *Country Landowner*, August, 1947.
[2] Letter from F. D. Smith and Barbara Wilcox, *Country Landowner*, February, 1952, p. 32.

cern (in some degree) all its members. An important example is town and country planning legislation as it bears upon compensation payments and upon the pressure on agricultural land.[1] The Association also took a large part of the credit for securing the Crichel Down inquiry of 1954, and thus for helping to reverse the post-war tendency towards state land acquisition. It is interesting that the Association's comments upon the Crichel Down case dwelled less upon administrative abuses than upon the political criticism that the Conservative Government had been unduly slow in reversing Labour policies.[2]

Thus the strength and harmony of the Association rests upon what may be accounted a mutually convenient arrangement between the two groups. Owner-occupiers value the Association largely for the services it provides and for its defence of certain limited interests. Doubtless some also enjoy the prestige of associating with the gentry, and in any case most of the 'small fry' are well content to leave questions of policy to their betters. If they want to express their own indignations, they always have the NFU. The estate owner, on the other hand, has more limited need of the Association's services. He or his agent normally knows quite as much about routine matters of landownership as the local secretary. The Association has been increasingly active in promoting discussion of general questions of estate management, and its annual courses on these matters are well attended. For the most part, however, estate owners see the Association as the body which protects their interests and traditions.

The organization of the CLA resembles the Workers' rather than the Farmers' Union in being considerably centralized. Subscriptions are paid to headquarters which makes grants to cover branch expenses, and which appoints and pays the branch secretaries. In the past the Association relied mainly on part-time branch secretaries, who were often land agents, but since the war these have mainly been replaced with full-time officers. However, the branch secretary does not enjoy the influence of the Workers' Union organizer, since he is serving persons of good education and experience in public affairs. An important part of his duties is the recruitment of new members, and a portion of his income depends upon the total membership he serves.

The county branches are not a force in county affairs to anything like the extent of the Farmers' Union branches, although they put forward views on a wide variety of topics. Each county sends from two to four members to the national Council, which is a large body

---

[1] The Association claimed to have secured forty amendments to the 1947 Town and Country Planning Bill (*Country Landowner*, Dec., 1953). It fought successfully together with other organizations for the abolition of development charge and for market value for compulsorily acquired land.

[2] 'Afterthoughts on Crichel Down', *Country Landowner*, August, 1954.

of about 160 persons. This Council meets quarterly and serves a function similar to that of the Council of the National Farmers' Union—that is, it keeps a general eye on the Association's activities, but leaves the real work to its executive and its officers. The land-owners too, have their annual meeting of delegates, but they do not seriously suggest that it is the place where policy is made. It is usually and accurately referred to as the Dinner.

The organizational genius of the Association resides in its pattern of leadership. Since 1925, with only one exception, each President has served for a two-year term. As a rule he has also now previously served for two years as Deputy-President and Chairman of the Executive Committee and before that for two years as Vice-Chairman. The Executive has fifteen elected members who retire every five years on a rotating basis, but who may then be re-elected (as they frequently are) after a year's interval. This system of regular but slow rotation nicely reflects the squirearchy's orderly ideas about the sharing of public duties. It is sensible and efficient when compared with the mixtures of long leadership and sudden fluctuations which have characterized the Farmers' and Workers' Unions. Supported by a most able secretary, the system has enabled the Association in recent years to make good use of its available talent.

Many of the landowners' leaders have been influential men in the Conservative Party. In the early 1950s, two chairmen of its Executive (Lord Carrington and Lord St Aldwyn) resigned in rapid succession to become Parliamentary Secretary to the Minister of Agriculture. One of its post-war Presidents (Major Sir Richard Proby) was simultaneously Chairman of the Conservative Party. There are about fifty CLA members in the House of Commons, but its stronger and easier parliamentary links are with the House of Lords.

These connections are by no means the political asset which might be supposed. The Labour Party and the Liberal Party too have long been hostile to country landowners, and this hostility is by no means dead.[1] Moreover, a considerable number of Conservatives are also reluctant to befriend in any way the landed aristocracy. The Association has good friends in the Conservative Party, but it does not officially support Conservatism and Conservatives in Parliament will not very willingly support it.

In consequence of this situation, the Association has emulated the Farmers' Union in paying great attention to the development of close consultative relations with Whitehall officials and with successive Ministers of Agriculture. The CLA, explains its brochure, is 'your key to the Government and official bodies'.

[1] See, in the case of the Labour Party, parliamentary debates on the 1958 Agriculture Act, and the critical comments on landlords in *Prosper The Plough* (Labour Party, 1958).

The views of the Association are regularly sought by the Government and its officially appointed committees on a wide variety of subjects connected with agriculture and forestry.[1]

This neutral and official approach may seem slightly strange for a body whose leaders are so naturally at home in Tory clubs and on the Tory front bench. Yet it was logical enough in the post-war context. The 1947 Agriculture Act which took so much from land-owners at least gave them a statutory right to consultation, and during the Labour period a strictly formal approach seemed also the wisest tactics. Subsequently the Association found that a moderate and well-argued case could be pursued more successfully in Whitehall than at Westminster, and had the advantage of reducing its dependence upon the always limited influence of its Tory friends in Parliament.[2]

Another critical question for the Association is its relationship with the National Farmers' Union. There is a considerable range of subjects, including taxation and rating, Government grants, and the protection of agricultural land, upon which the two organizations co-operate freely and to good effect. If there is a certain amount of overlapping in their activities and representations, at least this strengthens the agricultural case.[3] In the case of price reviews, marketing schemes, and certain other matters, however, the Association is always most careful not to question the Union's right to speak alone for agriculture. It confines itself to generalized support and to marginal comments on matters which particularly concern landlords. Finally, there are those matters such as rents where the interests of landlords and tenants directly conflict. Here the Association is in a weak political position because of the much greater political influence of the Union. Since 1945 the Association has made every effort to maintain friendly co-operation with the Union, and has advanced a contrary view only with great caution.

Individual landowners continue to provide leadership. A high proportion of the chairmen of wartime and post-war county agricultural committees have been landlords, as have many of the Minister's personal liaison officers who maintain contact with the committees.[4]

[1] CLA, *Your Land.*

[2] The Association's detachment from Parliament can be seen from the fact that by April, 1961, two years had elapsed since it had met the Conservative Agricultural Committee in the House of Commons.

[3] Examples of numerous cases of joint action are representations over grant aid for water supplies (*Country Landowner*, April 1950) and a deputation, together with the workers' unions, to protest at the development of agricultural land (*Country Landowner*, April, 1949).

[4] See Chapter VI, p. 141. In 1961 both the CLA President and the Vice-Chairman of its Executive were also liaison officers for the Minister.

Landowners have been prominent on important public bodies such as the Forestry Commission and the Agricultural Land Commission, and upon numerous official committees where they often act as chairmen. Now that his powers over his tenants have been so attenuated, the rural landowner has acquired a degree of impartiality which makes his traditional powers of leadership more acceptable. Yet the landowners' remaining traditions and influence depend upon the continuation of a still precarious system; and to patch this system up has required in recent times much ingenious effort from his Association.

3

The post-1945 prospects for agricultural landowners were, as we have seen, distinctly discouraging. There was little point in fighting the distasteful provisions of the 1947 Agriculture Act, and the Association wisely concentrated on wringing what advantages it could from its new consultative status and upon building up its strength. The latter aim was pursued with excellent results. Its membership, which was only 10,000 in 1945, rose rapidly to 25,000 four years later and stood at 34,500 in 1961. Its annual income increased over these sixteen years from under £8,000 to £104,000, and its staff grew from seven to sixty-one.[1] Still a dwarf among the major agricultural organizations, it nonetheless reaped the rewards of energetic recruitment and of a new sense of defensive solidarity among the owners of agricultural land.

In its uneasy relations with the Labour Government, the Association gained from one circumstance. The agricultural expansion programme created a need for re-equipment and land improvement. The Labour Government had shelved any immediate intention of land nationalization by 1949, and instead called upon landlords to play an active part in the provision of new capital.[2] This situation improved the landowners' morale, and also gave their Association an excellent argument for pressing on their behalf for tax concessions and participation in Government subsidies.

In the first post-war decade, as in the inter-war period, the Association's main achievements lay in this direction. Just before Labour won office, the Association had helped to secure most favourable treatment for agricultural land under the 1945 budget whereby the full cost of an improvement could be set against taxation in ten equal annual instalments, to which was added in 1954 an initial allowance of a further 10 per cent.[3] Labour maintained the general estate duty

[1] *Country Landowner*, December, 1960.
[2] See the 42nd. annual report of the CLA (1949), which gives an account of improved relations with Government.
[3] CLA *Jubilee History*, p. 36.

concession on agricultural land, which was converted by the 1949 Finance Act into an abatement of 45 per cent, while in response to CLA' arguments the large agricultural estates were treated with relative leniency under the Cripps' special levy of 1948. Landowners were offered substantial Government grants for improvements to water supply and land drainage, the building of farm cottages, and the rehabilitation of hill farms.[1] The Conservative Government continued and extended this assistance. Its culmination was the provision of a general grant of a third of the cost towards capital improvements under the 1957 Agriculture Act.

All this was helpful to landowners, but extremely illogical. At least part of the need for this aid derived from the very favourable treatment secured to tenants under the 1947 Act. The administration of this Act contributed to the continuation of the low agricultural rents of pre-war days. The average net rent (e.g. the sum received by landowners after expenditure on repairs, maintenance, and statutory charges) declined from 1938 to 1950, despite the considerable fall in money values and the increase in agricultural prosperity. Some estates were being run at an annual loss, and the yield on landlords' capital had become extremely low; by contrast, rent accounted for a greatly reduced proportion of farmers' expenditure.[2] This situation meant that landlords had hardly any rent income which could be reinvested, and Government grants and tax concessions became an indirect means of supporting a stagnant and ineffective system of land tenure.

The Agriculture Act of 1947 provided two methods by which a landlord could seek to remove an unsatisfactory tenant. He could apply to the County Committee for a certificate of bad husbandry against the tenant, or he could seek the committee's approval for a notice to quit. While the statutory grounds for the latter action were wider,[3] successful action by a landlord largely turned in practice upon his ability to demonstrate his tenants' incompetence. To a large extent the 1947 Act attempted to govern landlord-tenant relations by the same criteria as state-farmer relations, which meant giving to all farmers, whether owners or tenants, a strong measure of security

[1] The last was provided under the Hill Farming Act of 1948, over which the Association played an active part.

[2] Rents accounted for 11·3 per cent of total farm expenditure in 1939, for 8·1 per cent in 1944–5, for 5·6 per cent only in 1956–7. J. T. Ward, 'Farm Rents and Tenure', *Estates Gazette*, 1959, p. 24.

[3] A notice to quit could be granted if it was in the interests of good estate management or good husbandry, if the land was required for agricultural research or education or a non-agricultural use, or (in certain very limited types of case) if the landlord stood to suffer greater hardship than the tenant. The first condition was the most important, but the consideration of 'good estate management' was confined by judicial interpretation to the particular holding in question.

unless proven to be unfit. Chapter V pointed out that the committees were fairly lenient in their administration of the state's coercive powers, and it was not to be expected that they would support landlords against tenants with any greater degree of firmness.

During the ten years of the 1947 Act's operation the committees considered 6,765 applications for notice to quit and 934 applications for a certificate of bad husbandry. They gave their consent in rather less than two out of five notice to quit cases and in rather under half the bad husbandry cases. In many bad husbandry cases the committees initially chose to place under their own supervision a tenant whom they judged incompetent, rather than to issue the requested certificate; but this evasion (for such it was in terms of the Act) was later prevented by Government directive, after CLA representations. About a third of the notice to quit decisions between 1950 and 1958 were the subject of appeals to agricultural land tribunals. While two out of every five appeals by tenants were successful, only one out of four landlords' appeals were so.[1]

The depressed condition of landowning owed something at least to the attitudes of landowners themselves. Their Association continually urged them to take a responsible but business-like attitude towards the ownership of agricultural land,[2] but many were not really very interested in agriculture as a business. Landownership is still often valued for its social prestige and its incidental amenities, while in the post-war world it has carried considerable taxation advantages, from the viewpoint both of preserving capital and of spending surplus income in a pleasant way. Many traditional-minded landowners found it repugnant to take formal proceedings against their tenants or even to go to arbitration over rents. Landowners' nominees often leaned over backwards on the agricultural committees so as to avoid any impression of sectional attitudes. Privately, however, some would say that farmers had stolen a march on landowners while the latter were away at war.

The Association had an excellent case for arguing that, if the landlord-tenant system was to work at all, the 1947 arrangements over rents and tenure would have to be modified. Any change, however, would affect the interests of farmers, and their Union occupied the political sunlight while landlordism was still in shadow. The Association therefore had to walk delicately. It relied on a very moderate reiteration of its case, particularly through discussions at a not unsympathetic Ministry of Agriculture.[3] Eventually the repeal

[1] See Appendix C for more detailed figures. Information supplied by Ministry of Agriculture, Fisheries and Food.

[2] A good example is the critical polemics of 'Rusticus' in the *Country Landowner*. See 'Lazy landowners', *Country Landowner*, February, 1956.

[3] As early as 1953, 'round table duscussions' were reported between the Ministry, the CLA, and professional bodies. *Country Landowner*, October, 1953.

of sanctions in 1958 gave the Government an opportunity to introduce some complementary adjustments in the landlords' favour.

So far as tenure was concerned, the changes made by the 1958
Agriculture Act were very mild. The responsibility for hearing applications for notices to quit was removed from the committees and
vested exclusively in agricultural land tribunals. This accorded with
the general transformation of the committees' functions and with the
recommendations of the Franks' Committee. The Act stated the
grounds for consent in rather more positive fashion, and included the
managerial requirements of a whole estate as a valid reason for
terminating a tenancy;[1] but it also required that the application
should accord with the behaviour of a 'fair and reasonable landlord',[2]
and this qualification certainly means that hardship to the tenant
must still be considered. These adjustments were in fact agreed
between the Association and the Union, as the Government had
required before introducing legislation. They had a relatively small
effect in the first year of their application,[3] although it is fair to say
that the landlords' case was treated with slightly more sympathy.

The 1958 Act, however, also introduced, with minor qualifications,
the 'open market' principle as the basis upon which arbitrators
should determine new rents.[4] Even before the Act, rents had begun
to rise to a more reasonable level, and its effect will certainly be to
put agricultural landownership on a much more economic basis. The
Farmers' Union did not accept this part of the Act, and offered a
number of somewhat irrational criticisms.[5] Parliament was also uneasy but the Government stood firm. After a long period of uphill
struggle, the Association had at last achieved a major success.

4

Before the last war the Country Landowners' Association was rather
more like an aristocratic club than an organized interest group. Over
the last sixteen years it has spoken with a new and stronger voice,
calling on landowners to awaken from indifference and political
defeatism before it is too late. 'We shall meet new storms, but we
shall also meet fair weather; and in the new age into which we are
moving, there will be a place for you—different, perhaps, but no less

[1] Agriculture Act (1958), Section 3(2) (b). A landlord could, for example, seek
possession of farms in order to convert them into more economic units. In practice, such applications seem likely to be rare.
[2] Agriculture Act, Section 2.
[3] In the first full year of operation, there were 100 successful and 130 unsuccessful applications for notice to quit. *Country Landowner*, December, 1960.
[4] Agriculture Act, Section 2.
[5] For an interesting analysis of NFU criticisms, see Hallett, *op. cit.*, p. 62–72.

honourable, than the place of your fathers in the England of the past.'[1]

Landowners have accordingly been urged to seize the responsibilities of their position, 'and show the country that they are pulling their weight'.[2] They have been advised to put their estates on an economic basis and to take an active part in their management so that they will find a place in the 'new age'. They must demonstrate that they are good at the trade of land owning. More than that, they must see it as a trade and, like other trades, organize to protect their interests.

Since the craft guilds of the Middle Ages, collective negotiation has achieved much more than any individual by his own unaided efforts. Today, with many competing interests pressing their claims, the rights of the individual are in great danger of being submerged ... unless he has a professional association or Trade Union working on his behalf, acting as a buffer between himself and Government Departments, and if necessary, helping to fight his case in the courts.[3]

This approach has, as we have seen, met with considerable success. The Association has won a whole series of minor victories over taxation, Government grants, town planning, public acquisition of land, and security of tenure; as well as a major victory over rents and a striking political achievement in the Crichel Down case. It has done at least equally well in relation to forestry, a subject of considerable importance to estate owners but which raises too many separate issues to be discussed here.[4] Such failures as it has had may be accounted inevitable. Although the CLA presses every year for lower rates of estate duty, it can hardly hope to win further success here without a change of political attitudes to the whole question of death duties. It also realizes the impossibility of restoring more than a small fraction of the rights which landlords once possessed over their tenants. Its achievements have certainly been limited by political and social forces that are well beyond its control; yet it is fair to say that what the CLA could do it has done. It is perhaps ironical that

---

[1] *Journal of the Central Landowners' Association*, December, 1948, p. 143.
[2] *Ibid.*, June, 1949, p. 161.
[3] CLA. *Your Land*, p. 2.
[4] The CLA played a large part in settling the details of the dedication scheme (introduced in 1950) under which woodland owners could secure Government grants in return for following sound principles of management. It has been active over questions of timber marketing, control of fellings, and protection against imported timber, and has had close relations with the Forestry Commission. For various reasons an independent body (the Timber Growers' Association) was established in 1960 under CLA auspices to deal with the interests of woodland owners.

the landed gentry should prove so adept at trade union organization when at last persuaded to take it seriously.

Unfortunately, the Association's achievements cannot alter the fact that it is trying to rescue a precarious and weak system. It urges landlords to be more business-like, but the fact is that agricultural landlordism in Britain has become a most unbusiness-like institution, and that some of the Association's own successes have made it more so. Despite the stagnant level of rents, the capital value of tenanted farms increased threefold between 1938 and 1958,[1] and at least kept pace with most forms of industrial investment. This paradoxical situation is due largely to the social, taxation, and other incidental advantages that have become joined with the ownership of agricultural land. New investment in agricultural fixed equipment has been stimulated by Government grants and tax concessions, but even so it has been on a limited and probably inadequate scale when compared with the much larger investments in agricultural working capital. The more agricultural landlordism is propped up by Government support, the less justification it can claim as a source of private capital. It is possible, but not proven, that the rent increases which should follow from the 1958 Act will enable agricultural landlords to perform their functions more effectively and with less need for Government support.

Still more serious, perhaps, are the problems relating to the structure of landlordism itself. The agricultural landlord is conventionally thought of as the owner of a fair-sized estate, and both the social traditions and the economic advantages of landownership are associated with estates of this kind. The advantages of professional management, common services, and a comprehensive programme of agricultural improvements can only be realized on the larger estates. These estates also offer at least some opportunities for the improvement of farm lay-outs to suit modern conditions and for the amalgamation of uneconomic holdings, objectives which have become important in the context of modern agricultural policy but which are hard to realize.

In fact, however, a considerable proportion of tenanted agricultural land is held in small units of ownership, although no detailed figures are available.[2] The small landlord cannot realize any of the opportunities of the large estate owner, while he often has little

---

[1] The increase in the sale prices of farms offered without vacant possession was slightly less than 200 per cent, while that of farms with vacant possession was greater. Hallett, *op. cit.*, p. 57.

[2] For example, a survey of 13,044 acres in North Oxfordshire revealed that the average unit of ownership was only 116 acres, and that many farms had more than one owner. The area may have been in some respects exceptional, but similar results have been found elsewhere. See Agricultural Economics Research Institute, *Country Planning*, OUP 1944.

knowledge of agriculture and little capital to invest in improvements.[1] Fragmented ownership also makes the replanning of farm units still more difficult.[2] It seems at least probable that owner-occupation has more advantages in an agricultural sense than petty landlordism. At the same time, the larger private estates continue to decline. Statistics are again lacking, but a survey of landownership in ten eastern counties suggested that the number of estates with more than 2,000 acres had fallen by about a third between 1873 and 1941.[3] This decline has been slowed up not only by estate duty concessions, but also by the substantial interlocking of rural and urban wealth. Most of the larger landowners possess considerable non-agricultural wealth as well. By selling other assets they can retain their agricultural estates for a considerable time, although in fact their usual aim is to retain a balance between the two forms of wealth, each of which has its particular advantages.[4]

Although often greatly prized and skilfully defended, the private family estate seems bound to play a decreasing part in British agriculture. The most viable estates are those held by public, charitable, and educational bodies, and the continued existence of other estates would seem to require some form of corporate ownership. In this way the economic continuity of the estate system might be preserved, but its personal and family basis would be finally lost.

This situation provides the Association with its grimmest problem. In the modern world hereditary proprietorship of large estates has become an anachronism. It lingers on in British agriculture only because Governments have been merciful and because (short of the extreme expedient of land nationalization) no adequate alternatives to the old estate system have been created. Yet it is still this system which gives life and force to the landowning interest, which provides landowners with their traditions and with their leaders. The Association could not exist in its present form or with its present influence as an organization of owner-occupiers and petty landlords. It depends upon a system which cannot in fact be saved by the economic and business criteria to which it often appeals.

While giving considerable security to the husbandman, the (Landlord-tenant) system gives the landowner and his family a pride of ownership and a devotion to the land, which has been a prime cause,

[1] Ward, op. cit., p. 75.
[2] The Agricultural Land Commission recommended a compulsory reorganization of farm units in the Yetminster area of Dorset but was opposed successfully by the CLA.
[3] The survey was conducted by the University of Cambridge Department of Agriculture as reported in The Economist, September 17, 1949.
[4] See D. R. Denman, Estate Capital (Allen and Unwin 1958), for a full discussion of the finances of agricultural estates.

not only of social stability, but constructive leadership in the countryside. British landowners of the landlord and tenant system have inherited a living and a virile tradition which can stand without shame before the tribunal of history.[1]

It is this tradition, not death duties, rents, government grants, or tax concessions, which fundamentally concerns most estate owners. Whether the tradition is living and virile is a question; that it has been dealt a severe blow is certain; that it will die in the face of new social, economic, and political forces and ideas seems probable. Some landlords have abandoned this tradition and made themselves into farmers; others try to wish it back, or sit at their firesides, drinking good port (though not so good as before the war), and grumble. Those active in the Association have sought to meet the new circumstances through organization. But regardless of their success as a trade union—their success in maintaining the economic viability of the private agricultural landlord—there is little that they can do about the re-establishment or even the maintenance of what is left of the tradition associated with the great estate system. That fact throws a shadow over even their brightest achievements.

[1] CLA *Policy and Objectives* (January, 1955), p. 20

CHAPTER IX

THE POLITICS OF AGRICULTURE

1

THE consensus about agricultural policy which found expression in the 1947 Agriculture Act has endured surprisingly well. Agricultural policy-making has been in large measure apolitical, with the main decisions emerging out of consultation between Government and Farmers' Union. No powerful voice has been raised against this arrangement, nor (with the possible exception of the 'decontrol' controversy and the repeal of sanctions) have any of the basic issues of policy been tossed into the political arena. We must now enquire into the political basis of this consensus and *its* degree of durability. Can it really be that the ghost of a critical urban opinion, eager for cheap food and indifferent to agricultural welfare, has finally been laid? Has the conjunction between the interests of town and country, long thought so unlikely, after all been brought about? Or has the post-war prosperity and stability of agriculture rested upon special and temporary conditions?

In this chapter, we shall first consider the attitudes towards agriculture in Parliament and in the main political parties. In Parliament the status and strength of agriculture can be considered from two viewpoints. We can ask, first, how many Members sit for agricultural constituencies and what are their political affiliations. Secondly, we can consider the occupational representation of agriculturists in Parliament.

If by an agricultural constituency is meant one where agriculture forms the largest and most important source of employment, there are not many such in Great Britain. There were in 1955 six exceptionally rural constituencies (Leominster, Eye, Howden, Montgomery, Aberdeenshire West, and Kinross and West Perth) in which agriculture provided more than 40 per cent of total regular male employment. There were forty-eight constituencies with more than 25 per cent employment in agriculture, and 110 constituencies with over 15 per cent. This last group may be described as 'agricultural' constituencies in the limited sense that farming, while not always the most important activity, was undeniably of real importance. These 110 constituencies cover over 80 per cent of the total land surface and their representatives comprise just over one-sixth of the membership of the House of Commons.

AGRICULTURAL CONSTITUENCIES (1955)*

Agricultural Employment as Percentage of Total Male Employment (Age 15 and Over)	*No. of Constituencies*			
	ENGLAND	SCOTLAND	WALES	GREAT BRITAIN
15 to 19%	29	2	2	33
20 to 24%	19	6	4	29
25 to 32%	23	6	2	31
33 to 39%	6	5	0	11
40% and over	3	2	1	6
	80	21	9	110

* Figures in this and the next table are based on the 1951 Census of Occupations and the 1955 Register of Electors. See Appendix D for further details.

Ever since the decline of the Whig landed interest in the last half of the nineteenth century these constituencies have been heavily Conservative in their representation. In 1956, seventy-six of the eighty 'agricultural' seats in England were Conservative; seventeen of the twenty-one Scottish agricultural seats were Conservative; and so were all six of the rural seats in North Ireland which are not included in our tables. Only in the nine Welsh seats was there something like a balance between the three parties. Even in 1946, at the height of Labour's advance, the position was not greatly different, although an exact comparison is not possible because of changes in constituency boundaries. Allowing for this factor, it would seem that the Conservatives then held about three-quarters of the agricultural seats and that Labour held at the most twenty.

AGRICULTURAL REPRESENTATION (1955)
(After General Election)
No. of seats where Agricultural Employment
Exceeds 15 per cent of Total Male Employment

	ENGLAND	SCOTLAND	WALES	GREAT BRITAIN
Conservative	76	17	2	95
Labour	4	3	4	11
Liberal	0	1	3	4
Independent	0	0	0	0
	80	21	9	110

The occupational representation of agriculture in Parliament is a quite different matter. Most 'agricultural' seats are not represented by agriculturists, but on the other hand there is a sprinkling of other seats whose Members are or were farmers. The number of farmers in the House of Commons has increased since the war. Classifying Members by the principal occupation which they had held, J. F. S. Ross found an average of only ten farmers and stockbreeders for the inter-war period. The number rose to sixteen in 1945, twenty-five in 1950, and thirty-three in 1951.[1] The 1955 General Election returned thirty-six farmers to the House of Commons.[2] Since the war, more landowners have taken up active farming, and this partly accounts for the increase in farmers' numbers.[3] Not surprisingly all but a few of the farmer Members have been Conservatives, although the other parties have been putting forward an increasing number of agricultural candidates. At the 1959 General Election ten Labour candidates and thirteen Liberal candidates could be considered farmers, but only three Labour and no Liberal farmers won.[4]

The agricultural affiliations of Members of Parliament are too diverse to be easily classified. Apart from the active farmers, there are a fair number of business men and others who dabble in farming with greater or less zeal. Parliament reflects that linkage of urban wealth and rural sentiment which is so typical of prosperous English society. A study of Dod's Parliamentary Companion shows that a high proportion of Conservatives sitting for rural seats occupy 'farms', 'halls', or 'manors'. Many of these people consider themselves versed in agricultural questions, even though their own participation may be minimal. There are also a number of land agents, surveyors, and auctioneers, who are in close touch with agriculture.

Most of the active farmers occupy what are large holdings by British standards. Hardly any farm workers or 'muddy-boot' farmers have found their way into Parliament, although these groups account for over 95 per cent of the men on the land. This orientation towards size and wealth holds for the very few Labour farmers as well as the Conservatives.[5] There are plenty of Members who can speak with authority and feeling about large farmers' and landowners' problems, few who can do the same for farm workers. This is still truer if the House of Lords is included in the analysis, for many of their Lordships possess unrivalled technical knowledge about questions of estate and forestry management. Too much should not be made of

[1] J. F. S. Ross, *Elections and Electors* (Eyre and Spottiswoode, 1955), p. 433.
[2] D. E. Butler, *The British General Election of 1955* (Macmillan, 1955), p. 43.
[3] *Ibid.*, p. 42n.
[4] D. E. Butler and R. Ross, *The British General Election of 1959* (Macmillan, 1960), p. 127.
[5] At the 1959 General Election, Labour produced eleven farmer candidates and three candidates sponsored by the farm workers' union. Five of the farmers indicated the size of their holdings, which were 2,300 acres, over 2,000, 700, 440, and 'extensive'. *The Farmers' Weekly*, Sept. 25, 1959. Only three of these Labour farmers were subsequently elected, and of these two were 'hobby farmers'.

these sectional inclinations, however. Among agriculturally-minded Members, there is a strong commitment to the interests of agriculture as a whole and a sympathetic attitude towards the problems of smaller farmers and, to a lesser extent, of farm workers. Partly this reflects the active kind of squirearchical paternalism reinvigorated by the competition of similar sentiments among a tiny group of Labour 'squires'. Partly it demonstrates a strong acceptance, more evident among rural-minded Parliamentarians than in the agricultural organizations, that the interests of agriculture stand or fall together.

As this analysis has already indicated, the difference between the two main parties in respect of agricultural background and experience is extraordinarily wide. The Conservatives possess a large phalanx of rural-based or agriculturally-minded Members. Labour Members interested in agriculture are far fewer and less homogeneous. Since 1945 they have consisted of three small groups. There is a sprinkling of Members from rural or semi-rural constituencies; there is a group of Co-operative members concerned with the interests of food consumers and distributors; and there is the small group of Parliamentary leaders on agricultural matters, most of whom have also had administrative experience of agricultural problems. The composition of the last group strikingly illustrates the party differences. None of the five Labour Members who occupied agricultural posts in the 1945–51 Labour Governments were members of an agricultural constituency as defined above or had themselves, with one exception, worked on the land.[1] By contrast, Conservative office-holders generally come from agricultural constituencies and quite often have had farming experience. At a minimum, they wear tweeds naturally.

Agricultural debates in the Commons are almost monopolized, on the Conservative side, by the representatives of rural constituencies. Their speeches generally reveal a much more protectionist sentiment towards agriculture than their leaders, when in office, have been prepared to adopt. The majority of Labour speakers are equally sympathetic towards agriculture, being drawn either from the small rural constituency group or from the Parliamentary agricultural leaders who have become deeply committed to a pro-farmer programme. The only jarring note in this agricultural close-harmony is that of a few dissentient Co-operative and Labour members. Typically these are lone voices in debates where nearly all the speakers are

[1] To be fair, it should be added that three of the Members in question sat for constituencies which are partly agricultural, though not on our list: Mr G. A. Brown (Belper), Mr A. J. Champion (Derbyshire, South-East), Mr T. F. Peart (Workington). Mr Champion worked on a hill farm for five years. Junior Ministers from the House of Lords have not been included.

preoccupied with the producers' problems and requirements.[1]

A rather similar pattern holds in the Parliamentary party committees concerned with agriculture and food. These committees or groups are loosely organized forums in which interested organizations can be heard and party policy can be discussed. Again they are naturally weighted with the agriculturally interested, although the Labour group attracts an active core of consumer-minded and nutrition-conscious Co-operatives and others. As with most other Parliamentary groups of this kind, their influence on party policy is rather limited. Partly because of sporadic attendance, they are poor instruments for undertaking any careful or critical scrutiny of programmes and proposals. Definite group decisions are taken rarely and then may be reversed by the Parliamentary Party. However, the chairman of each group is usually an influential figure in agricultural politics. And the Conservative chairman in particular acts as a powerful spokesman for back-bench agricultural opinion when his party is in power. In opposition, the post is usually filled by the party's potential Minister of Agriculture.

2

Since the days of Disraeli's Young England movement, Conservatism has tended to identify itself with all that is best in rural traditions. It has assumed an almost organic connection between its own aims and those of rural dwellers and farmers. In 1948, Mr R. A. Butler gave voice to these old beliefs at the party conference at Llandudno.

In saving agriculture we are saving more than our own economy. We are saving a way of life in which the features are kindliness, freedom, and above all, wisdom. These are the qualities of the countryman and countrywoman. They are instinct with Conservative policy, they are vital to our existence.

Farmers may indeed 'instinctively' tend to think and vote as Tories where national issues are concerned; but where agriculture is concerned they have become a little sceptical about their instinctive ally. In the farmers' political vocabulary, the critical word has become 'security'—security against the impact of falling prices, fluctuating markets and foreign competition. Their Union's post-war policy statement was called, appropriately enough, 'The Basis of Economic Security', and the 'definiteness' and 'positiveness' of a party's programme became the yardstick for the farmers' approval. Con-

---

[1] Some of the Co-operative Members have become increasingly concerned with the problems of Agricultural Co-operatives, which is not of course the same thing as farmers' problems as presented by their Union.

versely their greatest source of anxiety was any suspicion of 'uncertainty' or 'drift' in government policy. These were the catchwords of the post-war agricultural debate.

The Labour Government had the satisfaction of passing the 1947 Agriculture Act, and of launching an expansion programme based upon generous guaranteed prices, measures which injected an element of party competition into agricultural policy-making for the first time in this century. Indeed, in some ways Labour had an ideological headstart in meeting the farmers' requirements, despite its almost complete lack of agricultural roots or experience. Its belief in state planning meant that it was much more inclined than the pragmatic Tories towards the use of fixed prices, production targets, and guaranteed markets. Of course planning of this kind could be used to impose stringent measures upon agriculture as well as to further its prosperity, but Labour in fact never adopted or threatened to adopt such methods.

The Conservatives responded by warmly endorsing the Agriculture Act in principle, emphasizing their own share in its formulation, but arguing that it did not go far enough in its assurances of security. They were particularly critical of the limitation of the farm guarantees to 'such part of the nation's food and other agricultural produce as in the national interest it is desirable to produce in the United Kingdom'. This clause was criticized in debates on the Bill, and it was also suggested that disputes over facts and figures at the price review should be referred for the opinion of an independent tribunal.[1] Subsequently the Conservative *Agricultural Charter* (Conservative Central Office, 1948) promised 'to give home agricultural production the highest priority, and to introduce a sense of urgency, of continuity and of certainty into policy'. Once in office, the Conservative Government abandoned production targets after a few years and availed itself, in the case of milk, of the very power to limit the size of the guaranteed market which the party had previously criticized. Conservatives could of course reasonably argue that times had changed, yet it was to provide for such changes that the Agriculture Act was cautiously drafted.

In opposition Labour moved at first towards an advocacy of more comprehensive planning coupled with a much greater sensitivity to farmers' wishes. *Challenge to Britain* (Labour Party, 1953) proposed that annual price reviews should be governed by five-year production plans, and that annual price changes should normally reflect only changes in costs until a fresh plan became due. This price proposal closely mirrored one put forward by the Union in 1951, and represented just the kind of Ministerial hand-tying which Labour when in

[1] See the proceedings of Standing Committee A on Clause Two of the Agriculture Bill, 1947. H. of C. O. R. Standing Committees, 1946–7, Vol. 2.

office had refused to accept. Despite increasing abundance *Full Harvest* (1955) still promised a definite expansion plan and a return to fixed guaranteed prices, which the Conservatives had partly abandoned, but was silent about the revision of price review procedure. *Prosper the Plough* (1958) favoured only a 'moderate increase' in output and its attitude to the price review was considerable more cautious. The 1947 Act as amended by the 1957 Act would be upheld and there would be a return to fixed guaranteed prices for some products. A heavy emphasis was placed throughout on the use of consultation with the Union.

One of the main obstacles to Labour's wooing of the farmers has been its ambivalent attitude towards agricultural marketing. The Co-operative section of the party holds strong views upon the wickedness of producer marketing monopolies and its distaste for the 1949 Agricultural Marketing Act, and for the Union-sponsored horticultural schemes which followed, led to some sharp interchanges within the party while Labour was in office. In 1953 the consumer champions in the party persuaded its Parliamentary Food and Agriculture Committee to oppose the Conservative Government's decision to raise horticultural tariffs. This decision was overturned in the parliamentary party itself at the insistence of Mr Tom Williams and a few colleagues who stressed the electoral danger of flouting the Union's wishes so openly. As S. H. Beer points out, this incident was a striking demonstration of the Union's power in view of the emphasis which Labour was then placing upon reducing the cost of living.[1]

In 1955 the Labour Party's prolonged internal deliberations upon agricultural marketing at last issued in a policy statement. The statement was a compromise between the proposals of the Lucas Committee for independent Minister-appointed commodity commissions and the demands of the Farmers' Union for producer-controlled boards.[2] The Lucas principle was favoured by the distributive unions and the Co-operative wing of the party, as well as by the Agricultural Workers' Union which had persuaded the 1954 Labour Party Conference to give a vague endorsement to the Lucas proposals. The compromise eventually adopted proposed to retain producer boards for milk, potatoes and wool, but to establish independent commissions for livestock, cereals, and eggs. It followed the general principle 'of preferring a Commission to a Marketing Board where activities are to be carried well forward along the marketing line'.[3]

---

[1] See Samuel H. Beer, 'Pressure Groups and Parties in Britain,' *American Political Science Review*, March, 1956, p. 13.
[2] See Chapter IV, pp. 90–94.
[3] *Agricultural Marketing. A Statement of Labour Party Policy*, January, 1955.

This document was unusually explicit and detailed for a party policy statement. Doubtless this reflected the conscientiousness with which Labour had threshed out the subject, but it was rather curious that the statement should appear during a by-election for the marginal seat of South Norfolk. Farmers' reactions to the proposals were clearly adverse.[1] Whether or not Labour would just have captured this marginal seat if it had remained silent cannot be known, but the pro-farmers in the party certainly stressed what they took to be the moral. In its next (1959) statement on agricultural and horticultural marketing, Labour went so far as to eliminate all proposals which might offend the Union. The Lucas-type commodity commissions virtually disappeared from the draft, which however stated that 'facilities under the Marketing Acts will be freely available' for the promotion of producer-controlled boards; and where the previous statement stated the safeguards for consumers in considerable detail, the 1959 one satisfied itself with one vague, inconclusive reference.[2]

It would be unduly cynical to assert that Labour simply tailored its policies to win farmers' votes. It would be truer to say that having found itself unexpectedly popular in agricultural circles, Labour concluded that farmers could be persuaded to change their traditional allegiances. For this to happen they must be persuaded that Labour 'planning' was preferable to Conservative 'freedom'; and Labour planning itself had perhaps to be adjusted a little to meet farmers' special tastes, for example over agricultural marketing. The old socialist panacea of land nationalization had also to be shelved, for nobody supposed that farmers liked it.

Labour had clearly gone on record in favour of land nationalization as recently as 1942, and the older party stalwarts were keen to keep the torch burning for their ideal. The issue was hotly debated at party conferences in 1949, 1953 and 1958, to the neglect of more pressing matters. In each case the leadership persuaded the party that the subject was better avoided while so many farmers' votes were (supposedly) hanging in the balance. Nationalization could wait until farmers were better educated. In 1958, Mr Tom Williams actually expressed doubts as to whether nationalization was even desirable. His main point, however, was that to upset farmers at this time would destroy Labour's prospect of victory at the coming election. 'I am convinced that anything in the nature of an unconsidered land nationalization proposal would not only wreck your chances at the

[1] See, for example, reports in the *Manchester Guardian*, January 4, 1955 and *The Times*, January 7, 1955.

[2] *Statement of Policy On Agricultural and Horticultural Marketing*. Labour Party, August, 1959. In view of Labour's agricultural record, it is rather startling that so authoritative a writer as Sir Ivor Jennings should still contend that 'Neither the Labour Party nor the Liberal Party is sympathetic to the chief aims of the Union.' *Parliament*, 2nd ed., 1957, p. 221.

next election but perhaps keep us in the political wilderness for a very long time.'[1]

At least from 1949, Labour party conferences accepted the notion that there were considerable and even decisive gains possible in rural constitutencies. Generally speakers were cautious about giving estimates, although in 1954 Mr Dye hazarded that twenty-four agricultural seats were within the party's reach and in 1958 Mr Crossman, speaking on behalf of the Executive, thought that *Prosper The Plough* might be a major factor in winning twenty to thirty seats.[2] The failure to make much headway in rural areas doubtless led some Labour supporters to agree with Mr Desmond Donnelly, M.P., that 'We have sold our birthright to the land for a mess of pottage, and we have not had the pottage so far'.[3] The majority, however, were prepared to follow the party leadership, which in turn had been persuaded by its small group of Parliamentary agricultural specialists that in due course Labour's seed would fall on fertile soil. It was just a matter of stressing Labour's positive advantages for agriculture, hushing up the unpalatable points, and waiting quietly.

With Labour wooing the farmers so vigorously, the Conservatives also had to strengthen their agricultural appeal. This seemed particularly necessary after a large Conservative majority was wiped out at a by-election in the heavily agricultural Torrington constituency in 1958. Correctly or not, it was widely believed that the victorious Liberal had benefited from a 'protest vote' against Conservative agricultural policy. Subsequently the Conservatives launched their small farmer scheme and set about explaining their agricultural policy more carefully.[4] The Liberals for their part, tried hard to overcome the impression of ambivalence which hung about their agricultural programme.[5] An observer in *The British Farmer* could assert, without boastfulness, that the three party conferences in 1958 had shown that the agricultural vote had 'a grotesque psephological importance'.[6]

---

[1] *Report of the 57th Annual Conference of the Labour Party*, p. 133.

[2] *Report of the 53rd Annual Conference of the Labour Party*, p. 146, and of the *57th Annual Conference*, p. 134.

[3] *Report of the 52nd Annual Conference of the Labour Party*, p. 144.

[4] See *Achievement in Agriculture* (Conservative Party, 1958).

[5] The fact that a Liberal not a Labour candidate won at Torrington had nothing to do with agricultural policy. The area was traditionally Liberal, and the previous incumbent was a 'National Liberal and Conservative' (which for Parliamentary purposes equals Conservative). For the 'new look' in Liberal agricultural policy, see *Policy for Agriculture*, 1959. This statement conceded that agricultural subsidies were necessary, at least until Liberal measures against monopolies and high industrial tariffs could be introduced. It also wanted cheap credit for farmers. Previous Liberal documents had been less clear, because of a split in the party itself, about the degree of support which farmers ought to have.

[6] Montague Keen, 'The Three Parties and Agriculture', *The British Farmer*, Nov. 1, 1958.

'Politicians,' wrote an observer of the 1955 general election, 'often exaggerate the significance of the genuinely agricultural vote and fail to realize that there are few, if any, constituencies in which farmers, farmworkers, and their dependents comprise even a quarter of the electorate.'[1] While this statement underestimates the agricultural vote—there were at that time nineteen constituencies which met this criterion—it is true enough that its numerical size is not very considerable. There were in 1955 only twenty-four British constituencies in which farmers, bailiffs, etc., as defined by the Census constituted even 5 per cent of the electorate. All workers in agriculture and their wives, estimated on the basis of certain assumptions, together constituted over 10 per cent of the electorate in 126 constituencies, over 20 per cent in thirty-seven, and over 30 per cent in eight.[2] This calculation suggests that there are a considerable number of constituencies in which the agricultural vote has some significance but few in which it is highly important.

The value placed upon the agricultural vote, however, depends not simply upon its numerical size but upon two assumptions: that it is potentially malleable and that it occupies a critical place in certain rural constituencies. These assumptions apply particularly to farmers themselves. Farmers are heavily dependent upon public policy for their prosperity, and they are well aware of forming a distinctive group within a mainly urban nation. As such they should perhaps be more responsive than most groups to party policies which bear upon their own welfare and interests.

The possible 'strategic' value of the farmers' vote derives from their key position within the rural economy. In general, the more agricultural a constituency the safer the seat for the Conservatives. The only exceptions relate to constituencies in the Celtic Highlands, which are traditionally Liberal, and in East Anglia, where the farm workers' union is strong. The eight agricultural seats outside these areas which Labour won in 1945 did not have a high proportion of agricultural employment and were also fairly industrialized.[3]

The strong Conservatism of rural Britain rests upon much wider foundations than the support of farmers. Retired people, wealthy ex-urbanites, clergymen, and the shopkeepers and professional men of small country towns all help to set the Conservative tone. Nonetheless, agriculture is still the economic backbone of the countryside, and the prosperity of farmers is generally accepted as the barometer of agriculture's well-being. If therefore a sizeable number of farmers

[1] Hugh Berrington in D. E. Butler, *The British General Election of 1955*, p. 130.
[2] See Appendix D for further details.
[3] These seats, in order of agricultural importance, were Derbyshire West, Maldon, Taunton, Lowestoft, Kidderminster, Thornbury, Faversham, Frome. None had over 20 per cent employment in agriculture.

could be persuaded to defect from the Conservative cause, other rural groups (it is assumed) may follow suit. Moreover, as hardworking toilers, farmers can be regarded as more probable and acceptable recruits to the Labour cause than the genteel, wealthy, and retired people who also live in the countryside. The fact that most 'agricultural' constituencies contain sizeable clusters of industrial, mining, or railway workers increases Conservative dependence upon the rural end of the constituency, and makes the loyalty of agriculture seemingly more crucial.

It is worth testing the plausibility of these assumptions by considering the immediate electoral effect of a substantial swing in the agricultural vote. A substantial swing can reasonably be defined as a decision by one in every four farmers, farm workers, and their wives to change their vote from Conservative to Labour. Since at any rate many farm workers already vote Labour and some farmers and workers abstain, a larger.turnover is difficult to envisage. If this switch had occurred at the 1955 Election, with all other votes unchanged, Labour would have won nineteen more seats.[1] The significance of this achievement would be less its immediate electoral effect than its general impact upon Conservative control of rural areas. Assuming that some shift in the same direction occurred among other rural groups, the Conservative hold upon its agricultural bailiwicks might become precarious.

These speculations have been introduced in the attempt to explain the peculiar political magnetism of the farmers' vote. It is not suggested that the reasoning is valid, and in fact it has so far proved false on the main points. Labour leaders themselves agree that they have not won over many farmers as yet. The theory that farmers will vote according to their distinctive interests has not held good. Many have certainly been persuaded that 'Labour is best for agriculture', while continuing to vote Conservative. Again, even if arguments about the farmers' indirect influence are true, the problem still remains that the most prestigious farmers are the least likely to vote Labour.

Even within the context of winning the agricultural vote, Labour's tactics have been curious. There are more farm workers than farmers, and only about a third of these are unionized. It might have been both more suitable and more profitable for Labour to have concentrated upon winning the support of the remaining farm workers or of the numerous class of small farmers. Yet Labour has generally pre-

---

[1] This calculation of nineteen electoral gains is rather similar to Labour's own hopeful expectations. Only twelve of these gains would have been in 'agricultural' constituencies, because the swing of even a small number of agricultural votes would have changed the results in certain other constituencies. For a study of the agricultural vote in marginal constituencies, see also J. Rowland Pennock, 'The Political Power of British Agriculture,' *Political Studies*, Oct., 1959.

ferred the farmers' to the farm workers' interest, and has proposed
nothing of special value to the small farmers. It seems almost to have
been hypnotized by the image of agriculture held up by the Farmers'
Union.

3

In seeking explanations for the apparent strength of the agricultural
interest in parties and Parliament since the war, it is natural to suspect the presence of a 'hidden hand' in the shape of some highly skil-
ful and pervasive pressure group. The National Farmers' Union
looks a likely candidate for this role, as its opinions are clearly very
influential and its demands have frequently been successful. However
its direct impact upon Parliamentary debates and party policies is
less than is often assumed.

Political studies frequently stress and sometimes list the connections between Members of Parliament and outside organizations.
S. E. Finer, for example, remarks that 'all organizations try very hard'
to get their own representatives into Parliament; and he goes on to
give a list of organizations, including the National Farmers' Union,
'which have, in some sense or other . . . "direct" representation in the
House of Commons'.[1] Many Members of Parliament do belong to
the Union—in one standing committee debate five out of six successive speakers declared their membership—but as the same debate
showed, membership of the Union is perfectly compatible with a
critical attitude towards its requests.[2] These members do not provide
the Union with direct representation in *any* meaningful sense. Indeed, leaving aside a few urban critics, some of the dryest Parliamentary comments on Union policy have come from one or two of its ex-
dignitaries. Most Union members in Parliament are, of course, Conservatives from rural constituencies. They often pride themselves on
their own independent agricultural knowledge and are much less
inclined than, for example, some Labour leaders have been to 'take
the Union's word for it'.

The Union definitely does not possess a Parliamentary lobby of
docile supporters, nor does it have, as it did before the war, any
special Parliamentary spokesmen. No candidate has received its
official endorsement since Mr (now Sir) Anthony Hurd in 1940,[3] and
no money has been spent from the political fund since 1945. Union
spokesmen sometimes present their organization's point of view,

[1] S. E. Finer, *The Anonymous Empire* (Pall Mall Press, 1958), pp. 40–41.

[2] H. of C. O. R. Standing Committees, 1956–57, Vol. I, cols. 27–37.

[3] Sir Anthony has continued to sit in the House of Commons, but he has not
been sponsored by the Union in recent elections and is certainly not its spokesman.

usually by invitation, at meetings of the Conservative and the Labour agricultural committees in the House of Commons, but they are careful to treat each group with equal care and respect. Circulars are also sent to the members of these committees and to others known to be interested, setting out the Union's position on current questions. There is, however, a strict avoidance of political partisanship, and the Union's approach to Parliament, especially during the early part of the post-war period, has on the whole been formal and cautious.

As Chapter II showed, the Union's first and basic aim since the war has been to reach agreement with the Government of the day, and with few exceptions it has carefully refrained from appealing to Parliament 'behind the Government's back' on any major matter. A good example of this policy was its attitude to the Agriculture Act, 1957. This measure did not altogether satisfy the Union, but the observations which it circulated to Members were careful to welcome the Bill in principle and to say no more about the new long-term assurances than that 'producers will inevitably reserve judgment' until their worth has been tested in practice.[1] In this case, despite the Union's mildness, the Opposition unbidden took up the cudgels on the farmers' behalf, arguing that farmers ought to have a much higher degree of price protection than the Union had obtained. Several Members professed to believe that the Union leaders had been incompetent—that, as Mr R. T. Paget (Lab., Northampton) put it, they 'have supinely connived at this attrition of their industry'.[2] They were restrained reluctantly from voting against the Bill by Mr Tom Williams who pointed out, as an ex-Minister of Agriculture might be expected to do, that it was after all an agreed measure with the Union.[3]

On the other hand, the Union is freely and copiously outspoken on matters of detail which will not upset its 'concordat' with Government. Such a relatively small matter as the Agriculture (Power Take-Off) Regulations, 1957, for example, received much fuller and more vigorous treatment for Parliamentary consumption than the important Agriculture Act, 1957.[4] There are always some Members ready to take up any points the Union cares to make, if only because they have none of their own; and the Union is sometimes successful in getting minor amendments accepted. However, in lesser matters the party temperature is sometimes lower and more objective attitudes prevail. This means that the Opposition has rather less use for

[1] Based on memorandum received by Members of Parliament.
[2] H. of C. R. Standing Committees, 1956–57, Vol. I, col. 79. Sir Leslie Plummer (Lab., Deptford), a Union county chairman, used similar language.
[3] *Ibid.*, cols. 70–71.
[4] Based on memorandum received by Members of Parliament.

Union-stocked ammunition and the Government is less defensively poised. There have been occasions when the Union's less rational arguments have received rather short shrift.

In criticizing the Hill Farming Bill of 1956, for example, the Union demanded the inclusion of hill dairy farmers in the scheme, although it was plainly uneconomic to encourage more milk production in the hills. It also wanted particular improvements to qualify for aid, without having to form part of a 'comprehensive' scheme, although the point of this provision was the sensible one of ensuring that the farm really could (after aid) yield a reasonable minimum income. Although some Members expressed sympathy with the excluded hill farmers, the Union's arguments received little support and were explicitly rejected by the concluding speaker for the Opposition. Mr Vane (Conservative, Westmorland) pronounced a fair judgment on the Union's views when he said that in this case Parliament had thought further ahead 'than many farmers and, for that matter, than many of their spokesmen'.[1]

Although the Union's political influence thus has its limits, there can be little doubt about the influence of its opinions when strongly expressed. Even Labour's attempts on occasion to outrun the Union have been tributes to its influence; and when the Union has openly disagreed with Government on a major issue the fact has been glee-fully exploited by the Opposition. In the 1956 price review debate, for example, held after the Union had repudiated the price settle-ment, seven of the nine Labour speakers made heavy play with what were alleged to be forty-eight votes of no confidence in Government policy from Union branches.[2] Similarly the Union's moderate dis-sent from the repeal of sanctions in 1958 was eagerly seized upon by the Opposition. *The Times* observed 'it would not be difficult to go through "Hansard" and single out the speeches that were based on the Parliamentary brief copiously prepared by the National Farmers' Union'.[3]

Unfortunately for the Union, Opposition support is a two-edged sword. It might jeopardize the Union's political neutrality. In 1958, for example, the President pointed out that the Opposition would 'be delighted' if the Union 'censured' Government price policy (rather than merely 'condemning' it!), but 'we have to play with either side. . . '.[4] Farmers have experienced the impotence of being identified with a particular party, and they have before them the examples of the Country Landowners' Association and the National

[1] H. of C. O. R., 1955–56, Vol. 556, Cols. 1617–20.
[2] H. of C. O. R., 1955–56, Vol. 552, Col. 32.
[3] *The Times*, March 24, 1958. See also H. of C. O. R., 1957–58, (Vol. 584), cols. 1128–9, 1141, 1154, etc.
[4] *The British Farmer*, April 5, 1958.

Union of Agricultural Workers. Generally each of these organizations can only hope to realize its aims when a particular party is in power; but that party, just because it need not fear the organization's disapproval, has less incentive to give these aims priority. The record of Labour Governments on the tied cottage issue and of Conservative Governments on landlords' control of their tenants show clearly that each party has been at least as concerned with the wishes of the uncommitted farmers as with those of its own special friends.

A second danger in arming the Opposition is that such tactics inevitably weaken the Union's strong consultative status. Indeed, one of the most helpful forms of Parliamentary support has to do not with substantive issues but with consultation. Parliament has been alert for any indication that Government discussions with the Union have been less than exhaustive, and it has become a routine parliamentary gambit to add the phrase 'after consultation with producers' at odd points in agricultural Bills, although there is seldom any doubt that consultation will take place.[1] While this Parliamentary vigilance may express no more than frustration at its own lack of control over delegated legislation, the Union clearly benefits from the implication that its concurrence is a major test of agricultural policy.

During the high point of its partnership with Government, the Union's political activities fell to a very low level. Its electoral like its Parliamentary voice was deliberately muted, in keeping with its great stress on the 'non-political' character of agricultural policy. Headquarters itself strictly avoided anything that might be construed as partisan activity. While Union leaders were sometimes consulted informally by party officials formulating agricultural platforms, the Union made no direct attempt either to influence party policy or as a rule to advise its members how to vote.[2]

As disagreements with the Government became more frequent, the Union took some steps to mend its Parliamentary fences. Similarly it encouraged county branches to step up their political activity, at least to the extent of seriously questioning candidates on agricultural issues and putting rather more pressure on rural Members of Parliament. This was a mild insurance policy. It was intended as a remote kind of pressure on the Government, a reminder that if unsatisfied with the results of policy administratively decided, farmers might again resort to direct political action. Any Government knows very well, however, that the Union remains loath to do so.

---

[1] Examples of provision for consultation, in minor agricultural measures are to be found in the Riverboards Act, 1948; the Food and Drugs, Milk and Dairies and Artificial Cream Act 1950; the Prevention of Damage by Pests Act, 1949; and the Agricultural Poisonous Substances Act 1952.

[2] As noted in Chapter II, an exception is sometimes made in the case of the Liberal Party.

THE STATE AND THE FARMER

4

In the last fifteen years politicians seem mainly to have wanted only to outdo one another in their favours to agriculture. It is true that their ardour was keenest when the responsibilities of office were most remote, but all the same agriculture has come a long way since the time when it considered itself ignored by both main parties, the one confident that it had nothing to lose, the other sure that it had nothing to gain.

This chapter has thrown some considerable doubt, however, upon the extent to which agriculture can maintain its political position. That position depended in large measure upon three conditions, all vulnerable to change. There was the national need for additional agricultural production, which indirectly enhanced the farmers' political standing. There was the cult of the farmers' vote, which hinged upon the belief of one major party that this vote was the key to a sizeable block of Parliamentary seats, and upon its willingness, in an evenly balanced party situation, to pay a high price for farmers' support. There was finally the factor of a strong farmers' organization, wielding influence upon the basis of administrative partnership and political neutrality.

The first of these conditions has passed, at least for the time being. The second is probably passing because of Labour's difficulties in wooing the farmers successfully and because of deeper shifts in the political balance which may make the agricultural vote of much less account. The third condition has been affected by the increased interest of Governments in loosening their ties with the Union and by the fact that the Union can do little to stop the process. If it takes its case to the parliamentary and political arena, it further weakens its consultative status.

On the other hand, British agriculture has acquired some political advantages which should prove more durable. One is its improved position within the national economy. Twenty years of fair prosperity have built up the importance of agriculture to other industries. Suppliers of machinery and fertilisers, for example, have a clear interest in maintaining a large and prosperous agriculture. Such important industrial firms as Imperial Chemical Industries and Fisons have recognized their stake in the welfare of agriculture. Both provide advisory services to farmers. I.C.I. sponsored in 1956 an important agricultural conference, whose general conclusions recognized the necessity of continuing agricultural aid.[1] In 1956 Fisons treated the public to a series of newspaper dialogues between a town mouse and a country mouse in which the latter had much the better of the argument.

[1] *Agriculture In The British Economy*, Imperial Chemical Industries (Central Agricultural Control), 1957.

A more weighty factor has been the Union's influence within the Federation of British Industries which it joined after the war. On several occasions it has persuaded the Federation to support the farmers' case over matters in which the interests of industrialists, particularly those seeking export markets, might have been supposed different. For example, the Union persuaded the Federation that agriculture ought to be excluded from the 1957 plan for a European free trade area, and also that the agricultural support programme should be omitted from Federation criticisms of excessive government spending.[1]

If the economic prosperity of agriculture should decline, a different factor comes into play in the shape of the welfare state's concern with problem sectors of the economy. The political and economic thinking which no longer accepts the necessity of mass unemployment is equally unlikely to countenance a repetition of severe agricultural depression. Complete abandonment of agriculture by the state can definitely be ruled out. The trouble with this welfare concern, from the farmers' point of view, is that it operates only if an industry is ailing.

Union leaders saw early that the political position of agriculture was likely to deteriorate as Britain's economic position improved and that in the meantime public opinion should be cultivated. 'The tide is with us now,' *The British Farmer* editorialized in 1950, 'but time is not on our side.'[2] Agricultural policy is finally judged at the bar of a largely urban public opinion, and it was desirable if possible to keep the judge favourably inclined. As Laurence Easterbrook put it, 'The greatest hope of security for farming lies not so much in legislation as in a convinced public opinion. We shall be safe when the great British public says, as a matter of course, "Well, whatever happens, we mustn't let agriculture go to the wall".'[3] The difficulty was knowing how such a convinced public opinion might be fostered.

The English love of the countryside and appreciation for the values of rural life seem to put agriculture in an advantageous position, but Union leaders have been wary of these attitudes, which they regard as fickle, sentimental, and extremely ambiguous. Love of the countryside does not necessarily mean love of the countryman or support for his political programme. Indeed, the countryside might be more beautiful if farmed less intensively, and some of the special virtues of farming might be stimulated by moderately hard times. At any rate, the Union has been intensely suspicious of any friendly opinion which seemed to have at its root a fondness for quaint, inefficient old 'Farmer Giles'. In 1946 the Union journal remarked emphatically

[1] National Farmers' Union *Yearbook*, 1958, pp. 7–18.
[2] June 30, 1950.
[3] *The British Farmer*, September, 1953.

on the need 'to dispel the time-honoured and case-hardened illusion that [subsidies] are paid to preserve farming and the countryside as a "way of life", rather in the style of an allowance to decayed gentility: as though it were a charming but out-of-date and inefficient luxury to be "kept going" on sentimental grounds'.[1]

Instead the Union has consistently based its case on 'hard' economic and strategic grounds.

We need to kill, once and for all, the false and damaging suggestion that farming is a sort of lame duck among industries and, as such, is in a special position of privilege. The charge is damaging because the British sense of fair play rightly resents any section of the nation being singled out for special favour. It is false because farming, so far from being in a position of privilege, is engaged, in co-operation with the Government, in a pioneer attempt to gear a great industry directly into the nation's over-all economic strategy while keeping the conduct of the industry in the hands of the individual enterpriser.[2]

The difficulty with this approach is that the economic value of agriculture is much harder to demonstrate than is its sentimental value, particularly when large subsidies are overtly paid out to agriculture each year. The Union's rejoinder has been to point out repeatedly that many other industries also receive substantial state support, often through the 'back door' of high tariff protection. While, up to a point, this contention is just, it does not provide a very satisfactory argument. The fact that, comparatively speaking, farmers are somewhat less well-protected than appears is a rather sophisticated point to convey to public opinion.

Behind this type of issue lies the problem of a continuing ambivalence in British public opinion. The farmers' economic problems are not in fact too well understood by townsmen. Without doubt many townsmen do believe that farmers are 'featherbedded', in the untrue sense that they lead a comfortable well-paid existence. The facts that bankruptcy is still much more frequent in farming than in most industries and that the average level of farm earnings is quite modest are not widely appreciated. Again, the notion that farmers must be extremely inefficient to need so much help is perhaps natural, but is at most a half-truth.

The Union assisted in the formation of the Association of Agriculture, which tries to foster better understanding between town and countryside, and its branches cultivate connections with local Chambers of Commerce. It also has a staff of regional publicity officers. Nonetheless the Union's publicity department has regularly

[1] *NFU Record*, May, 1946, p. 159.
[2] *The British Farmer*, June 30, 1950.

received considerable internal criticism for not putting the farmers' case vigorously enough or for showing too little vigilance in refuting criticism. This department has undergone several reorganizations in an attempt to improve its effectiveness, and prestigious outsiders have been called in to lend weight to the Union's publicity programme. In 1960, for the first time, the Union sponsored a nationwide advertising campaign, with the theme, 'Agriculture Serves the Nation', which attempted to combine the rugged, old-fashioned approach which comes naturally to a farmers' organization with the sophistication of modern public relations. The Union's difficulties may be conceded, but there is a limit in any case to the possibilities of public relations. The declining political influence of agriculture makes it all the more vital that the case that it presents to the nation be a reasonable one that will reconcile the interests of agriculture with the broader interests of the country as a whole.

CHAPTER X

AGRICULTURE AND THE PUBLIC INTEREST

1

OUR intention in this conclusion is to consider the 'partnership' between the state and the farmer in the light of the public interest. There is a strong tendency in the literature on interest groups to regard any such attempt as altogether quixotic, and it is therefore necessary to consider briefly the grounds of such an evaluation as we here propose. Throughout this book we have sought to approach agricultural politics as directly, as little burdened by fashionable 'conceptual schemes', as possible. Of course we have employed concepts, but they are concepts found in political life. The most important of these is the 'public interest', but prior to that is the notion of 'interest' itself. In this section we present, not a theory of interest or the public interest, but some elementary, if often overlooked, reflections about the meaning of these words as they are used in political life.

Generally writers in this field try to define interest objectively. Thus for S. E. Finer, interest groups are those with 'a social or economic "stake" in society', and for Harry Eckstein they are distinguished 'chiefly by objective characteristics' such as income or occupation. In contrast, both writers refer to a different type of group whose values are subjective. Finer calls these 'promotional bodies' which are concerned with some cause, and Eckstein talks of 'attitude groups' whose goals reflect 'purely subjective values'.[1] The main point of these distinctions is to draw a line between groups seeking some hard material advantage on the basis of a common objective interest and groups which are held together only by common ideals or policies.

This distinction certainly has some utility, but it may be misleading. It suggests that interest groups are wholly or mainly guided by considerations of gain (generally material gain) of a sort that can be deduced from their circumstances. In fact, however, most such groups are also concerned with something wider than such private advantage. Finer concedes that the National Union of Teachers 'has a genuine faith in Education'.[2] But is this, as Finer implies, the excep-

[1] Finer, *Anonymous Empire*, pp. 3–4; Harry Eckstein, *Pressure Group Politics* (George Allen and Unwin, 1960), pp. 9–10.

[2] S. E. Finer, 'Interest Groups and the Political Process in Great Britain', Henry W. Ehrmann (ed.) *Interest Groups on Four Continents* (University of Pittsburgh Press, 1958), p. 117.

tion, or is it not rather the rule? The National Farmers' Union certainly has a genuine faith in Agriculture, and so, one supposes, has the Federation of British Industries in Free Enterprise and the British Medical Association in Health. The faith or concern of these bodies in their respective fields is of course closely connected with (and sometimes only a cover for) the advantage of their members; but it is certainly part of their 'interest'. The point is that their interest is ambiguous, and one function of interest group studies, it seems to us, is to attempt to elucidate and understand that ambiguity, not to define it away.

Moreover an objective interest is not just given by the facts. It has to be recognized, and unless society is viewed as wholly deterministic, the questions of what mutual interests men recognize and to which ones they give priority are themselves important questions of choice. For example, small farmers in Britain might have formed a separate organization or joined with farm workers; or large farmers might have made common cause with landowners; or tenant farmers might have separated themselves from owner-occupiers. While economic facts may make some choices of organization more likely, they do not automatically exclude other alternatives.[1]

Nor, once a group has organized, can its policies and activities simply be deduced from the common objective characteristics of the members. It is for this reason that we find too restrictive the term, 'pressure group', which is now in rather general use in Britain.[2] 'Pressure group' stresses the methods of these groups to the exclusion of their ends. These methods are certainly important, and the use of the term is reasonable in this limited context. However, organized interest groups do more than promote their interests; they also have to discover and define what their interests are.

This is not so easy a task as is sometimes assumed. In the first

[1] Thus Eckstein says that 'in interest groups there exists a high probability that political purposes will be pursued collectively, and normally this is the case in groups sharing objective characteristics.' (*Pressure Group Politics*, p. 9). But at most this is 'normally' the case only in groups sharing certain *kinds* of objective characteristics, such as (to use Eckstein's examples), income and occupation. It is not normally true of children, red heads, 37 year olds, etc., all of whom share objective characteristics. The crucial point is that the distinction between those objective characteristics that are politically relevant and those that are not is based on what Eckstein would have to call 'subjective' or 'value' grounds. It was partly in recognition of this difficulty that David Truman reduced 'interest' to 'attitude', thus obliterating altogether the distinction under consideration here. See his *The Governmental Process* (New York: Alfred A. Knopf, 1953), pp. 33ff.

[2] S. E. Finer does not like either 'interest group' or 'pressure group' and suggests instead 'The Lobby'. This has the disadvantage, among others, of suggesting activities aimed at the *legislature* which, in Britain at least, seriously misplaces the emphasis. It is also of some importance that the representatives of influential organizations such as the National Farmers' Union spend very little time waiting in anyone's lobby.

place, interests cannot be viewed simply as the wants or appetites of individuals or groups. Groups do not usually advance claims which they know to be completely unreasonable or socially unacceptable, even though they often engage in special pleading. As Plamenatz puts it, 'what they [men] ask for and insist upon having is partly determined by their conceptions of justice'.[1] It is for this reason that the notion of interest, as used in ordinary language, tends to be ambiguous. It refers partly to the actual articulated demands which individuals or groups put forward; but it also refers to the social principles which they invoke to support their claims. Shorn of the second factor an interest would be lacking any reason for social acceptability. This is not to presume a complete correspondence of group interest and general interest. On the contrary, in modern democratic societies it is recognized that interests clash and that up to a point it is reasonable to fight for the distinctive interest of one's own group. We can say that it is even the duty of group leaders to advance the distinctive interests of their groups, so long as this is accompanied by an adequate recognition of the wider social interests within which their claims ought to be defined. This is the meaning of the distinction in ordinary speech between statesmanship and politics, a distinction which has the same significance at the group as at the national level.

In the second place, however cunning or stupid special interest groups may be, they almost invariably recognize the elementary fact of their own partiality—as we do when we called them 'special' interests or 'sectional' interests. They are parts of some whole, and their conception and promotion of their own interest must be based on *some* view of that whole. This is the reason why interest groups do not simply make demands, but frequently also put forward arguments about the public interest. Very often these arguments are not taken seriously by students of politics because it is assumed that they are only 'rationalizations' of private or sectional interests (or 'attitudes'). It is certainly true that these arguments will overstate the importance of the special interest to the interest of the community, and that they will often be motivated less by a genuine concern for the public interest than by a shrewd awareness of the need to secure general support. Any schoolboy knows that—and government officials and the representatives of interest groups themselves certainly know it—but it is a superficial kind of 'realism' that stops here. It is as unrealistic to assume that the process of government consists of nothing but political pressure as it would be to assume that it consists of nothing but pure reason.

[1] John Plamenatz 'Interests', *Political Studies*, February, 1954. See also the interesting analysis by S. I. Benn, 'Interests in Politics', *Proceedings of the Aristotelian Society*, January, 1960.

The National Farmers' Union stresses repeatedly its concern for the general or public interest. Sometimes its claims are so exaggerated as to raise a smile. 'We are met here,' said its President on one occasion, 'to defend not an industry but a nation.'[1] More soberly, its journal described post-war Union policy in the following terms:

The Union set about conveying the urgency of its vision to the Government and to the nation, placing before the people the need for a full employment of our land and its resources as the solid foundation of economic security. Had the Union been actuated in this by no motive other than that of benefiting the farmers of this country it need not have been ashamed. In fact, however, the Union was moved by considerations far wider than the interests, however, valid, of any single section of our community; the future of the whole nation, not of our farmers only, was, as it still is, at stake in this issue.[2]

Exaggerated and one-sided as it is, this statement certainly reflects the beliefs of Union leaders. They are sure that the development and economic security of agriculture serves the interests of the nation as well as of farmers; and they are not unwilling to abate their claims if an injury to the public interest can be persuasively demonstrated.

It is often asserted, however, that it is not meaningful to talk about the public interest, since there is no way of giving it a clear definition or one to which general assent will be given. Curiously the denial that there is a public interest typically goes along with an assumption that there certainly are special interests. But the former is at least as real as the latter. One trouble with the argument that apparently demolishes the public interest is that it likewise demolishes the group interest.

The special interest may be easier to perceive, but the difference in this respect should not be overemphasized. J. D. Stewart, for example, says that 'the sectional interest, as represented by the group is clear';[3] but that is by no means always the case. It is not clear where the farmers' interest lies with respect, say, to price supports *versus* direct grants. It is not easy for farm workers to see where their interests lie when they are pulled one way by their links with farmers and another way by their links with the Labour movement. It is not easy for landowners to see where their interest lie in a changing post-war Britain which seems to have no place for the old landowning tradition.

[1] *The British Farmer*, January 31, 1952.
[2] *Ibid.*, August, 1952.
[3] J. D. Stewart, *British Pressure Groups, OUP, 1958*, p. 244. It should be noted, however, that in other respects Stewart's conclusions are not unlike those presented here.

Moreover the public interest is often at any rate as clear as that of any special interest. It was relatively easy to see that an increase in domestic food production was required after the war. Nor was it so difficult even for farmers to see the case for reducing the level of agricultural support in the late 1950's. Of course there are important questions about the public interest where there is much doubt and darkness. Few would venture to assert with unbounded confidence, for example, where the public interest lies with respect to the social value of small farms. But in principle such questions are no more obscure or difficult than those which have already been raised in relation to the interest of special groups. Indeed they are usually the same questions, asked from the viewpoint of society as a whole instead of from the viewpoint of farmers or farm workers.

Yet there does seem to be one important sense in which the interests of the parts are more obvious than those of the whole. Under conditions in which the state is prepared to dispense economic support and other favours, such groups as farmers are in a position to band together to demand benefits without having to accept equivalent costs. The citizens of a state possess no such unilaterally advantageous direction of interest. Each citizen's interest as a tax-payer, for example, is balanced in various ways by his interest as a consumer of state services, with the equation working out differently for every individual. It is of course this situation which creates the distinctive character of 'pressure group politics' where clearly-defined special interests compete for special privileges. Even in terms of sectional advantage, however, the interests of a group are not necessarily well served by a single-minded pursuit of the favours of the state. The result may be not only to leave the group dangerously exposed if those favours are modified or withdrawn, but to inhibit voluntary measures and mutual cooperation which might well prove of more lasting benefit than state assistance.

The concept of the public interest raises broad questions of political philosophy which cannot be adequately treated in this book. It is, however, necessary to state at least the broad problems that arise with respect to the relationship between a modern democratic state and special or sectional interests within it. These problems are of two kinds. There is first the need to relate the claims of special interests to the general welfare of the community. Second, there is the state's concern with the equitable adjudication of conflicts between and within groups.

It is well to be explicit about the implications of our statement of the first of these problems. First, it implies, as already suggested, that there are numerous overlapping, more or less well-organized interests in modern societies and that they are not *per se* illegitimate. We take it that there would be little disagreement with the proposition that, given their present conditions, the health of political societies like Britain is not to be found in the elimination of special interest groups but in their reconciliation with one another and with the public interest.[1] The statement implies, in the second place, that the special interest and the public interest are, as a general rule, reconcilable but that there is no automatic natural harmony; the reconciliation is the product of art as well as nature. Finally the statement implies that in case of conflict, the public interest must prevail. This is not to adopt a simple 'monistic' as against a 'pluralistic' view, for the priority of the whole does not preclude a very considerable amount of vigorous, self-directed activity in the parts; indeed, the public interest lies partly in just such vitality.

The prevalence in the USA of a school of 'group theory', which attempts to reduce the whole process of government to the interaction of special groups, can be explained partly by a historical absence of pressing national problems. When A. F. Bentley wrote the first important study of modern group pressures,[2] the American people as a whole seemed to have little need to concern themselves with collective problems of defence, foreign policy, world trade, or the conservation of natural resources. Today, the American position is wholly different, although the group theorists do not seem to have realized it yet. In British political life, nobody doubts the existence of a public interest in such matters as physical security, foreign trade, financial solvency, economic growth, and other matters. This point would hardly need making, were it not that some writers on the political process, influenced by American group theory, seem to forget that public interests, although much broader, are fully as 'objective' and discernible as those of special groups.

Public interest in this sense refers to the needs, rather than to the wants, of a particular community. In a democracy the wishes of a majority may be accepted as providing a *prima facie* indication of the public interest, but they do not provide a final or unqualified verdict. Nor is the public interest adequately defined as an accommodation of special interests. This is generally understood in Britain, where political institutions and conventions foster the screening of sectional

[1] Whether they are desirable in principle is a question which it is impossible to consider here. Fortunately, that is not necessary for our limited purposes. Special interest groups are one of the conditions of modern life; this condition may be modified but not fundamentally altered. It is a mistake, we think, to move too quickly to the theories of, say, Rousseau in a discussion such as this. Relevant as Rousseau certainly is to a full treatment of interest group theory, it is important to recognize (as he did) that his ideal state depended upon certain special, and rare, conditions.

[2] A. F. Bentley, *The Process of Government* (Evanston, Illinois: The Principia Press, 1949; first published in 1908). For an excellent brief essay on American group theory see W. J. M. Mackenzie, 'Pressure Groups: The "Conceptual Framework",' *Political Studies*, October, 1955.

claims by reference to notions of the general interest. In our view, however, the basic soundness of British political life has misled some observers into undue complacency about the character and consequences of group pressures upon Government.[1]

Since the strength of special interests has developed *pari passu* with a growth in the range and importance of public interests, the defence of the latter against the former becomes both more important and more difficult; while the transference of much of the process of adjustment of interests from the political to the administrative level reduces public awareness of the issues at stake. These developments throw an increasing burden of responsibility upon the guardians of the public interest, the Ministers of the Crown and the senior civil servants who advise them. Neither their capacity to exercise this responsibility wisely nor the public's willingness to support them can be taken for granted. Moreover, that view of politics which ignores or subordinates the government's custody of the general interest is not confined entirely to American students. Harold Laski's comment that 'the making of policy . . . is the more successful the larger the number of affected interests consulted in its construction,'[2] is closely related to American 'group' theory, both in its theoretical foundation and in its effect on political life.

Especially important for the treatment of sectional economic groups is the public interest in economic growth and welfare. Thus the claims of farmers are generally reviewed in terms of two standards: that of utility (e.g. their contribution to the national economy) and that of equity (e.g. their right to a fair share in the wealth of the community). The standard of utility rests upon the presumption that the maximization of real or 'consumable' wealth is inherently desirable and that it is in the State's business to further this goal. Leaving aside the formidable difficulties which arise in measuring the wealth of a community, it is enough to note that the desirability of raising the total wealth and average living standards of the community is rarely questioned and that this objective constitutes a general standard by which sectional claims must expect to be tested.

There is of course no necessary reason why this should be so. A

[1] For example *The Political Quarterly's* special number, 'Pressure Groups in Britain' (Jan.–March, 1958), contains interesting material on the workings of groups, but most of the authors simply assume that these groups can be satisfactorily assimilated into the workings of the British constitution, without producing any special problems. Harry Eckstein (*Pressure Group Politics*, Ch. 7) concludes that if the private negotiations between the Government and the British Medical Association had led to undesirable decisions on important matters, the public would have heard about it and action would have been taken. We see no reason for this conclusion. S. E. Finer (*Anonymous Empire*, Ch. 9), ends on the other hand with an appeal for 'more light' on group activities, without however explaining what kind of action might need to follow.

[2] Harold Laski, *A Grammar of Politics* (Allen and Unwin, 1941, 4th ed.), p. 375.

society might quite reasonably attach greater weight to other values and less to the value of material wealth. While Britain's vulnerable trading position does limit the extent to which the public interest can be defined in non-material terms, this emphasis upon economics should not obscure the importance or validity of other types of standard. The public interest is often invoked to defend or to promote certain cultural values. A good example is the protection given to green belts, national parks, and areas of 'outstanding scenic beauty' under town and country planning legislation. Such action generally involves a considerable frustration of individual wishes, and often adds to the costs of economic development. It is by no means certain that it would be supported by majority opinion, nor is it usually justified in those terms. The justification is that certain aspects of human experience and cultural heritage ought to be safeguarded against permanent destruction or injury. This opinion is of course open to challenge, both in principle and (still more) in application; but the idea that there is a public interest involved in such matters is very widely understood and accepted. The significance of cultural factors in the case of agriculture is considered in the next section.

In addition to the problem of reconciling group with public interest, the State is also concerned with the equitable adjudication of conflicting claims between and within groups. While the government's responsibility is less active in the latter case, it is scarcely necessary to say that there is no sharp line dividing these two spheres. Indeed, the most important point is that the relations between particular groups are a matter of public interest. There are, it is true, some very limited matters in which this interest is negligible, except in the sense that the public is always interested in fairness between parties. Such, for example, is the question as to whether and under what conditions farmers should be permitted to pay their workers by cheque rather than in cash. The weak bargaining position of the individual worker and the inconvenience to him of having to negotiate a cheque has led to a requirement by Government that he be paid in cash. But if representatives of farmers and workers can agree to some modification of this rule, the public may reasonably leave it to the parties immediately concerned. And if they cannot agree, the public interest requires no more than that the inconveniences on both sides be fairly balanced.

Similar considerations apply to the choice by groups of their representatives, although here the public interest is more immediate. If the Government accepts the claim of a single organization, such as the National Farmers' Union, to speak for an entire industry, the ability of lesser organizations to recruit support or to press their views will be severely handicapped. The dominance of one main organization may also cause politicians and administrators to attach excessive importance to the views of its leaders. These drawbacks do not necessarily outweigh the advantages of the arrangement, but they do illustrate the public interest in equitable representation.

Generally, however, the public interest is directly involved even in what presents itself as wholly a dispute between sectional interests. The claim for equal treatment or for 'fair shares' has a kind of limited *prima facie* validity, especially where the state makes extensive use of economic regulation and aid. But when such a claim is made the question immediately arises whether, under given circumstances, equal treatment is equivalent to *fair* treatment, and this question requires recourse to the public interest. For example it might be accepted as in the general interest that no section of the community should fall below a certain minimum level of economic welfare, just as a similar rule is accepted in the case of individuals. This might then justify the provision of minimum guaranteed prices for farmers, and minimum wages for farm workers, even if this necessitated a degree of state aid not extended to other industries.

To take a somewhat different kind of case which presents itself as merely a dispute between parties, we might consider the question of how much security of tenure should be given to agricultural tenants. This is a question in which the public has a direct interest, bearing as it does upon farming standards, the cost of support, and the ability of newcomers to enter farming. Under such circumstances, agreement between the parties immediately concerned is an insufficient guide. One of the dangers of the weight that is now placed upon consultation with affected parties, an emphasis which is especially prominent in agricultural policy, is that politicians and civil servants are likely to regard their tasks as completed when accommodation between the parties has been reached. They tend to lose sight of their broader obligation which is not only to accommodate the interests of conflicting parties but to search out and to promote the broader public interest.

2

Questions of the public interest are relevant to agricultural policy in three principal ways. First, there is the problem of balancing the economic welfare of farmers with that of the nation. Second, there is the question of whether agriculture possesses any special cultural values of a kind which call for measures of aid or protection. Third is the question of what general types of farming system the State should seek to promote, and what steps it should take for improving the general functioning of agriculture. Necessarily, our review of these questions must be brief and restricted. Our excuse for undertaking it is that any conclusions about the post-war experiment in agricultural 'partnership' will hinge upon some judgments about these matters. It is preferable, even if it is rash, to make these explicit.

A full answer to the question of whether agriculture is more protected and subsidized than other industries would require an elaborate study, but a broad conclusion can be safely given. Agriculture does not enjoy the same degree of tariff protection as many industries. Several important foodstuffs enter duty-free, while others pay varying but generally low rates of duty.[1] On the other hand, price subsidies to British agriculture between 1950 and 1960 provided equivalent protection to a substantial tariff.[2] In addition, agriculture received considerable support from direct grants and subsidies, and it is completely exempt from local rates. Farmers also benefit from the subsidization of rural electricity by urban consumers, and from special Government grants for rural water supplies, drainage, cattle grids and several other purposes. On balance, it cannot be doubted that agriculture received more State aid during this period than any other major industry.

The importance of Government aid to farmers themselves needs less stressing. It is a curious and disturbing fact that Government support to agriculture in the period since rationing ended has been equivalent to over two-thirds of the total net income received by farmers during this period. The result has not been to keep many farmers in feather-bedded affluence. The average farmer's income by 1960 was no more than about £1,200, and if interest on his working capital were deducted from this figure, the net earnings left to himself and his family for their work would be closer to £900.[3]

As we have seen, farmers' actual incomes fluctuate very widely indeed, and the state has taken the risks out of farming only to a very limited extent. What it has ensured, all things considered, is a fair general level of stable prosperity to agriculture throughout the last twenty years, including a recent period in which the fortunes of agriculture would otherwise have veered sharply downwards.

From the viewpoint of the national economy, the principal value of an expanded and more prosperous agriculture has been its con-

[1] For details, see Economist Intelligence Unit, *Britain and Europe* (1957, Ch. 4).

[2] According to one calculation, it would seem that an additional average tariff of about 30 per cent would have been necessary to give British farmers equivalent protection to that provided by price subsidies in 1954/5. E. F. Nash 'The Competitive Position of British Agriculture', *Journal of Agricultural Economics*, June, 1955.

[3] These calculations are derived from dividing the aggregate farming net income of £360 million among the 300,000 full-time farmers of the United Kingdom. In fact, a small part of these earnings went to part-time farmers and ought properly to be deducted. If some allowance is made for this factor, and if 5 per cent interest is allowed on the £1,500 million estimated investment in livestock, crops, and machinery, the average farmer's income becomes about £900.

tribution to the national balance of payments. This contribution is the result of an increase in net output since pre-war of 70 per cent by 1960, which is estimated to be worth some £300 million a year. Besides its direct contribution to food supplies, the expansion of agriculture is said to be helpful in keeping down the average cost of food imports, by reducing the volume which is required, with a consequent beneficial effect on the nation's terms of trade.[1]

However, it is very questionable whether these savings have really been worth the cost of the subsidies from a national economic standpoint. The Government itself has repeatedly stressed the uneconomic nature of the support which has been given to certain products, such as pigs, eggs, and milk. The argument about the indirect contribution of agriculture to the terms of trade (in so far as it is true at all) is also open to a converse argument of equal significance. The autarchic policy pursued by Britain has dissuaded other countries from developing their agricultures faster in order to supply the British market. A good example is the fact that the production of lamb and dairy products could be increased much more economically in New Zealand than in Britain, and New Zealand would have been fully prepared to extend its trade with Britain if allowed to do so.[2]

So far as the future is concerned, British agriculture faces problems which are general to economically advanced countries. In such countries, the technical progress and development of agriculture is rapid, but the demand for food expands more slowly because the population is already reasonably well fed.[3] It is true that there is still plenty of scope for further dietary improvements in Britain. Although the demand for some foods will be static or declining there should be a considerable increase in the consumption of poultry, meat, eggs and certain fruits and vegetables.[4] British agriculture is quite capable in a technical sense of supplying most of this

[1] This is the view of the Government as expressed in *Agriculture*, Cmd. 1249 (1960), p. 3.

[2] The expectation that industrialization in such areas as Australasia will reduce the food available for export overlooks their great agricultural potential. Since the marginal costs of agricultural expansion are generally much lower than in Britain, many food exporting countries have good reason to develop agriculture as well as industry so long as markets are available.

[3] E. A. G. Robinson, for example, has estimated that an increase of 30 per cent in total personal consumption might cause increases of 15 per cent in food expenditure and of 12 per cent in the quantity of food consumed. (*Agriculture In The British Economy*, pp. 22/3). Changes in the income elasticity of demand for food, however, tend to vary in both directions at different stages of development and raise many complex issues.

[4] In 1955 27 per cent of total calory consumption in Britain took the form of animal products, while the figure in the USA was 33 per cent. See Dr N. C. Wright, *Ibid.*, p. 72. The attainment of American standards of nutrition would therefore require a considerable increase in the consumption of animal products.

expanding market. In economic terms it is not well equipped to do so.

Food can ot course only be imported to the extent that sufficient export markets are developed and maintained. The uncertainties of world trade probably justify special encouragement to British agriculture, so long as the extra cost seems reasonable in terms of the foreign exchange which is thereby saved. British agriculture had developed by 1960 to a point where it accounted for almost 50 per cent by value of the nation's food supplies, and for as much as 66 per cent if tropical products, which cannot be grown in Britain, are excluded from the calculation.[1] The scope for 'import-saving' had been correspondingly reduced. Under the existing system of support, marginal output was a great deal more costly than imported supplies, and also entailed considerable expenditure upon imported feedingstuffs, fuel, and other requisites. In these circumstances, there seems to be no national economic case for any further extension of autarchic policies. This means that any further increase in the total size of British agriculture must probably depend upon improvements in its competitive performance.

This analysis has not taken account of the various national contingencies or emergencies which might require sudden changes in agricultural policy. Farmers' leaders are quite right to insist that a long-term view should be taken of national agricultural requirements, but the inferences drawn from this proposition are frequently unjustified. A collapse of export markets or an unexpected worsening of the terms of trade might suddenly necessitate the production of more food in Britain; and the same situation might occur through an outbreak of war. The basic requirement for dealing with such situations is that agriculture should be capable of rapid expansion. For this purpose, it is desirable for buildings and equipment to be kept in reasonable repair and for the land to be itself in good heart. These objectives do not necessitate a high or comprehensive level of support; indeed in an emergency some forms of production now subsidized, such as eggs or pigmeat produced from imported feedingstuffs, would be an obvious liability. Such emergencies could be prepared for in various ways; for example, through guaranteed prices for certain particularly important commodities, direct grants for the encouragement of good cropping routines and grassland management, and an advisory-sanctions programme of the kind provided for in the 1947 Agriculture Act but subsequently abandoned.

Programmes such as these, together with provision for spare-time holdings and allotments (which have cultural as well as 'survival' values) could, it is true, provide only a limited kind of insurance, and one which would take some time to come into effect. Probably the

[1] *Agriculture*, Cmd. 1249, 1960, p. 3.

only practical direct insurance against extreme military disaster is to be found, not in agricultural policies at all, but in a food storage programme.[1] If the British nation really had to feed itself for an extended time, possibly under harassing circumstances, the system and methods of agriculture would have to be revolutionized in ways which nobody, least of all farmers themselves, at present contemplate or would willingly accept. Yet the limited preparations that might be made for such an emergency have been hampered by the failure of the farmers' leaders and, to a lesser extent, political leaders to see that it is both impracticable and undesirable to attempt to prepare for the possibility of another war by keeping agriculture on the footing of the last one.

We turn next to the special cultural and social values associated with agriculture. Traditionally, rural life has been characterized by a low level of public services, social facilities, and cultural opportunities; its compensations have resided in superior physical and probably mental health,[2] and in access to the countryside and rural pursuits. However, the differences between rural and urban life are steadily narrowing. Rural public services have been greatly improved in the last two decades, and improved transport will increasingly bring the more specialized urban facilities within reach of all but the most remote rural dwellers. Conversely, drawbacks of urban life such as overcrowding and atmospheric pollution, and the poor health conditions to which they give rise, are being reduced. Public policy is playing a large part in equalizing the conditions of urban and rural life, and probably will continue to do so.

Yet in spite of the development of modern means of communication, the farmer enjoys (or endures) one of the rarest commodities of modern life, a modicum of privacy. There is ordinarily some considerable space between him and his fellows, and he is often alone. One must beware, of course, of romanticizing this mixed blessing; but it would be equally absurd to ignore its real value, especially in the crowded civilization of Britain.[3] Moreover, even under conditions of mechanization, agricultural work requires a varied range of skills and provides direct functional contact with the processes of nature. Good husbandry requires careful attention to the rotation of crops, to the breeding of livestock, and to the maintenance of soil fertility. Even if farming has no special economic value in terms of

[1] See H. T. Williams (ed.), *Principles for Agriculture Policy* (Oxford University Press, 1960), Part IV.

[2] *Report and Evidence of the Royal Commission on the Distribution of the Industrial Population* (Barlow Report), Cmd. 6143, 1940, paras. 106–31.

[3] A favourite subject of the women's pages of the farming journals is whether the lot of the isolated farmers' or farm workers' wife provides an opportunity to enrich the mind and soul, or only oppressive loneliness. made tolerable by hard work and the light programme.

its contribution to the total satisfaction of consumers' demand, it can reasonably be regarded as a more satisfying and rounded occupation than the highly routinized and monotonous activities of many workers in industry and commerce. There is no reason to doubt the conclusion of a recent study that 'as far as satisfaction in his work is concerned, the farmer and farm worker is likely to remain more favoured than the town worker'.[1] It is not necessary to regard the farmer as the embodiment of the complete man to recognize that agricultural employment embodies some desirable qualities which most modern occupations conspicuously lack.

Many individuals understandably choose agriculture for these reasons, despite its financial drawbacks. Intrinsically, there is nothing absurd or mistaken in the exercise of a similar preference by society as a whole. The maximization of real incomes and consumption standards has become the conventional objective of most modern societies; but a society which laid less emphasis upon the product of work and more upon the creative value of the work itself might well be wiser and happier.

It does not follow, though, that the state should subsidize or protect agriculture for these reasons. In the first place, a democratic government cannot simply overrule the valuations placed upon work and consumption by a large majority of citizens. In Britain there is a sense of the value of agricultural pursuits, and this has some effect upon public policy; but it hardly constitutes a major deviation from the general interest of society in the maximization of wealth. Farmers and land workers themselves share the general belief in technological improvement and economic advance. This is why they tend to reject, sometimes mistakenly, any ascription of special value to agricultural work as 'sentimentality'. The increasing approximation of their living and working conditions to those in towns is generally prized, although its incidental consequences for traditional ways of life is often deplored. Farmers generally want state support, but they do not want it provided on social or cultural grounds.

Secondly, in modern states generally and pre-eminently in Britain, agriculture can in any event occupy only a small minority of the population. Special aid to agriculture might increase this proportion slightly or, to speak more realistically, might check its decline. Such a policy would make little or no difference to the ways in which well over nine-tenths of the population earn their living and conduct their lives. The only realistic way of providing widespread contact with soil or countryside is through the development of spare-time activities, whose importance will steadily increase. Arguments about the quality of modern life and the need for more creative leisure-time opportunities have important consequences for town and

[1] *Principles for British Agricultural Policy, op. cit.,* p. 237.

country planning. They strengthen the case for population dispersal, for the provision of spare-time holdings and allotments, and for improved access to the countryside. But they have virtually no consequences for agricultural policy as such.

It is not only the values associated with agriculture generally that need to be considered, but the advantages of particular agricultural *systems*. Since Aristotle much has been heard of the peculiar virtues of agricultural owners, a status which did not, in classical writers, imply actual toil. In modern times more weight has been attached to the special qualities of peasant proprietors or family farmers. John Stuart Mill, for example, considered that the English system of land tenure and large estates was inferior to the system of peasant proprietorship in certain Continental states. Whether or not this preference was justified, Mill and others have been able to argue quite convincingly that under certain conditions the ownership of a small farm tends to stimulate industry, to train intelligence, and to promote forethought and self-control.[1]

As Mill himself recognized, however, the deliberate encouragement of small-scale farming becomes wasteful and self-defeating if carried too far. It results in holdings which cannot provide a satisfactory living for their occupants, and on which the self-reliant thrift which he so admired gives way to poverty, backwardness, and excessive dependence upon public charity. The French policy of deliberately nourishing a large peasantry has produced merely a large group of poor and dependent persons. The Jeffersonian theory of the existence of some peculiar connection between farm ownership and political sanity has also fared very badly by practical tests. As A. Whitney Griswold has demonstrated, the several million small farmers who still exist in the United States of America cannot possibly be regarded as the heirs of American political wisdom and democratic virtues. The question, as he rightly concludes, is not whether the family farm will save American democracy, but whether American democracy is prepared to save the family farm.[2]

British experience is different, inasmuch as the old independent yeomanry of Britain was destroyed, with Parliamentary support, by the enclosure movement. In the last fifty years, however, a steady increase in the number of owner-occupiers has occurred, while the rights and functions of agricultural landowners have declined. Indeed, as the estate system has been weakened, the distinction between individual proprietors and tenant farmers has lost almost all of its social as well as a large part of its economic significance, and

[1] J. S. Mill, *Principles of Political Economy* (Longmans, Green and Co., 1891), Book 2, chs. 6 & 7.

[2] A. Whitney Griswold, *Farming and Democracy* (*New York*: Harcourt, Brace, and Co., 1948).

is now mainly important for the finance of capital improvements. Another fact of importance is the steady decrease in the manpower required by British agriculture. In the last decade (1950–1960), the number of regular hired workers fell by no less than a quarter. While mechanization on farms may now proceed more slowly in view of its exceptionally rapid development since the war, manpower requirements will certainly continue to diminish.

The future of family farming in Britain has to be considered in the context of these conditions. There is no longer much room for the farmer with small capital resources or indifferent abilities; nor is there much scope for real small-scale, full-time farming.[1] But while modern agriculture requires much more capital, rather larger units, and more technical ability than previously, the efficient family farm can still claim many of the virtues connected with individual proprietorship. Agriculture can continue to offer peculiarly satisfying and interesting opportunities for individual enterprise, so long as the size of the farm and the abilities of the farmer suffice for their realization.

We can now turn to the interest of the state in improving the general performance of agriculture. Under the 1947 Agriculture Act, this interest was primarily conceived as a matter of supervising or dispossessing incompetent farmers. Instead of being abandoned, these powers of control might have been placed on a modified basis which would have helped to keep agricultural land and equipment in a satisfactory condition against future emergencies. Even had this been done, the interest of the state in the functioning of the agricultural system was bound to become wider than the maintenance of mild supervisory powers. The state's main impact upon agriculture comes through the extensive economic aid which it provides. This aid is costly, yet it has failed to help the weaker farmers really effectively, or to overcome the structural and competitive weaknesses of British agriculture.

It might be possible for the state to embark upon a comprehensive reconstruction of the agricultural system as a condition of its support. With the decline of private landlordism and the large estates, problems of inadequate capital, fragmented ownership and bad farm lay-outs have become in some ways harder to solve at a time when their importance has increased. This situation creates the case for the comprehensive replanning of agriculture in larger, better laid-out, and more uniformly equipped units which was advanced

---

[1] As a spare-time activity, it should be repeated, the importance of small-scale farming, in conjunction with employment in decentralized industries, may well grow. On both strategic and social grounds such development deserves Government support and certainly seems preferable to any attempt to maintain a considerable class of subsistence-level farmers.

before the war by such authorities as Sir Daniel Hall and Dr C. S. Orwin. The advantages of this programme may not, in fact, be so great as its advocates assumed, since the economies of large-scale units tend to be increasingly offset by problems of management. But the greatest difficulty with such a programme is that it would depend upon a new enclosure movement carried out through the agency of the state. Given the powerful conservatism of the countryside and the formidable difficulties in the way of establishing a large state enterprise which would act effectively, so radical a measure of agricultural reconstruction seems unlikely in the near future to be tried or, if tried, to succeed.

It may be suggested that the state ought next to turn its attention to four objectives, rather different from those which have prevailed during the last sixteen years. The first is the provision of a more limited, but not lightly altered, foundation of basic support, restricted to a smaller number of commodities. The second is to take out an insurance policy against future contingencies by encouraging good conditions of farm maintenance and soil fertility, which might be linked with a re-introduction of modified supervisory powers, at least over farmers receiving special aid. The third aim is to give a certain amount of special aid, as well as technical and economic advice, to smaller farmers who can reasonably improve their positions. A start in this direction has been made with the small farmers scheme, which has also barred those small farmers who cannot attain the requisite standards from receiving this particular form of aid. This programme may need to be expanded, and an extended and improved advisory service is required if small farmers are to be persuaded and instructed to use their opportunities to good effect.

The fourth aim is to improve the general performance of agriculture by way of a few general stimulants to its efficient development. While some forms of special aid will still be necessary, there is a limit to the efficacy of piecemeal intervention. The numerous specific grants now available tend to submerge the farmers' economic judgment beneath intricate calculations of special benefit, and it would probably be more satisfactory if most of them were replaced by the provision of agricultural capital and credit on more favourable terms than is now available.[1] A very important field for improving the general performance of agriculture is that of marketing, and the

---

[1] For many years the Conservative Government has insisted that favourable rates of interest have a distorting effect upon the economy and has consequently preferred to offer direct grants. In both psychological and economic terms, however, the provision of low interest capital and credit has more to commend it where agriculture is concerned. State programmes of providing agricultural credit and special aid to small farmers could also be designed to provide more encouragement for the amalgamation of uneconomic holdings, although a major attack on that problem would no doubt require direct Government intervention.

Government could profitably direct more of its assistance towards agricultural co-operatives and farmers' organizations seeking to improve the quality of farm products and the methods of their distribution.[1]

At the same time, new issues of agricultural policy have made their appearance. Foremost among these are the problems for agricultural support which arise in connection with the various possible schemes of European integration. We have not discussed this subject in this book, because it belongs rather to the future than to the past and because so many diverse possibilities exist at the time of writing.[2] The Union has so far successfully insisted that British agriculture should be excluded from such schemes or insulated from their consequences. It is doubtful whether the farmers' influence will remain strong enough, however, to dissuade the Government indefinitely from participating in any European plans which are generally advantageous to Britain.

Any closer association of Britain with the European community will require not only the methods but also the aims of state support to be changed. British agriculture is in general more technically and economically advanced than the agricultures of most European states, with the notable exceptions of Holland and Denmark. On the other hand, the incomes, services, and amenities enjoyed by British farmers are much closer to those prevailing in urban occupations than is the case in other European countries, where very wide disparities in these matters still exist. Indeed, the civilized amenities of the English countryside are a source of wonder to most foreign visitors. While some British farmers could certainly maintain their higher incomes in competition with other European producers, it seems unlikely that the majority can do so. This situation increases the need for the Government to stimulate the economic performance of agriculture, and to tackle the problems of uneconomic holdings, if British farmers are to keep their relatively favourable position.

In making these suggestions, we have ventured a short way into a very large field. Plainly, it would be impracticable to deduce from any general considerations exactly how much support agriculture should receive and how this aid should be provided and allocated. These questions have to be settled in the light of changing circumstances, and there is plenty of room for different opinions even within a framework of agreed general principles. However, the emerging

[1] The Government made a start in this direction by offering a small amount of assistance for such schemes at the 1961 Price Review. *Annual Review and Determination of Guarantees*, Cmnd. 1311, p. 10.

[2] Also outside the scope of this discussion is the important question of whether agricultural support should continue to be financed by taxation, or whether its cost should be transferred to consumers as is now generally proposed for 'Common Market' countries. Britain prefers the former course.

problems of British agriculture make still more necessary what agricultural policy-making in the post-war period has largely lacked: serious deliberation and well-grounded political decisions about the long-range objectives and methods of the agricultural support programme.

3

We turn finally to the system of 'partnership' between Government and agricultural interests. How well has this system served the best interests of agriculture and nation?

Its mainspring has been the relationship between the National Farmers' Union and successive Governments. Even for a period in which Government and interest groups have been drawn closely together, this relationship has probably been unique in its range and its intensity. In following the common practice in describing this relationship as a partnership, we do not, of course, imply that the partners are equals. In the last resort the right and the duty of the Government to determine agricultural policy has never been in question. In practice, however, almost every issue of agricultural policy has been settled by mutual adjustment and compromise, and only in the last few years has the Union been simply overruled on subjects which it judged important. The relationship has been closer to a true partnership than its constitutional status of consultation would suggest.

There is no easy answer to the question of whether a democratic Government ought ever to concede an exclusive franchise for consultation and co-operation to a single organization.[1] Clearly this status cannot be claimed as a right, and ought, in any event, to be withdrawn if the organization in question ceases to be sufficiently representative. These qualifications, however, do not solve the questions of what circumstances justify such an arrangement, how the representativeness of the organization is to be tested, how broad and absolute the recognition should be.

There are weighty reasons for permitting an exclusive relationship of this type in certain circumstances. If the Government had to decide its policy in consultation with a number of separate farmers' organizations, it might have greater scope to decide for itself what the general interests of farmers required; but it would also have the difficult task of balancing a variety of specialized and probably extreme claims. By contrast, a single broadly-based organization, if such exists, has itself to hold the balance between the various farming groups, whose claims are then subjected to a real and quite

[1] For an American view in the negative, see Paul Appleby, *Big Democracy* (New York: Alfred A. Knopf, 1945), pp. 116–117.

possibly wholesome measure of internal self-discipline. Because of its more comprehensive dealings with Government, it should also become better aware of broad considerations of public interest, and it may tend towards a position which is more moderate, more conservative, and more responsible than that of more specialized and limited organizations. Considerations such as these led one American observer 'to favour (not exclusively, but on balance) the general farm organization over the special purpose association'.[1]

The consultative monopoly accorded to the National Farmers' Union can certainly be justified, up to a point, by reference to these considerations. From the viewpoint of Government, close co-operation with the Farmers' Union had great advantages during the period when the availability of food supplies was closely dependent upon the efforts and the morale of British farmers. The Union kept the Government well-informed about farmers' needs, and lent its support to the achievement of Government objectives. Advantages of this kind have, of course, diminished, but they remain important. Moreover, there can be little doubt of the broadly representative character of the Union which is demonstrated by its very high figures of membership, by the vitality of its county and local branches, and by the absence of any important competing organization. Although the Union's rise was certainly helped by its recognition by the Government as sole spokesman for the general interests of farmers, it has to be remembered that the desire for effective representation was one of the main reasons why farmers joined it; they reasoned that unity was strength.

Recognition achieved, the Union has worked hard to maintain the cohesiveness of farmers' interests. This aim has certainly imposed some internal discipline upon the demands of sectional groups, but it has also induced a rather rigid formulation of the Union's claims. Once the conventions of the price review had been firmly established, a permanent allocation of Government aid according to set formulae seemed the safest course for the Union to pursue. It was loath to consider differential schemes of aid to smaller farmers, not because it grudged them extra support, but because it did not want support provided in ways which would upset existing arrangements and divide farmers into competing groups; and it therefore preferred the illogical course of trying to help smaller farmers through demanding special support for those commodities of most importance to them. Equally, the Union's marketing policy basically reflected a conservative adherence to methods which had satisfied farmers in the past, and an anxiety not to deprive any group of the possible benefits of a marketing scheme. The Union's exclusive franchise made it in

[1] Charles Hardin, *The Politics of Agriculture* (Glencoe, Illinois: The Free Press, 1952), pp. 262–3.

some ways moderate and responsible, but it has not encouraged flexible or progressive policies.

This book has given many examples of the undesirable effects of Union influence upon Government policy. In the case of the price review, the Government was slow to explore more flexible and more selective methods of support for which the Agriculture Act provided, because of the Union's strong opposition to any departure from the conventions which it had managed to get established. It was only in 1957 that an overdue simplification of review procedure was introduced, and only in 1958 that the Small Farmers Act marked a significant but still minor departure from the tradition of generalized support to agriculture as a whole. In the case of marketing, the Ministry of Agriculture's predilection for the kind of statutory marketing schemes which existed before the war helped the Union's proposals to be sympathetically received; but this fact caused a narrow view to be taken of the public interest in agricultural marketing. The closeness of the Government's relation with the Union also inhibited it from developing a satisfactory relationship with the County Agricultural Committees.

It would be misleading to suggest that the Ministry simply succumbed to Union pressure, or developed anything like the dependent relationship upon a specialized clientele which characterizes, for example, some American government agencies. The Ministry of Agriculture was no more than the 'responsible department', administering Government policy under the supervision of the Cabinet and its adjunct of Treasury control. When concessions were made to the Union on such matters as prices, they were made with the authority of the nationally-responsible Cabinet. What is true is that continuous contact with one powerful organization induced a defensive posture in the Ministry which allowed the Union to set the pace —or to hold it back. The Union's views were not opposed by any other organized interest of comparable strength and access to a Government Department. Indeed, the Union's only important opponent in the early post-war period was, curiously, another department, the Ministry of Food. Because of the pervasive effects of partnership, the political process at this time was neutralized and dormant as a source of alternative agricultural policies and programmes.

It is not only public policy, however, that has been endangered by this close partnership; the representation of the agricultural interest is also affected. In the first place, while the Union may reasonably be regarded as fully representative of producers over such general issues as the price review, the case is rather different with more specialized questions. For example, the Poultry Association of Great Britain contains many fewer egg producers than does the Union, but it is still a sizeable enough body for its views on egg marketing

to be important. In fact, however, the Government has been somewhat reluctant to bring such bodies into consultation or to accept
their representative status, even for limited purposes; and while the
Union is anxious enough to assist specialized groups, it wants to do
so through its own machinery. Several examples have been given of
how smaller agricultural organizations have had to put up with the
Ministry's cold shoulder and with the Union's hard one.

Partnership also affects the Union itself. The view that the Government is frequently a victim of Union 'pressure' has its counterpart in
the opinion of some Union members that their leaders are prisoners
of the Government. It is easy to see how this belief arises. The Union
has had so comprehensive and important a consultative status that
its own freedom of action and expression has inevitably been reduced. Once Union leaders have reached a settlement with the
Government, they naturally represent it as the best obtainable and
are often impatient to secure its endorsement. Thus the view gained
ground that the Union was 'almost part of the executive of the
Government' and was so 'friendly' with the Government that it
could not adopt an independent position.[1] This opinion never became the prevailing one. The Union leadership has been so generally
trusted and so obviously competent that most farmers have believed
that on balance their interests have been well served by close ties
with Government. However, it is not only the rank and file, but even
the leaders themselves who have sometimes wondered whether the
relationship was not rather *too* close.

It has, indeed, been the closeness rather than the exclusiveness of
the Union's relationship with Government which has had harmful
effects. The Union has balanced the interests of its members reasonably well, within the framework of its general strategy, but the heavy
pre-occupation of its leaders with political and administrative bargaining has caused too little attention to be paid to other possibilities
for improving farmers' welfare. The tendency of the close concordat
has been as much to debilitate the Union as to hamper the Government.

In recent years the character of agricultural partnership has been
subtly changing. Although a close consultative relationship still
exists, and was reaffirmed in the White Paper of December, 1960,[2]
it seems slowly to be taking on a more flexible and limited character.

The Government's partial withdrawal was facilitated by changing
economic conditions and by the amalgamation of the Ministries of
Agriculture and Food. The Agriculture Act of 1957 was an agreed
measure between the new Ministry and the Union for tightening and

[1] *The Farmers' Weekly*, December 12, 1952. Many such comments are to be
found in the columns of this journal.
[2] *Agriculture*, Cmd. 1249/1960.

simplifying the statutory basis of agricultural support. The Union's leaders welcomed the measure because it increased farmers' legal rights, although they did not fully foresee and certainly did not like the Government's subsequent behaviour. Farmers having been given somewhat greater formal security, the Government felt itself free to adopt a firmer position at annual price reviews. It became much less anxious to secure the Union's endorsement and began to experiment with new forms of support which were not greatly to the Union's liking. The Union found that its scope for bargaining and pressure at the review table was considerably reduced.[1]

Should Britain become a member of a wider European community, the significance of the annual price review will be further reduced. European governments are pledged to give continued support to their farmers, and any form of European agreement seems certain to include flexible arrangements for guaranteed minimum prices. Nonetheless, the British Government would no longer have a free hand in determining these prices, which would have to be related to agricultural conditions throughout Europe. It is probable that the guarantee arrangements of the Agriculture Act of 1957 would prove insufficiently flexible for this purpose and would have to be amended. The National Farmers' Union would have to seek allies among other European farm organizations instead of relying on its close relationship with the British Government. This prospect explains the Union's distaste for European integration and its energetic efforts (still successful at the time of writing) to maintain the established conventions of the price review.

A growing dissatisfaction with the fruits of partnership led the Union to investigate some new possibilities even before Whitehall's attitude had cooled. Its leaders, however, are most reluctant to abandon beliefs on which they have acted at least since 1945. They were convinced that the prosperity of agriculture depended almost entirely upon Government action and that their own efforts were best directed towards influencing that action. While they always paid lip service to the principle of self-help, it did not occupy a prominent place in their thinking. So long as they conceived their task as being primarily political, there was little reason (and little time) to concern themselves closely with questions of technical and economic development as such.

[1] Since 1957, the National Union of Agricultural Workers and the Country Landowners' Association have had brief discussions with the Ministry before the opening of the price review proper. These discussions have been merely an informal exchange of views on 'the prospects for agricultural production and guarantees' (*The Land Worker*, March, 1957, p. 3), and they do not affect the Union's prerogative to speak for agriculture in the subsequent formal discussions. However, this widening of consultative arrangements is in accordance with the reduced importance of Government-Union negotiations.

As the Union has become less well able to get its way at the annual price review, it has begun to shift its objectives. The Union always expected the Government to put pressure on farmers to cut costs and to improve efficiency, but for a long time it sought to ease this pressure rather than add to it. By January, 1958, however, its President was suggesting that farmers could 'aspire to this removal of the Exchequer liability—and thus, at the same time, reduce the liability of the farming industry to political whim'.[1] There was a time when even to 'aspire' to this goal would have seemed not only impracticable, but almost treasonable. Later in the same year *The British Farmer* editorialized: 'We have to intensify our knowledge of the commercial problems. In the past we equipped ourselves with first-class economic and political know-how, and it was the basis of our influence. Knowledge will be power in other fields, too.'[2]

Doubtless there is a large measure of rhetoric in these statements. Farmers still lean very heavily upon Government support and they know it. Nonetheless, the Union's successful launching of a commercial company, the Fatstock Marketing Corporation, gave its leaders more confidence in their ability to attack farmers' problems directly rather than through the Government. It is significant, of course, that this venture was undertaken reluctantly and was regarded as an inferior alternative to the statutory marketing scheme for which the Union had hoped. Nonetheless, once done, the achievement suggested the possibility of other measures of agricultural self-help; and in recent years the Union has taken a number of small and tentative steps in this direction.

The Union has greatly expanded its own staff of technical specialists and has set up its own Marketing Development Section to engage in market research.[3] Together with the marketing boards and the Fatstock Marketing Corporation, it established a British Farm Produce Council to co-ordinate publicity and information programmes on behalf of British agricultural products.[4] In 1959 it incorporated an Agricultural Credit Corporation, whose most significant feature is that loans are guaranteed to farmers only 'on evidence of need for the satisfactory execution of a farm management programme'.[5] Superficial, but not entirely insignificant evidence of the Union's more commercial approach is also provided in its journal, *The British Farmer*. The journal's principal aim is still to make its

[1] *The British Farmer*, January 18, 1958, p. 2. See also December 21, 1957, p. 8; February 6, 1960, pp. 14–15.

[2] *Ibid.*, May 31, 1958, p. 3.

[3] *Ibid.*, July 16, 1960, p. 8; November 5, 1960, p. 26; January 7, 1961, p. 26.

[4] *Ibid.*, November 5, 1960, p. 45.

[5] J. Howard Morgan, 'Management Advice and Essential Credit', *Ibid.*, October 10, 1959, p. 65; see December 3, 1960, p. 17.

readers more reliable Union members, but it increasingly attempts to make them better farmers as well.[1]

These various innovations are not very important in themselves, but they may be the beginning of larger changes in the Union's aims and methods. As yet, this question cannot be answered. For example, in spite of headquarters' greater support of voluntary co-operation, its basic reliance on statutory marketing boards has been only slightly modified. Farmers' leaders have talked freely in recent years of the need for bold new ventures, particularly in the marketing field, whereby farmers can demonstrate their commercial ability and extend their collective assets; but the Union's ability to enter these new fields effectively remains unproven. 'The NFU', said its president in 1961, 'is the only body that can represent the economic and commercial as well as the political interests of farmers in this country'.[2] But the Union's power is rooted in its political success, and its monolithic character and cumbersome machinery hardly provide an easy springboard for successful commercial ventures, especially as these cannot be combined with the close sympathy for producers' attitudes and prejudices that has always typified Union behaviour. Certainly the Union can do much more than it has to help farmers to help themselves, but it will indeed be fortunate if it can combine the functions suggested by its president.

The ending of the close partnership between Government and Union could only be welcomed. This does not, of course, imply that the state should abnegate its new-found responsibilities for the general welfare of British agriculture, but it needs a freer hand to discharge this task well. Equally, the Union's future course will depend upon how well it has learned the lesson that leadership of the agricultural industry requires more than hard political bargaining for a share of the public purse. The Union's views will certainly and rightly continue to influence Government policy, but that does not imply that the two parties must feel habitually constrained to proceed always by agreement. Government cannot, consistently with its responsibility to the public interest, bind itself by such a partnership with any sectional interest.

[1] *The British Farmer* introduced descriptions of the successful application of time and motion, or 'work study', principles to farming, and in 1960 the Union established its own Work Study Consultancy Service, making available on a fee basis the services of a professionally trained work study officer.

[2] *NFU News*, March 6, 1961.

APPENDIX A

GOVERNMENT SUPPORT TO AGRICULTURE (1959–60)

	£ million
A. Price guarantees:	
Wheat and rye	20·4
Barley	25·2
Oats and mixed corn	12·8
Potatoes	1·0
Eggs, hen and duck	33·1
Cattle	3·4
Sheep	25·3
Pigs	22·2
Milk*	8·5
Wool	2·8
TOTAL A	154·7
B. Farming grants and subsidies:	
Fertilisers' subsidy	29·4
Lime subsidy	11·0
Ploughing grants	9·4
Field drainage grants	2·6
Water supply grants	0·7
Improvement of livestock rearing land	1·5
Marginal production assistance	1·7
Bonus payments under the tuberculosis (attested herds) scheme	9·0
Calf subsidy	16·5
Hill cattle and hill cow subsidies	4·1
Silo subsidies	1·4
Grants for farm improvements	6·6
Grants to small farmers	1·1
Miscellaneous grants	0·1
TOTAL B	95·1
Administrative expenses	5·9
Contribution to Northern Ireland	1·2
TOTAL SUPPORT	256·9

* Excluding school and welfare milk.

SOURCE: *Annual Review and Determination of Guarantees* (Cmnd. 1311, 1961), p. 18

APPENDIX B

SUPERVISION AND DISPOSSESSION

(Action Taken Under The Agriculture Act, 1947, Part 2)

(Figures supplied by the Ministry of Agriculture, Fisheries and Food)

Action	1948 (ten months)	1949	1950	1951	1952	1953	1954	1955	1956	1957	TOTAL
Estate management supervision orders made under s. 12 (1)	25	73	159	163	186	122	53	18	12	—	811
Husbandry supervision orders made under s. 12 (1)	530	838	724	608	812	421	183	51	30	3	4,200
Dispossession on grounds of bad estate management*	—	—	1	9	1	5	5	1	1	—	23
Dispossession on grounds of bad husbandry†	1	23	64	69	112	82	19	6	—	1	377

* Certificates made under s. 16 enabling the Minister to purchase the land compulsorily
† Orders made under s. 17 terminating an occupier's interest or occupation

APPENDIX C

LANDLORDS' CONTROL OF TENANTS
(England and Wales)

Notices to quit
IN the ten years of the operation of the 1947 Agriculture Act (March 1, 1948—
February 1, 1958) a total of 6,765 applications for notice to quit were heard by
county agricultural executive committees acting on behalf of the Minister of
Agriculture, or by the Minister himself. Consent was given in 2,490 cases and
refused in 4,269 cases.

Detailed figures relating to appeals are available only for the eight years from
March 1, 1950 to February 28, 1958. In this period, 4,543 applications were heard
by county committees or the Minister, and appeals by county committees or the
Minister to agricultural land tribunals were lodged in 1,534 cases. There were
639 appeals by tenants against approval of a notice to quit, of which 257 were
successful. There were 895 appeals by landlords against refusal to grant a notice
to quit, of which 175 were successful.

Certificates of bad husbandry
In the ten years, March 1, 1948—February 28, 1958, 934 applications for certi-
ficates of bad husbandry were heard by the county committees or Minister.
Certificates were granted in 439 cases and refused in 495 cases. There were a total
of 176 appeals, of which sixty-four were successful. Source: Information from
Ministry of Agriculture, Fisheries and Food.

APPENDIX D

THE FARMERS' VOTE

THE figures in the first two tables of Chapter 9 are based on the 1951 Census of
Occupations and the 1955 Register of Electors. The Census of Occupations
distinguishes five agricultural groups which include farmers, farm workers,
horticulturists, gardeners, forestry workers, and workers in certain ancillary
occupations. Our definitions of agricultural employment and agricultural voters
include all these groups, so that some persons are included who do not identify
their interests with those of agriculture. The Census provides no satisfactory basis,
however, for excluding such persons.

In the period between the 1951 Census and the 1955 Register, agricultural
employment declined slightly, so that our results marginally overstate the size of
the agricultural vote in 1955. (It should also be remembered that the agricultural
vote has continued to shrink since 1955). The Census figures are based on local
government divisions in England and Wales, and in some cases the figures had
to be adjusted to allow for the different boundaries of parliamentary constituencies. These adjustments were relatively minor and do not affect the general
reliability of the figures. In Scotland, however, the Census figures were obtainable
only for counties, and not for urban and rural districts, so that calculations had
to be approximate and the results are considerably less reliable.

The estimates of agricultural voting power later in the chapter (p. 202) involved
a different calculation. To estimate the size of the farmers' vote and the total
agricultural vote for each constituency, it was necessary first to eliminate all
employed persons who were under voting age. It was then possible to express the
Census category of 'farmers, farm managers, farm bailiffs and farm foremen'
as a proportion of the electorate of each constituency. Not surprisingly perhaps

the 'farmers' vote' itself, as thus defined, proved to be extremely small. It exceeded 5 per cent in thirty-nine constituencies and 10 per cent in only one constituency.

However, if voters are to be classified on an occupational basis, it is necessary to make allowance for the wives and other adult dependants of voters. For this purpose, we have added in the estimated number of wives of workers in agriculture, but ignored other adult dependants whose numbers are harder to calculate. While the results cannot pretend to be accurate, they give some indication of the probable significance of the agricultural vote.

SIZE OF THE AGRICULTURAL VOTE (1955)

No. of Constituencies

Percentage of Total Electorate	Farmers, bailiffs, etc. and wives.	All agricultural voters and wives.
0 – 10	263	161
10 – 20	23	89
20 – 30	1	29
Over 30	0	8

In general this analysis tends, for reasons which have been given, to exaggerate slightly the size of the agricultural vote. We have undertaken this modest statistical exercise, despite its limitations, because of the considerable political importance attached to the 'farmers' vote' during the post-war period.

APPENDIX E

NOTE ON SOURCES

A LENGTHY bibliography would be inappropriate in a work of this kind, since many books touch only marginally on subjects we have discussed and since much of our material cannot be derived from books at all. This note explains some of the sources which have been helpful in writing this book, but it is highly selective and does not include the large number of articles, political pamphlets, etc. upon which we have drawn. References to these can be found in the appropriate chapters. We have not included a section on interest groups, since little of this literature deals with agriculture specifically and an adequate list would be long.

(1) British Agriculture
The general history of British agriculture is well described in Lord Ernle, *English Farming Past and Present* (5th edition revised by Sir A. D. Hall, Longmans, Green & Co., 1936), and C. S. Orwin, *A History of English Farming* (Thomas Nelson and Sons, 1949). The economic problems of state intervention in agriculture are dealt with in Anne Martin, *Economics and Agriculture* (Routledge and Kegan Paul, 1958) and Edith H. Whetham, *The Economic Background to Agricultural Policy* (Cambridge University Press, 1960) while a good brief introduction is provided by Chapter 13 of Kenneth E. Boulding, *Principles of Economic Policy* (Staples Press, 1959). E. M. Ojala, *Agriculture and Economic Progress* (Oxford University Press, 1952) is also very relevant.

The economic structure of British agriculture is described in numerous reports and studies published by University departments of agriculture. *Agriculture in the British Economy* (Imperial Chemical Industries, 1957) provides a fairly recent review of economic problems and prospects, and Viscount Astor and B. Seebohm Rowntree, *British Agriculture* (Penguin Books, 1939) is still of interest. Recent economic history from 1956 is fully covered by the volumes of *The Agricultural Register* (New series: Agricultural Economics Research Institute, Oxford). For farmers' incomes, see the Ministry of Agriculture series *Farm Incomes in England and Wales.* (HMSO).

The life of the small farmer is described in *The Small Farmer* (ed. H. J. Massingham, Collins, 1947). Rural attitudes are depicted in W. H. Williams, *The Sociology of an English Village* (Routledge and Kegan Paul, 1956). Lord Ernle, *The Land and its People* (Hutchinson & Co., n.d.) contains some still interesting reflections upon the social and political history of agriculture.

(2) Agricultural Organizations
There are virtually no studies of British agricultural organizations, except for some short 'official' histories. An exception is A. H. H. Mathews, *Fifty Years of Agricultural Politics* (P. S. King & Son, 1915) which gives a full history of the Central Chamber of Agriculture. Reg. Groves, *Sharpen the Sickle!* (The Porcupine Press, 1949) gives a polemical history of the Farm Workers' Union. Tom Tiffin, *The Origins of the National Farmers' Union* (Lincolnshire Chronicle, 1949) deals only with the Union's early history.

Important sources for the activities of the agricultural organizations are their own official journals: *The British Farmer* (National Farmers' Union), *The Land Worker* (National Union of Agricultural Workers), *The Country Landowner* (Country Landowners Association). Other useful sources are the NFU's Year Books and, among independent journals, *The Farmers Weekly.*

(3) Government Organization
Sir Francis L. C. Floud, *The Ministry of Agriculture and Fisheries* (C. P. Putnam's Sons, 1927) is now only of historical interest. Organization and problems in the second world war are dealt with from contrasting viewpoints in two volumes of the UK civil series of official war histories: *Agriculture* by Keith A. H. Murray (HMSO 1955) and *Food: The Growth of Policy* by R. J. Hammond (HMSO 1951). A personal record is supplied by Anthony Hurd, *A Farmer In Whitehall* (Country Life, 1951).

Government organization and activities since 1945 have been the subject of several official reports and inquiries, including:
11th R. from the Select Committee on Estimates: Agricultural Services 1948–9.
Reports of the Agricultural Improvement Council for England and Wales, 1944 and 1950.
R. of the (Ryan) Committee appointed to review the organization of the Ministry of Agriculture and Fisheries (1951).
5th R. from the Select Committee on Estimates: Agricultural Research, 1953–4.
Public Inquiry ordered by the Minister of Agriculture into the disposal of land at Crichel Down, Cmd. 9176, 1954.
R. on the National Agricultural Advisory Service; the first eight years, 1946–54. 1955.
R. of the (Arton Wilson) Committee appointed to review the provincial and local organization and procedures of the Ministry of Agriculture, Fisheries and Food. Cmd. 9732. 1956.

(4) Agricultural Policy
Government agricultural policy is set out in a variety of White Papers and statements in the House of Commons. The former include the annual series (1951 and after) of price review documents, the explanatory memorandum on the 1947

Agriculture Bill (Cmd. 6996), the 'decontrol' White Paper of 1953 (Cmd. 8989), and 'Assistance for small farmers' (Cmd. 553, 1958).

Important public reports on agricultural policy issued by the Ministry of Agriculture, Fisheries, and Food include:

R. of the (Lucas) Committee to review the working of the Agricultural Marketing Acts, 1947.

R. of the (Williams) Committee on milk distribution, 1948.

R. of proceedings under the Agricultural Wages Acts, 1937–50, 1952.

R. of the proposed British egg marketing scheme, Cmd. 9805, 1956.

R. of the (Bosanquet) Reorganization Commission for pigs and bacon, Cmd. 9795, 1956.

R. on Agricultural Marketing Schemes for the years 1938–55, 1957.

R. of the (Runciman) Committee on the marketing of horticultural produce, Cmnd. 61, 1957.

Interesting studies of particular fields of policy are provided by G. R. Allen, *Agricultural Marketing Policies*. (Basil Blackwell, 1958) and Graham Hallett, *The Economics of Land Tenure* (Land Books, 1960). A general approach is provided by H. T. Williams (ed.), *Principles for Agricultural Policy* (Oxford University Press, 1960).

INDEX

For Product Safety Concerns and Information please contact our EU
representative GPSR@taylorandfrancis.com
Taylor & Francis Verlag GmbH, Kaufingerstraße 24, 80331 München, Germany